Digital Methods for Social Science

Digital Methods for Social Science

An Interdisciplinary Guide to Research Innovation

Edited by

Helene Snee
Lecturer in Sociology, Manchester Metropolitan University, UK

Christine Hine
Reader in Sociology, University of Surrey, UK

Yvette Morey
Research Fellow, Centre for the Study of Behaviour Change and Influence, University of the West of England, UK

Steven Roberts
Senior Lecturer in Sociology, Monash University, Australia

Hayley Watson
Senior Research Analyst, Trilateral Research and Consulting, UK

First published 2016 by
PALGRAVE MACMILLAN

Palgrave Macmillan in the UK is an imprint of Macmillan Publishers Limited, registered in England, company number 785998, of Houndmills, Basingstoke, Hampshire RG21 6XS.

Palgrave Macmillan in the US is a division of St Martin's Press LLC, 175 Fifth Avenue, New York, NY 10010.

Palgrave Macmillan is the global academic imprint of the above companies and has companies and representatives throughout the world.

Palgrave® and Macmillan® are registered trademarks in the United States, the United Kingdom, Europe and other countries.

ISBN 978–1–137–45365–5

This book is printed on paper suitable for recycling and made from fully managed and sustained forest sources. Logging, pulping and manufacturing processes are expected to conform to the environmental regulations of the country of origin.

A catalogue record for this book is available from the British Library.

Library of Congress Cataloging-in-Publication Data
Digital methods for social science : an interdisciplinary guide to research innovation / [edited by] Helene Snee, Christine Hine, Yvette Morey, Steven Roberts, Hayley Watson.
    pages   cm
Includes bibliographical references and index.
ISBN 978–1–137–45365–5 (hardback)
1. Social sciences—Methodology.   2. Social sciences—Research—Data processing.   3. Internet research.   4. Digital media.   I. Snee, Helene, editor.
H61.D546 2015
300.285—dc23   2015021880

Contents

Figures and Tables

Figures

Tables

Foreword

There is still no consensus about what digital social methods are. Some argue that social research methods have been digital for a long time, as computational devices entered the social research toolkit many decades ago, in the form of punchcards, and the range of quantitative and qualitative software packages that social researchers have been trained to use from the 1970s onwards. Others argue that the long-standing process of 'digitization' is taking a new form today, as digital devices are currently transforming social life in ways that precisely render it available for social research in unprecedented ways. Many agree that developments such as the rise of social media, the proliferation of mobile devices and the uptake of digital analytics across professional practices are giving rise to a new apparatus for researching social life. They also have as a practical consequence that 'social methods' are becoming ever more prominent or 'mainstream' in our societies and cultures: today, users of digital devices are almost de facto researching communities, measuring influence and so on. Social media platforms such as Facebook routinely rely on methods of social network analysis to suggest new profiles to 'friend'. And well before the rise of 'social' media, the research paper introducing the search engine Google cited the sociologist Robert Merton as an important source of inspiration in the development of computational methods for analysing the 'reputation' of web pages.

Of course, whether or not the analytic measures that have been built into digital infrastructures qualify as social research methods – whether they deserve to be called by that name – is something that we can debate and disagree about. Some social scientists insist on the difference between computational methods and the dominant methodological repertoires of the social sciences (interviews, surveys). By contrast, others have highlighted the many overlaps between methodological traditions of the social sciences and computing: methods for the analysis of conversations, networks and discourse have been developed across fields, and they have both a computational and a sociological dimension. But whatever one's view on this matter, the project of the 'mainstreaming' of digital methods raises important questions for social research. As computational methods are deployed by industry to gain insight into social life, where does this leave 'social research' as an academic, public and everyday undertaking? As the contributions to this volume help to make clear, it is highly implausible to expect digital platforms themselves to take on all the various tasks of social research, as these platforms are increasingly configured to serve the rather narrow purposes of marketing and advertising research, leaving it partly to academic and public social researchers to develop the research designs and wider methodology that we need in order to make digital data, tools and methods work for social enquiry.

But someone has to make the first move, and the contributions to this volume show that academic, social and cultural researchers are very much up to this task. They help us to understand just how much it takes – in terms of practical astuteness and methodological investment – to make Internet-based and Internet-related methods work with other social research methods. Intellectual scepticism about digital methods – and about digital industries – is not necessarily unfounded, but it too often serves a placeholder for an unwillingness to do this work. Yes, the type of social research that is facilitated by digital platforms and the kind of 'knowledge about society' pursued by social researchers are in many ways at odds, but this only means that we must do the work of making digital data, tools and methods serve the ends of social inquiry. This volume provides many examples that demonstrate how to do this.

In the process, the contributions also show us that digital methods are not just another set of methods or just another toolkit. To be sure, social research methods have long had a computational dimension. But what we are facing today is a much wider re-negotiation of social research methodology across academia, industry and society. If something unites those who 'do' digital methods, it is perhaps that they are prepared to recognize the importance of technology and socio-technical arrangements to how we gain knowledge about social life. They recognize that digital technologies, settings as well as digital user practices and the 'research situation' all inform the 'method' we end up using in our research. As we learn how to research social life 'with the digital', we then inevitably come to re-specify what participates in the composition of method: machines as much as people, ideas and situations. How to do it? This is as much a practical as an intellectual question, and this is what makes digital methods so exciting and the willingness to engage with them so important.

Noortje Marres
Goldsmiths, University of London, UK

Acknowledgements

This collection started life following the 'Digital Methods as Mainstream Methodology' research network and events. The editors would like to thank Rose Wiles and her team at the ESRC National Centre for Research Methods, who funded the network through the Networks for Methodological Innovation programme (2012). Thanks also to the bursary awardees Lorenza Antonucci, Ibrar Bhatt, Nell Darby, Jo Hope, Carole Kirk and Victoria Tedder for all their hard work and contributions. We are grateful to our event speakers: David Beer, danah boyd, Axel Bruns, Christine Griffin, Rachel Gibson, Noortje Marres, Eric Meyer, Mike Thelwall and Sue Thomas; the 'pecha kucha' presenters Temitayo Abinusawa, Amy Guy, Jeremy Knox, Evelyn McElhinney and Eve Stirling; and all of the attendees who participated. Their contributions are summarized in the final report of Digital Methods as Mainstream Methodology (Roberts et al., 2013); we have drawn on these insights in our concluding chapter. Thanks also to the University of the West of England, the British Library and the University of Manchester for hosting the events.

An additional thanks to MovieStarPlanet ApS for giving permission to reproduce the screenshot of MovieStarPlanet in Chapter 7 and to Catherine Talbot for her assistance in preparing the manuscript.

Contributors

Jonathon Adams has been working as an English language specialist at the English Language Institute of Singapore, Ministry of Education, since 2013. His main area of work involves providing support for learning in different school subjects through classroom-based research and developing resources. His research draws on systemic functional linguistics, multi-modal interaction analysis and mediated discourse analysis to investigate the construction of multi-modal meanings made with mediating digital texts.

Stuart Agnew is a senior lecturer at the Faculty of Arts Business and Applied Social Science, University Campus Suffolk (UCS), UK. He is course leader for the BSc (Hons.) Criminology course and Deputy Director of the Institute for Social, Educational and Enterprise Development (iSEED) at UCS. He is a Fellow of the Higher Education Academy and a highly committed academic with a passion to create and deliver teaching of the highest quality. His research on using technology to enhance learning has been presented at the Assimilate Conference at Leeds Beckett University, UK, and at the European Association for Practitioner Research for Improving Education, Biel, Switzerland. A case study, co-authored with Emma Bond, regarding the use technology to support M-level students programme has been published by the Scottish Higher Education Enhancement Committee as an example of exemplary practice from an international perspective. His other recent research projects include investigating the prevalence of urban street gangs in Birmingham, educational experiences of young people in Suffolk, youth unemployment in Ipswich and evaluation of a diversionary programme for Suffolk Youth Offending Service.

Julie Barnett is Professor of Health Psychology at University of Bath, UK. She works across a range of areas in social and health psychology with particular focus on public appreciations of risk, risk communication, health technology, food allergy and intolerance, and using big data and social media in the context of evidence-based policy making. Over the last ten years, she has been principal or co-investigator for a range of largely interdisciplinary projects funded by the Engineering and Physical Sciences Research Council, the Economic and

Social Research Council (ESRC), FP7 (Seventh Framework Programme of European Union), UK Government Agencies and Departments and the Wellcome Trust.

Ibrar Bhatt is a senior research associate at the Department of Educational Research, Lancaster University, UK. His research and publication interests lie at the intersections of literacy studies, educational technologies, socio-material theory and digital methods. His recent research investigates the digital practices of curricular assignment writing and the dynamics of academics' knowledge creation through writing. In addition, he has prior experience of project management, research and teaching in higher and further education, as well as in private companies.

Emma Bond is an associate professor at University Campus Suffolk, UK, and she is also Director of iSEED (The Institute for Social, Educational and Enterprise Development). She has 14 years of teaching experience on social science undergraduate and postgraduate courses and PhD supervision. She has extensive funded research experience and is a senior fellow of the Higher Education Academy and a visiting senior fellow at the London School of Economics. Her research interests focus on the everyday interactions between people, society and technology, and she is especially interested in developing both innovative and accessible methodologies in research which foster participation with marginalized groups. Her research on virtual environments has attracted much national and international acclaim, and she has been interviewed for *BBC Breakfast*; *The Today Programme* on Radio 4; *Woman's Hour* on Radio 4; Channel 4's *The Sex Education Show*; and for various national media channels in the United Kingdom, America and Canada. Her book *Childhood, Mobile Technologies and Everyday Experiences* (published by Palgrave Macmillan in 2014) was nominated for the highly prestigious BSA Philip Abrams Memorial Prize for the best first and sole-authored book within the discipline of Sociology. Her research interests have a strong focus on qualitative methods, including innovative, creative and virtual methods, and include risk and everyday life; self-identity, especially gendered and sexual identities; technology and higher education; and young people's use of media.

Phillip Brooker is a research associate at the University of Bath working in the emerging field of social media analytics. His research interests include sociology, science and technology studies, computer-supported cooperative work and human–computer interaction. He has previously contributed to the development of a social media analytics data collection and visualization suite – Chorus (www.chorusanalytics.co.uk) – and currently works on CuRAtOR (Challenging online feaR And OtheRing), an interdisciplinary project which focuses on how 'cultures of fear' are propagated through online 'othering'.

Axel Bruns is an Australian Research Council Future Fellow and a professor at the Creative Industries Faculty at Queensland University of Technology (QUT), Brisbane, Australia. He leads the QUT Social Media Research Group. He is the author of *Blogs, Wikipedia, Second Life and Beyond: From Production to Produsage* (2008) and *Gatewatching: Collaborative Online News Production* (2005) and a co-editor of *Twitter and Society* (2014), *A Companion to New Media Dynamics* (2012) and *Uses of Blogs* (2006). His current work focuses on the study of user participation in social media spaces such as *Twitter*, especially in the context of news and politics.

Jean Burgess is Professor of Digital Media and Director of the Digital Media Research Centre (DMRC) at QUT. Her research focuses on the uses, politics and methods for studying social media platforms, and she is currently involved in several externally funded research projects that apply computer-assisted methods to the analysis of large-scale social media data. Her co-authored and co-edited books include *YouTube: Online Video and Participatory Culture* (2009), *Studying Mobile Media: Cultural Technologies, Mobile Communication, and the iPhone* (2012), *A Companion to New Media Dynamics* (2013), *Twitter and Society* (2013) and *Handbook of Social Media* (for publication in 2016). Over the past decade, she has worked with a large number of government, industry and community-based organizations on addressing the opportunities and challenges of social and co-creative media. She collaborates widely, with international research partners in Brazil, Germany, Canada, the United Kingdom, the United States and Taiwan.

Timothy Cribbin is a lecturer at the Department of Computer Science, College of Engineering, Design and Physical Sciences at Brunel University London. He has research interests and expertise in information visualization, visual text analytics, scientometrics and search user interfaces. He is the founder and lead of the Chorus project, which began as a sub-project of FoodRisc (EU FP7) and was conceived to support longitudinal and corpus-based analysis of discourse around a food infection (*E-coli*) outbreak. He was a co-investigator on the recently completed Multidisciplinary Assessment of Technology Centre for Healthcare (MATCH) project at Brunel where he further developed and applied the Chorus tool suite to explore how social media analysis can bring about a better understanding of user needs relating to medical devices.

Roberto de Roock is a researcher and designer at the Center for Games and Impact, Arizona State University, USA. In his research, he bridges the fields of New Literacy Studies and the learning sciences through qualitative and design-based research studies of digitally mediated literacy practices. He is committed to promoting the equitable impact of digital media and has spent the last 16 years collaborating with marginalized communities as a language arts teacher, digital arts facilitator and educational researcher.

Adolfo Estalella is an anthropologist and postdoctoral researcher at the University of Manchester, UK. His two research fields are anthropology of knowledge and science and technology studies. One of his research lines investigates the various intersections between digital cultures, activism and the city; a second research line is focused on the methodological reinvention of social science, specifically on the transformation of methods with the incorporation of digital technologies and the development of forms of collaborative research.

Jorge Fábrega is an assistant professor at Adolfo Ibáñez University, Chile, and an in-house social scientist at Statcom/Datavoz (a public opinion research firm). His primary research interests are in the mix of social diffusion of information, political economy, institutional formation and Internet as a digital public arena. He has several publications on the diffusion of information and group formation along social networks platforms.

Claire Hewson is Lecturer in Psychology at The Open University, UK. She has a wide range of publications on Internet-mediated research methods, including *Internet Research Methods* (2003; second edition forthcoming). She was the convenor and editor for the recently published British Psychological Society guidelines on ethics in Internet-mediated research (2013). Her research interests include online research and assessment methods, common-sense understandings, particularly folk psychology, and related issues in philosophy of mind and cognitive science.

Christine Hine is Reader in Sociology at the Department of Sociology, University of Surrey, UK. Her main research focuses on the sociology of science and technology. She also has a major interest in the development of ethnography in technical settings and in 'virtual methods' (the use of the Internet for social research). In particular, she has developed mobile and connective approaches to ethnography which combine online and offline social contexts. She is author of *Virtual Ethnography* (2000), *Systematics as Cyberscience* (2008), *Understanding Qualitative Research: The Internet* (2012) and *Ethnography for the Internet* (2015) and editor of *Virtual Methods* (2005), *New Infrastructures for Knowledge Production* (2006) and *Virtual Research Methods* (2012).

Jo Hope holds a PhD from the University of Surrey, UK. In her research, which was funded by ESRC, she explores the use of online peer support within the wider caring practices of parents with a rare syndrome. Her research interests include the sociology of health and illness; parenting; mixing modes and methods; digital, health and social inequalities; digital sociology; disability, evaluation and digital methods. She has supervised Sociology and Criminology undergraduates at Kingston University, UK; tutored students in methodological and sociological courses; run day courses in social research; worked as a research assistant at the University of Surrey; and provided evaluation support and advice to statutory partners as an independent evaluation consultant.

Emma Hutchinson has recently completed her PhD, entitled 'Performative Identity and Embodiment: An Online Ethnography of Final Fantasy XIV', at the Department of Sociology, University of Warwick, UK. Her work concerns the performative relationship between identity and embodiment online in the context of online gaming. This research maps how performative identity and embodiment via an avatar can be enacted within an environment that is structured by social norms including heteronormativity and racism. The research also charted different ways of researching online gaming using qualitative methods including participant observation, asynchronous interviewing and forum observation. Her research interests include digital sociology, digital social research methods and visual sociology.

Jeremy Knox is Lecturer in Digital Education at the University of Edinburgh, UK, and a core member of the Digital Cultures in Education (DiCE) research group in the School of Education at Edinburgh. His research interests include open and digital education, higher education and museum and gallery education that are grounded in critical approaches to pedagogy, technology and culture. He works with the theoretical areas of posthumanism, new materialism and the socio-material, as well as the way these ideas might help us to understand education in the digital. He is currently working on projects funded by the Arts and Humanities Research Council (UK) to develop mobile applications for gallery education and by the National Research Foundation (South Africa) to develop renewed critical pedagogical practices in higher education, as well as the ESRC Code Acts in Education seminar series. His background includes teaching, education technology and software development, and he currently teaches on the MSc in Digital Education, a fully online postgraduate course from the University of Edinburgh. He also developed and taught the innovative and pioneering 'E-learning and Digital Cultures' massive open online course (MOOC) with the University of Edinburgh in partnership with Coursera, one of the first of such courses in the United Kingdom. Jeremy has published widely in the area of MOOCs and open education and is regularly invited to speak at national and international conferences.

Noortje Marres is Senior Lecturer in Sociology at Goldsmiths, University of London. Her work investigates various intersections between technology, environment, knowledge and the public. She has a background in the social studies of science and technology, and her recent work is mainly concerned with the role of devices, environments and things in the enactment of participation (in public life, innovation, research, change). She was part of the team that built the Issuecrawler, an online platform for the location and analysis of issue-networks, and is currently developing Issue Mapping Online. She is convenor of the MA/MSc in Digital Sociology and is Director of the interdisciplinary research centre CSISP (Centre for the Study of Invention and Social Process) at Goldsmiths.

Yvette Morey is a research fellow at the Centre for the Study of Behaviour Change and Influence, University of the West of England, Bristol. She conducts interdisciplinary research on young people and well-being; risk and participation in online and offline communities, cultures and networks; and the use of digital methodologies in the social sciences. Her publications have appeared in the *International Journal of Market Research*; *Sociology*; *Young*; and *Addiction, Research & Theory*. Her recent co-authored article 'Online and Digital Research: The Issues for Researchers from a Qualitative Psychology Perspective' has appeared in the British Psychological Society's quarterly publication *The Psychologist*.

Steven Roberts is Senior Lecturer in Sociology at Monash University, Australia. He has diverse research interests, but they centre around the youth stage of the life-course. Within this field, his key areas of focus are how social class and gender shape, influence and constrain young people's transitions to adulthood independence and their experiences of education, employment, consumption and the domestic sphere. He has published widely in international journals and is co-/sole editor of three volumes with Palgrave Macmillan.

Javier Sajuria is a postdoctoral research associate in the School of Government in Public Policy, University of Strathclyde, UK. He is part of Parliamentary Candidates UK. His primary research interests are comparative political behaviour, social media and quantitative methods. His work has focused primarily on social capital in online contexts.

Sanjay Sharma is a senior lecturer at the Department of Social Sciences, Media and Communications, Brunel University London. His recent work includes exploring the pedagogy of racialized representation and affect as well as technologies of race. In particular, he is interrogating the materialities of digital race and networked racisms and currently is completing a project examining online discourses of racism denial. He is the author of *Multicultural Encounters* (Palgrave Macmillan) and is a co-founder/editor of the open access *darkmatter Journal*.

Helene Snee is Lecturer in Sociology at Manchester Metropolitan University, UK. Her research explores stratification and socio-cultural change with a particular focus on young people, cosmopolitanism and class. Her interests also include online methodologies and ethics and how these illuminate wider questions for the social sciences. She is the author of *A Cosmopolitan Journey? Difference, Distinction and Identity Work in Gap Year Travel* (2014), which was shortlisted for the BSA Philip Abrahams Memorial Prize for the best first- and sole-authored book within the discipline of Sociology. She has also published on the methodological and ethical issues associated with blog analysis.

Eve Stirling is Senior Lecturer in Design at Sheffield Institute of Art, Sheffield Hallam University, UK. Her research interests include technology and higher education, the use of social media in higher education and the pedagogical impacts of these. She is also interested in design thinking and its influence on the research process, ethnographic research methods and social media as a research tool and research site. She holds a PhD from the School of Education, University of Sheffield, UK.

Victoria Tedder holds a PhD in Sociology from the University of Kent, UK. She is working as a community development research consultant, bringing her understanding of digital methods into evaluation techniques. Her research interests are diverse and include nostalgia, domesticity, gender, skill and social movements.

Hayley Watson is a senior research analyst at Trilateral Research & Consulting, a niche research and advisory consulting company bringing together strategy, technology and policy. Her main areas of expertise include the role of technology including social media in relation to security, and she is particularly interested in the ethically and socially responsible use of information and communications technology in crisis management. She is actively involved in ISCRAM (Information Systems for Crisis Response and Management) community and co-chairs the ELSI (Ethical, Legal, and Social Issues) Working Group at ISCRAM. She is author of several book chapters, articles and popular press pieces relating to the role of social media in crisis management, citizen journalism and crises and the publicity of terror.

1
Digital Methods as Mainstream Methodology: An Introduction

Helene Snee, Christine Hine, Yvette Morey, Steven Roberts and Hayley Watson

Introduction

This book explores exciting innovations in the field of digital social research. The growing significance of 'the digital' for contemporary social life is undeniable; nevertheless digital methods have yet to be fully accepted into mainstream social science. By presenting a range of work by social scientists from a variety of disciplinary backgrounds, it is our aim to highlight digital methods as a valuable and increasingly integral part of the social research toolkit. They offer the chance to access, generate and analyse new kinds of data on the social world in novel ways and address new research questions, as well as providing different approaches to long-standing questions. In this collection, we define digital methods as *the use of online and digital technologies to collect and analyse research data*. Our concern is not only with research that explores online phenomena, but also with a broader interest in utilizing digital methods to engage with all aspects of contemporary social life.

In each of the chapters that follow, the contributors consider two central questions:

- How do the methods described supplement or extend the existing methodological repertoire of the discipline?
- How far do these digital methods contribute to or transform understanding of a 'mainstream' issue?

This collection therefore embraces digital technologies for what they offer in terms of methodological innovation and conceptual insights. However, we also recognize the practical and ethical challenges of digital methods, and we offer critical reflections on establishing these tools as viable, rigorous and effective sets of methodologies.

In this introductory chapter, we set the scene for the innovations that follow by providing a contextualizing literature review of the emergence of digital social research. We outline the growth and changes in Internet use and the response by social science and then discuss the developments in digital methods – from ethnographies to 'big data' analysis – that the chapters in this book build upon. Following this overview, we discuss some of the challenges in bringing digital methods into the mainstream, before outlining the contributions to this collection. In this book, we hope to contribute to important debates across social science disciplines concerning how digital data augment, enhance and problematize our conventional methods of research. Such debates raise fundamental questions over who is researched, what is researched and how research is conducted.

The emergence of digital methods in social science

Since the Internet became a mainstream phenomenon in the mid-1990s, it has been clear that it provides both a fascinating resource for doing social science and a significant opportunity to develop and build upon some established modes of social science research. Following an initial early phase of scepticism about the social potential that computer-mediated communication offered, it subsequently became widely apparent that online interactions were of sufficient intensity and significance for their participants that social scientists could study them and in fact needed to take them seriously (Jones, 1995, 1997). Following this recognition, a burgeoning literature has explored the specific qualities of online social spaces, often in a pioneering spirit that has stressed the need for social scientists to adapt their techniques to the specific qualities of new phenomena (Hine, 2005a).

Since its initial emergence as a phenomenon of significance for social science, much has changed about the Internet and digital social science. Successive waves of the Oxford Internet Survey (Oxford Internet Institute, 2014), Pew Research Center studies of Internet use (Pew Research Center, 2015) and the World Internet Project (World Internet Project, n.d.) have documented the growth and diversity of the Internet-using population. A very important qualitative and quantitative shift in online activity has been occasioned by the growth and broadening out of user participation in the creation of online content, fed by the emergence of social networking sites and the development of modes of contribution which require little technical skill from users. This emergence of Web 2.0 (O'Reilly, 2005; Beer and Burrows, 2007) or what is known as the participatory web (Blank and Reisdorf, 2012) reflects the input of an ever-widening segment of the population and changes the nature of what is said online. In 2015, We Are Social reported that there were approximately 2.078 billion active social media accounts; Europe alone contributed 387 million accounts (Kemp, 2015). Social networking sites offer a 'platformed sociality' (Van Dijck, 2013) which provides a simple means for users to connect with one another and, in the process, to leave persistent traces of their activities. The potential of the 'big data' – data which is 'high-volume, high-velocity and/or high variety' (Gartner, 2013) – generated by social media, for instance, to offer new ways of doing social science is one of the themes explored in this collection.

As the Internet-using population has broadened out, so too have the aspects of everyday life reflected on the web. The wider population has become accommodated to the idea of the Internet as a site where information is accessed and a space where their own daily lives may be played out, both in moments of drama and crisis and in more mundane ongoing practice. Among academic researchers, there has been a subtle, but nonetheless important, shift in emphasis within the literature, with the growing recognition that the Internet, rather than acting as a transcendent phenomenon which offers a separate form of social space, is instead embedded in multiple contexts of everyday life (Wellman and Haythornthwaite, 2002). This 'contemporary Internet' has become a complex and multifaceted arena which both reflects and reshapes everyday life, subtly remodelled by the platforms which provide options for sociality and the algorithms which circulate data and personalize our online experience (Beer, 2013). It has become increasingly difficult for social scientists across a wide range of domains to ignore the role that digital technologies, and online interactions in particular play in the forms of life that they are studying. Interest in digital methods has therefore spread far beyond those researchers who are interested in the Internet for its own sake. As online interactions have burgeoned, and as social science ambitions for taking account of these online interactions have broadened out, the complexity of the methodological challenges has also increased. The multi-platform embedded in the Internet poses a new set of demands on established research methods, as we seek to find ways to keep up with new technologies that provide platforms for sociality, to map the connections between online and offline space and to analyse diverse forms of data.

This collection focuses on an assorted array of approaches across the social sciences using digital methods to address 'mainstream' issues. The authors focus on digital phenomena, but they do so in full recognition that such phenomena are not to be considered as 'merely' digital or qualified as *only* online forms of sociality. Rather, these researchers study digital phenomena because they are social, and as such, deserving of attention, and significant within the overall concerns of their home disciplines. These researchers are faced with the specific demands placed upon them by the contemporary Internet as a complex and embedded phenomenon, but they do so building on the tradition of online research and a wide array of established research methods. This collection focuses on contemporary challenges and develops its strategies out of a strong heritage of qualitative and quantitative research into online phenomena. The remainder of this section will, without attempting a comprehensive overview, outline some of the key foundations of online methods which this collection builds upon.

The development of digital methods

The question of how to do research in online spaces has been a recurring theme for collections and handbooks over the years as the Internet itself has developed (e.g. Jones, 1999; Mann and Stewart, 2000; Hine, 2005b; Fielding, Lee and Blank, 2008). The web has been used extensively to reach research participants by both qualitative and quantitative researchers. Web-based surveys (Dillman, 2007), for example, have become a much-valued resource, allowing for flexible delivery to broad samples at relatively low cost and access to hard-to-reach populations (Coomber, 1997). Online interviewing and focus groups have become routine, both in asynchronous mode and in real time (Kazmer and Xie, 2008; James and Busher, 2009; Salmons, 2009; Salmons, 2011). Interviewing online can offer a safe space for participants to address sensitive issues (Illingworth, 2001; Orgad, 2005; McCoyd and Kerson, 2006) and provide for inclusion of those who might find face-to-face interviews hard to fit into their lives (Madge and O'Connor, 2002; Nicholas et al. 2010).

Some qualitative researchers have used data from online discussion groups and forums, preferring to draw on this naturally occurring data for its capacity to explore how participants formulate issues in their own words and for the low burden placed on participants. Systematic comparisons have established that such data compare favourably in quality with the conventional interview (Seale et al., 2006; Seale, Ziebland and Charteris-Black, 2010). Computer-mediated discourse analysis (Herring,

2004, 2011) uses techniques from linguistics to explore the specifics of online language use and conversational structure. Other uses of online 'found data' take a larger-scale quantitative approach to the analysis of emergent patterns of discourse (Thelwall, 2009; Bruns and Stieglitz, 2012) or exploit the underlying structure of hyperlinks to explore the emergence of issues across the landscape of the web (Rogers and Marres, 2000; Thelwall, 2004). Digital data offer a readily available resource for exploring social patterns on a large scale.

Researchers have also extensively used ethnographic approaches to explore the specificities of the online cultural space. The development of participant observation techniques tailored to online spaces, such as virtual ethnography (Hine, 2000), cyberethnography (Teli, Pisanu and Hakken, 2007), netnography (Kozinets, 2009) and digital ethnography (Murthy, 2008), has entailed extensive reflection on what it is to be present in an online space and how ethnographers can plausibly represent themselves as developing a robust knowledge of those who inhabit them. Moving on from this notion of discrete online cultural space, and reflecting the move towards the comprehension of a complex, multiply embedded Internet, those conducting ethnographic studies of online spaces have increasingly found themselves drawn to explore complex connections between online and offline in an effort to understand the multiple ways in which the Internet is localized (Postill, 2008). Digital anthropology (Horst and Miller, 2013) explores online spaces in their own right and also navigates the broader cultural territory within which being online has become a way to experience being human. Hine (2015) advocates a multi-sited form of ethnographic practice which addresses the Internet as embedded, embodied and everyday. Postill and Pink (2012) discuss the 'messy' web which emerges from ethnographic attempts to track the online and offline activities of social movements.

There is, therefore, a rich heritage of methods that both celebrate and interrogate the specific qualities of digital forms of interaction and seek to situate them within a broader social context. Savage and Burrows (2007) feared that social science faced a crisis, as its traditional techniques were increasingly sidelined by the emergence of a wealth of data and the tools to interrogate it largely developed in commercial settings. Instead, it appears that social scientists have risen to the challenge, developing new techniques designed to celebrate the qualities of digital data (Rogers, 2013). Social science has to some extent embraced a new era of big data, although this has not occurred without critical examination. As Manovich (2011) discusses, it is important not to take digital data as transparently reflecting what people do and think. Marres and

Weltevrede (2013) reflect on the need to critically reflect on the assumptions inherent within data generated by tools developed for commercial purposes. Elsewhere, boyd and Crawford (2012) argue for the need to retain qualitative approaches alongside and in dialogue with the seductively large scale of analysis offered by big data. The status of digital methods in the social sciences remains a rich site for reflection on the wider goals and strategies of social scientists striving to keep pace with each new development.

Digital methods as mainstream methodology: The challenges

Social researchers adopting digital methods therefore face some epistemological dilemmas, concerning what the online phenomena that we study actually represent in social science terms and what assumptions we may make when adopting new tools and new research practices. In addition to these epistemological issues, social researchers in digital territories face a considerable array of practical challenges. Each technological development in the Internet, and each new platform, may require different techniques for data collection, new forms of data analysis and innovations in publication format. This pace of change may mean that social science can lag behind engaging with what has already become 'mainstream' in the commercial or public sphere. Moreover, the economic value of digital data means that access is increasingly controlled by corporations and can be expensive (see Bruns and Burgess, Chapter 2 in this volume). One challenge is that the technical proficiency to access and analyse data may require skills not routinely offered to social scientists as part of their methods training. Digital social research is the subject of specialist courses, conferences and journals, but does this create silos rather than embedding these methods and tools into broader disciplinary concerns? A key priority is to support the work of PhD students and early career researchers in this area, but how do we embed such efforts into 'mainstream' social science? Alternatively, innovation, collaboration and interdisciplinary work are undoubtedly crucial and could be fostered through carving out common ground across disciplinary boundaries. There is also much potential in working outside the mainstream at the 'interface' of digital media and digital social research in order to drive forward methodological development in challenging ways (Marres and Gerlitz, 2015). Yet, as Hewson (see Chapter 13 in this volume) considers, there are also considerable challenges in applying the ethical standards of critical social science to new and rapidly changing environments. The chapters in this collection attest the vital importance of adopting theoretically grounded and reflexive approaches to digital tools and methods, recognizing that their production and use are part of wider political, social and cultural processes (Lupton, 2015). We will return to these themes in our concluding chapter.

Outline of the book

This text is divided into four parts, each with three chapters organized around broad themes. We introduce each of these parts with an overview of the key methodological issues raised across the three chapters and some advice for researchers working in similar territory.

Part I considers not only quantitative and qualitative analysis of social media, addressing the contemporary concern with 'big data', but also the rich or 'thick data' available online. Chapter 2 by Bruns and Burgess seeks to highlight the challenges associated with access to data from social media stemming from Twitter as well as some of the tools that can be used for analysing Twitter data. Chapter 3 by Brooker, Barnett, Cribbin and Sharma examines the technical aspects of computational applications for capturing and handling social media data from Twitter that can impact the researcher's reading and understanding of the data. Lastly, Chapter 4 by Stirling provides an insight into her own first-hand experience as a researcher conducting a 'digital' ethnography with the help of the social networking website Facebook.

Part II provides examples of research that has sought to explore digital methods through comparing and combining these with 'offline' or traditional approaches. In Chapter 5, Hope describes research aimed at understanding the use of online support by parents of people with the rare condition Rett syndrome. This chapter provides an exemplar of an approach to exploring sample and data biases across online and offline modes of administering surveys and interviews, and it gives advice on potentially problematic issues when combining data from different modes in the same research project. In Chapter 6, Sajuria and Fábrega continue this theme of comparing different modes of data collection with their exploration of Twitter data. Their case study focuses on discussions surrounding the Chilean presidential election of 2013. Sajuria and Fábrega summarize the problematic status of Twitter as an apparent barometer of public opinion against the surveys more conventionally used to explore the issue. In Chapter 7, De Roock, Bhatt and Adams explore a complex, multi-modal setting which requires them not just to compare different forms of data but to work across them and explore the ways in which their participants do the same. The situation which they focus upon is an ethnography in a physical learning environment (classroom or lecture room), but within this site work goes on in both online and offline spaces. De Roock et al. share their experiences of capturing and analysing the multi-modal practices and events that occurred within the classrooms and the online spaces with which they connected.

Part III provides case studies that are innovative in their use of new, existing and combined methods. The chapters in this part question the nature of innovation and are concerned with what is left out in the drive to discover new methods. In Chapter 8, Estalella draws on a period of ethnographic observation at Medialab-Prado – a collaborative space for the creation of prototypes stemming from experimentation with software, hardware and raw materials. Chapter 9 by Hutchinson draws on research conducted on the online identity and embodiment of players of the massively multiplayer online role-playing game Final Fantasy XIV. The chapter focuses on photo elicitation, specifically the use of photos and screenshots of avatars in online asynchronous interviews with gamers, to argue that existing research methods should be extended and repurposed for use in the digital terrain rather than continually seeking new digital methods. Drawing on research with crafters and gardeners, Chapter 10 by Tedder highlights a gap in the digital methods literature with regard to skills, in particular how skills are transmitted and learned in digital environments. The exploration of skill transference in digital environments highlights components of this process that are often overlooked (haptic, visual, sensory, etc.).

Part IV develops some of the key challenges in mainstreaming digital methods, including debates in educational research; in research with young people; and the ethical issues that digital/social researchers face. In Chapter 11, Knox explores the under-theorized emerging research on massive open online courses (MOOCs) and suggests socio-material theory as key to understanding relationships between humans and technology as MOOC research moves into the mainstream. Chapter 12 by Bond and Agnew provides insights into and reflections on the use of digital methods to engage children and young people, drawing on creative methodologies and the use of virtual environments and social media not only to encourage participation but also to provide an online space for participants to share their views. Lastly, in Chapter 13, Hewson provides an extensive discussion on the key debates and approaches to ethical practices in online research and the growing consensus over a situational approach to digital/social ethics.

We bring the text to a close in Chapter 14, which emphasizes the blurring of boundaries when discussing digital social research. We consider the insights from the chapters in the collection regarding access and gatekeeping; disciplinary boundaries and internal constraints; analytics and tools; methods and concepts; and research ethics. Although we highlight the drivers of innovation, and stress the need to overcome barriers to the adoption of digital methods and digital tools, we also suggest that the binaries between mainstream and marginal, and between digital and conventional data, should not be too readily taken as real distinctions. Instead, we argue that as the digital becomes increasingly part of mainstream *social life*, mainstream *social science* will undoubtedly be required to engage with these contemporary forms of sociality.

References

Beer, D. (2013) *Popular Culture and New Media: The Politics of Circulation*. Basingstoke: Palgrave Macmillan.

Beer, D. and Burrows, R. (2007) 'Sociology and, of and in Web 2.0: Some initial considerations', *Sociological Research Online*, 12(5), www.socresonline.org.uk/12/5/17.html

Blank, G. and Reisdorf, B.C. (2012) 'The participatory web', *Information, Communication & Society*, 15(4), 537–54.

boyd, d. and K. Crawford (2012) 'Critical questions for big data: Provocations for a cultural, technological, and scholarly phenomenon', *Information, Communication & Society*, 15(5), 662–79.

Bruns, A. and Stieglitz, S. (2012) 'Quantitative approaches to comparing communication patterns on Twitter', *Journal of Technology in Human Services*, 30(3–4), 160–85.

Coomber, R. (1997) 'Using the Internet for survey research', *Sociological Research Online*, 2(2), www.socresonline.org.uk/2/2/2.

Dillman, D.A. (2007) *Mail and Internet Surveys: The Tailored Design Method (2007 Update with New Internet, Visual, and Mixed-Mode Guide)*. Hoboken, New Jersey: Wiley.

Fielding, N.G., Lee, R.M. and Blank, G. (2008) *The SAGE Handbook of Online Research Methods*. London: Sage.

Gartner (2013) 'Gartner survey finds 42 percent of IT leaders have invested in big data or plan to do so within a year', *Gartner: Press Release*, http://www.gartner.com/newsroom/id/2366515, date accessed 24 February 2015.

Herring, S.C. (2004) 'Computer-mediated discourse analysis: An approach to researching online behavior', in S.A. Barab, R. Kling and J.H. Gray (eds.) *Designing for Virtual Communities in the Service of Learning*. New York: Cambridge University Press, pp.338–76.

Herring, S.C. (2013) 'Discourse in Web 2.0: Familiar, reconfigured, and emergent', in D. Tannen and A. M. Tester (eds.) *Georgetown University Round Table on Languages and Linguistics Discourse 2.0: Language and new media*. Washington, DC: Georgetown University Press, pp.1–25.

Hine, C. (2000) *Virtual Ethnography*. London: Sage.

Hine, C. (2005a) 'Internet research and the sociology of cyber-social-scientific knowledge', *The Information Society*, 21(4), 239–48.

Hine, C. (ed.) (2005b) *Virtual Methods: Issues in Social Research on the Internet*. Oxford: Berg.

Hine, C. (2015) *Ethnography for the Internet: Embedded, Embodied and Everyday*. London: Bloomsbury Publishing.

Horst, H.A. and Miller, D. (2013) *Digital Anthropology*. London: Berg.

Illingworth, N. (2001) 'The Internet matters: Exploring the use of the Internet as a research tool', *Sociological Research Online* 6(2), www.socresonline.org.uk/6/2/illingworth.html

James, N. and Busher, H. (2009) *Online Interviewing*. London: Sage.

Jones, S.G. (ed.) (1995) *Cybersociety*. Newbury Park, CA: Sage.

Jones, S.G. (ed.) (1997) *Virtual Culture*. London: Sage.

Jones, S. (ed.) (1999) *Doing Internet Research: Critical Issues and Methods for Examining the Net*. Thousand Oaks, CA: Sage.

Kazmer, M.M. and Xie, B. (2008) 'Qualitative interviewing in Internet studies: Playing with the media, playing with the method', *Information, Communication & Society*, 11(2), 257–78.

Kemp, S. (2015) 'Digital, Social and Mobile Worldwide in 2015', *We Are Social*, http://wearesocial.net/blog/2015/01/digital-social-mobile-worldwide-2015/, date accessed 24 February 2015.

Kozinets, R.V. (2009) *Netnography: Doing Ethnographic Research Online*. London: Sage.

Lupton, D. (2015) *Digital Sociology*. Abingdon: Routledge.

Madge, C. and O'Connor, H. (2002) 'Online with the e-mums: Exploring the Internet as a medium for research', *Area*, 34, 92–102.

Mann, C. and Stewart, F. (2000) *Internet Communication and Qualitative Research: A Handbook for Researching Online*. London: Sage.

Manovich, L. (2011) 'Trending: The promises and the challenges of big social data', in M.K. Gold (ed.) *Debates in the Digital Humanities*. Minneapolis: University of Minnesota Press, pp.460–75.

Marres, N. and Gerlitz, C. (2015) 'Interface Methods: Renegotiating relations between digital social research, STS and sociology', *Sociological Review* (forthcoming). DOI: 10.1111/1467-954X.12314.

Marres, N. and Weltevrede, E. (2013) 'Scraping the social? Issues in live social research', *Journal of Cultural Economy*, 6(3), 313–35.

McCoyd, J.L.M. and Kerson, T.S. (2006) 'Conducting intensive interviews using email', *Qualitative Social Work*, 5(3), 389–406.

Murthy, D. (2008) 'Digital ethnography', *Sociology*, 42(5), 837–55.

Nicholas, D.B., Lach, L., King, G., Scott, M., Boydell, K., Sawatzky, B.J., Resiman, J., Schippel, E. and Young, N.L. (2010) 'Contrasting Internet and face-to-face focus groups for children with chronic health conditions: Outcomes and participant experiences', *International Journal of Qualitative Methods*, 9(1), 105–21.

O'Reilly, T. (2005) 'What is Web 2.0? Design patterns and Business Models for the next generation of Software', http://oreilly.com/web2/archive/what-is-web-20.html, date accessed 10 February 2011.

Orgad, S.S. (2005) *Storytelling Online: Talking Breast Cancer on the Internet*. New York: Peter Lang.

Oxford Internet Institute (2014) *The Oxford Internet Surveys*, http://oxis.oii.ox.ac
.uk, date accessed 9 June 2015.

Pew Research Center (2015) *Internet, Science and Tech*, http://www.pewinternet
.org, date accessed 9 June 2015.

Postill, J. (2008), Localizing the Internet beyond communities and networks', *New
Media & Society*, 10(3), 413–31.

Postill, J. and S. Pink (2012) 'Social media ethnography: The digital researcher
in a messy web', *Media International Australia Incorporating Culture and Policy:
Quarterly Journal of Media Research and Resources*, 145, 123–34.

Rogers, R. (2013) *Digital Methods*. Cambridge, MA: MIT Press.

Rogers, R. and N. Marres (2000) 'Landscaping climate change: A mapping technique for understanding science and technology debates on the World Wide
Web', *Public Understanding of Science*, 9(2), 141–63.

Salmons, J. (2009) *Online Interviews in Real Time*. Thousand Oaks, CA: Sage.

Salmons, J. (2011) *Cases in Online Interview Research*. Thousand Oaks, CA: Sage.

Savage, M. and Burrows, R. (2007) 'The coming crisis of empirical sociology',
Sociology, 41(5), 885–99.

Seale, C., Charteris-Black, J., MacFarlane, A. and McPherson, A. (2010) 'Interviews and Internet forums: A comparison of two sources of qualitative data',
Qualitative Health Research, 20(5), 595–606.

Seale, C., Ziebland, S. and Charteris-Black, J. (2006) 'Gender, cancer experience
and Internet use: A comparative keyword analysis of interviews and online
cancer support groups', *Social Science & Medicine*, 62(10), 2577–90.

Teli, M., Pisanu, F. and Hakken, D. (2007) 'The Internet as a Library-
of-People: For a Cyberethnography of Online Groups', *Forum Qualitative
Sozialforschung/Forum: Qualitative Social Research*, 8(3), http://www.qualitative
-research.net/index.php/fqs/article/view/283.

Thelwall, M. (2004) *Link Analysis: An Information Science Approach*. Amsterdam:
Elsevier.

Thelwall, M. (2009) *Introduction to Webometrics: Quantitative Web Research for the
Social Sciences*. San Rafael, CA: Morgan and Claypool.

Van Dijck, J. (2013) *The Culture of Connectivity: A Critical History of Social Media*.
New York: Oxford University Press.

Wellman, B. and Haythornthwaite, C. (eds.) (2002) *The Internet in Everyday Life*.
Oxford: Blackwell.

World Internet Project (n.d.) *World Internet Project*, http://www.world
internetproject.net, date accessed 9 June 2015.

Part I
Big Data, Thick Data: Social Media Analysis

Introduction to Part I

The problem: What are the challenges of social media research?

As time progresses, so does the way in which individuals communicate with one another, where they interact with others and the means with which they do so. It seems something of an understatement to note how central social media are to these developments. As we discussed in Chapter 1, a significant number of individuals across the world are using and engaging with social media on a daily basis, and often throughout the day as a result of the advances in mobile solutions. Bruns and Burgess (Chapter 2) suggest that social media are 'truly public', with billions of people using these accounts to share and communicate with a global network.

Following breaking news, for instance a terrorist attack, hundreds of thousands of individuals, groups and organizations flock to social media websites such as YouTube, Flickr and Twitter to gain further information of an unfolding event and to view latest images from the scene. For those on the ground of an incident, social media provides a means of sharing insights with others – as was the case with the 2014 Boston Marathon bombings. This is not restricted to crises; we are seeing extensive uses of social media for a vast range of purposes, including teaching, recruitment, event planning, selling and day-to-day social interactions (to name only a few).

For the social sciences, such a development has significant implications for research activities and the nature of the data social data in particular. As we noted in the Introduction, a key development in digital social science is the new era of social media 'big data'. To put the volume of big data into perspective, public opinion polls run by the European Commission in the form of large-scale surveys involve the gathering of data from 27,000 respondents, whereas tweets produced during Hurricane Sandy in 2012 in the United States numbered more than 20 million (Meier, 2013). Big data are also high-velocity data, that is, the speed with which they are produced. For example, over 2,000 tweets per second were generated following the 2011 earthquake and tsunami in Japan (Meier, 2013). Data are not just restricted to large amounts, but these are also of considerable variety; with social media sites such as Twitter, data may be in the form of text, images, video and meta-data (i.e. data that contain identifying material such as who it was posted by, the time and location it was posted). With such a vast amount of data to be studied for such varied purposes, what are the various challenges and solutions that digital social scientists face?

Considerations for social scientists engagement with big 'social' data vary greatly: from battling the contested area of digital research ethics to more practical considerations concerning skills and tools for capturing, analysing and visualizing data. The present volume aims to provide some insights into how researchers have managed these challenges, providing some key lessons for others.

Big data, thick data: Social media analysis

Part I begins with an insightful contribution by Axel Bruns and Jean Burgess who seek to highlight the increasingly precarious nature of Twitter research. Against the backdrop of engaging with social media data within the disciplines of journalism, media, communication and cultural studies, their chapter provides the reader with an insight into the challenges associated with access to this big data. Focus is placed on interactions with commercial entities, including the Twitter Application Programming Interface (API) that provide researchers with access to public data but which is increasingly coming at a cost. They also provide some useful guidance on some of the tools and methods available for analysing Twitter data.

Chapter 3 by Phillip Brooker, Julie Barnett, Timothy Cribbin and Sanjay Sharma examines how the technical aspects of computational applications for capturing and handling social media data can impact researchers' reading and understanding of the data. Their examination of this challenge is also focused on data stemming from Twitter.

Taking a critical stance to the study of Twitter data, they emphasize that researchers need to recognize the limits of such data in terms of what can be studied and surmised. They focus on two practical issues: first, the limits of the Twitter API and its impact on data gathering and, second, spatial mapping algorithms in Twitter data visualization. Through the use of illustrative examples, their study promotes the approach of 'assemblage', a way of conducting research that 'draws together various social and technical (and other) factors into a unified research process'.

Lastly, Chapter 4 by Eve Stirling provides an insight into the first-hand experience of conducting an ethnography situated in both digital and physical environments. The study explored the everyday use of Facebook by first-year undergraduate students in their transition to university. The self-reflection by Stirling provides the reader with an overview of the various perspectives on online ethnography and then proceeds to providing a discussion of key elements of her multi-sited study, including participant observation, field notes, ethical considerations and the challenge of moving away from the field. Here, social media provides 'thick', rich data.

Combined, these chapters provide the reader with some key lessons regarding the study of social media within the social sciences:

- Prior to conducting a study on social media, it is necessary to consider how you will access the data. Consider what restraints are there, what costs, what software and skills are required. Such an acknowledgement suggests a need for enhanced skills in the computational component associated with social media analytics.
- Investigate how to analyse social media data. Consider the tools that may assist you in this domain, including data-gathering techniques and visualization software.
- Recognize and acknowledge the limitations associated with big data analytics in social media.
- Research involving social media analysis still requires attention to ethics; be sure to conduct a thorough ethical assessment of your study and complete any required ethical reviews.
- In qualitative work, consider your 'field site'. If you are studying behaviour, you may wish to consider multiple field sites involving both the digital realm and the non-digital world that people occupy (and bear in mind that the division between the two is not necessarily clear).

• Consider how you will record your insights and notes in studies involving 'digital' participant observation.

References

Meier, P. (2013) 'What is big "Crisis" data?', *iRevolution*, http://irevolution.net /2013/06/27/what-is-big-crisis-data/, date accessed 19 February 2015.

2
Methodological Innovation in Precarious Spaces: The Case of Twitter

Axel Bruns and Jean Burgess

Introduction: Social media analytics and the politics of data access

The contemporary social media moment can be understood in terms of a 'platform paradigm' (Burgess, 2014) – one in which the private, interpersonal and public communication of a significant majority of users is being mediated via a small number of large proprietary platforms like Facebook and Twitter, and those platforms are redefining how such communication can be monetized and analysed. In this current conjuncture, the data generated either directly or indirectly by user practices and interactions are at the centre of such platforms' business models – user data analytics are used to power advertising and personalize newsfeeds, and user-created social media content is in itself a commodity to be mined commercially for business insights, public relations crisis aversion and even stock market prediction. Alongside such commercially motivated developments, the social and behavioural sciences as well as the digital humanities have been developing ever more sophisticated and large-scale methods for analysing social media data, often motivated by different questions but relying on similar tools to access and analyse data as the commercial players, and thereby operating in ways that entangle scientific practice with the evolving markets in user data. To complicate matters, as the power and uses of social data analytics have grown, so too has the social anxiety around surveillance, exploitation and user agency.

While such multiple interests intersect, compete and conflict in and around the issue of access to and use of social media data (Puschmann and Burgess, 2014), here we are most interested in those uses which are explicitly framed in terms of *research*, and therefore for the purposes of clarity in this chapter, we concentrate on key differences between commercial, market-oriented research and scholarly, scientific research. Commercial research is frequently centred around three main themes: approaches which enable platform providers themselves to better understand their users and ensure that further technological enhancements meet their needs and interests; approaches which allow the advertisers and marketers that contribute to the platforms' revenues to more effectively target specific interest groups within the overall user base; and approaches which enable corporate players and other institutional actors to understand and improve the ways their customers are engaging with them as a brand or as a company. Scientific research using social media data has expanded beyond the early interests of computer and information scientists on the one hand and pockets of the humanities and social sciences on the other to include a wide range of social, behavioural and even physical science disciplines interested in how 'naturally' occurring social interaction data can be mined to understand the dynamics of self-organizing systems, information diffusion and social influence. In the field of communication, large-scale, data-driven social media research tends to be motivated by questions about the systemic communicative processes which are evident within a large and diverse user population and interested in investigating how such processes respond to specific short-term events within and beyond the social media platform itself. There are also considerable points of connection between scientific and commercial research interests, of course, and in spite of potentially substantial differences in the ethical and organizational frameworks which govern their research and the very real conflicts that these differences can produce – as the Facebook 'emotional contagion' controversy demonstrates (Kramer et al., 2014; also see Hewson, this volume) – fruitful collaborations are possible.

Regardless of the commercial or scientific orientation of individual research projects, the fundamental point must also be made that social media research as such is genuinely important for a variety of reasons. Social media have now become a major form of public communication in their own right. Indeed, they are one of the few truly *public* forms of communication currently available, in the sense that they enable billions around the world to publicly express their thoughts, ideas, interests, ambitions, likes and dislikes within a shared global communications environment. This does not mean that all such voices are equally audible, of course, but it is precisely the dynamics of how specific issues, themes and memes emerge to prominence from this globally distributed conversation, and what impact they may come to have well beyond individual social media platforms themselves, that has become a key object of study for social media researchers across fields from political through crisis to enthusiast and everyday communication.

Increasingly central to both the commercial and scientific research agendas, therefore, has been the development of social media analytics methodologies which are able to draw on large and potentially real-time datasets that describe the activities (or at least those activities which are publicly visible to other participants) of a large number of social media users. The current generation of social media platforms is distinct from its predecessors in part due to its greater focus on the multi-platform use and embeddability of its content, enabling users to use a range of official and third-party tools to access their social media feeds across different devices and operating systems as well as allowing various parties to embed relevant social media feeds and functionality within websites, smartphone and tablet applications (apps), as well as other contexts. Such functionality is supported by modern social media plat-forms chiefly through the provision of a unified and well-documented API: an interface which constitutes an access point that, on request, provides structured data in a standard format which does not prescribe the context or form in which such data are made available to the end user. While such APIs are used mainly by popular social media end-user clients from the official Facebook and Twitter apps to Tweetdeck and Hootsuite, they also provide an exceptionally useful point of access to social media data for researchers. Using APIs it becomes possible to retrieve the public profile information and public updates posted by specific users or containing given keywords or hashtags, for example; processed effectively, such data become the raw material for social media analytics.

At the most basic level, analytics approaches which draw on the APIs provided by leading social media platforms are necessarily limited by the range and amount of data available through APIs. APIs rarely provide unrestricted access to the totality of all data about users and their activi-ties that may be available internally; for example, data about private (i.e. non-public) messages exchanged between individual users are available generally only to these users themselves and to the API clients to which they have provided their authorization codes. Such restrictions result in considerable differences in what social media analytics approaches are able to investigate for different social media platforms, then: on Facebook, for example, few posts (except for posts and comments on public pages and posts on user profiles whose visibility level has been explicitly set to 'public') are truly globally public, while a majority is visible only to the sender's 'friends' or 'friends of friends'. Unless it has been authenticated by a user within such a friendship circle, such semi-private posts will remain invisible to a tool gathering social media data. Twitter, on the other hand, uses considerably more limited privacy settings: its accounts are either 'public' (meaning that all of their tweets are globally public and visible even to non-registered visitors to twitter.com) or 'protected' (tweets are visible only to followers of the account whom the user has explicitly approved). Since only a small and shrinking minority of Twitter accounts are set to be 'protected' in this way, the activity data potentially available through the Twitter API therefore constitutes a considerably more comprehensive reflection of the totality of Twitter activity than is the case for Facebook, where a dataset of globally public posts would contain only an unpredictable (and certainly unrepresentative) mixture of deliberately and accidentally 'public' messages.

In spite of Twitter's smaller global user base – as of July 2014, it claimed 271 million 'monthly active users' (Twitter Inc., 2014), compared to Facebook's 1.23 billion (PR Newswire, 2014) – social media analytics methodologies for Twitter, especially where they draw on large datasets tracking the activities of users, are therefore arguably more developed than those for Facebook. These methodologies have begun to generate new and important insights not only into how Twitter itself functions as a social media platform, but also into how the patterns of user activity found here can be seen as exemplary for the adoption, adaptation and use of new digital communications technologies more generally.

But Twitter's APIs are far from neutral and transparent tools. Rather, APIs are an essential means for the platform provider to encourage some uses of user data and to regulate or even prohibit others – affecting the research agenda and business plans of all those who would make use of user data. Second, in addition to constraining and enabling particular *kinds* of data use, the Twitter APIs have changed over time as the business imperatives of the platform have changed, often in ways that are misaligned with third-party developers and other actors in the Twitter 'ecosystem'. Twitter's APIs therefore mediate between, and are the site of friction between, competing uses and understandings of Twitter as a platform and changes to how they work have been accompanied by controversy and debate; as Taina Bucher has argued in work that reports on interviews with third-party developers working with Twitter data, APIs are 'objects of intense feeling' (Bucher, 2013, n.p.).

As data-driven Twitter research began to grow in scope and in the stakes attached to it, such shifts have also become increasingly politicized and materially significant for the scientific community. Academic researchers have been no less frustrated and entangled with the politics of these APIs, which sit alongside other practical and ethical challenges in doing data-driven social media research (see Lomborg and Bechmann, 2014, for an excellent overview).

Consequently, this chapter focuses substantively on the changing affordances of Twitter data, as well as the tools and methods for analysing it, with reference to questions of methodological advancement in our core disciplines of journalism, media, communication and cultural studies. But at the same time, this story can reveal as much about the political economy of the new digital media environment as it does about the pragmatics of scientific research in this environment. This chapter contributes to such an understanding via a short history of the uses of Twitter data for media, communication and cultural research; the methodological innovation that has taken place over this time; and the stakeholder relationships and socio-technical arrangements that have both supported and constrained such work.

Phase one: Building the Twitter ecosystem

Although some early Twitter research drew on more primitive methods for gathering data from the platform – such as taking regular screenshots or using generic HTML scrapers to regularly archive the Twitter feeds of selected users – the considerably greater utility of instead connecting to the API to gather data in a standardized and reliable format soon led researchers to pursue that avenue. At first, the tools used to gather data from the API were mainly developed ad hoc and in house at various research institutions; for the most part, they focused initially on gathering the tweets posted by selected accounts, or containing specific keywords or hashtags. (Our own contributions to this effort, building on open-source technologies, are gathered in Bruns and Burgess (2011c), for example.)

The Twitter API imposes a number of restrictions on its users, relating to the number of users and search terms which may be tracked through a single API request and to the volume of data which is returned. At the time of writing, for example, the open API only returns up to 1 per cent of the total current volume of tweets being posted. This means that if, this hour, Twitter users around the world were posting 1 million tweets in total, a keyword search for 'twitter' would return only up to 10,000 tweets during that hour, even if more tweets had contained the term 'twitter'. The API will also notify its client about how many tweets had been missed, however. In a variety of contexts, such restrictions pose significant complications: research which tracks common keywords such as 'flood' or 'earthquake' to extract early indicators of impending natural disasters would be severely limited by the throttling of its data access at 1 per cent, for example, especially at times when one or more severe disasters coincide. However, current literature which studies the uses of social media in crisis communication by drawing on Twitter datasets largely omits any discussion of this potentially crucial limitation.

Both to address such issues and to more generally encourage the development of innovative Twitter analytics models, Twitter Inc. therefore instituted an API whitelisting system for developers and researchers. By contacting Twitter support staff, interested third parties could request a lifting of API access restrictions for the data-gathering tools they developed. With whitelisted access made available ad hoc and relatively speedily, this supported the emergence of a number of popular Twitter clients for professional end-users (such as TweetDeck or Hootsuite), as well as the development of a range of research initiatives which aimed to work with larger Twitter datasets than were commonly available to API users. Twitter Inc. itself recognized the importance of this growing 'ecosystem' of developers and tools which drew on and enhanced the central platform; indeed, the research outcomes enabled by this early, explorative phase of Twitter analytics also contributed substantially to demonstrating the importance of Twitter as a platform for public communication in contexts ranging from second-screen television viewing (see e.g. Highfield et al., 2013 on Twitter and the Eurovision Song Contest) to political activism (see e.g. Papacharissi and de Fatima Oliviera on Twitter in the Egyptian uprising, 2013), and this served to establish Twitter as one of the most important global social media platforms.

Finally, this early phase of research innovation also resulted in a first trend towards methodological consolidation, as several leading tools for gathering Twitter data emerged. These included stand-alone tools such as 140kit and TwapperKeeper as well as the Google Spreadsheets extension TAGS (see Gaffney and Puschmann, 2014). The growing use of such publicly available tools in preference to in-house solutions meant that the datasets gathered by different researchers and teams were now more immediately comparable, and this enabled the development of a range of standard analytical tools and metrics building on common data formats (Bruns and Stieglitz, 2013). This also considerably enhanced the level of scholarly rigour in social media analytics by enabling researchers to replicate and test each other's methodological frameworks. The availability of such tools as free hosted services, or as software released under open source licences, also contributed significantly to such methodological innovation and evaluation: the open availability and extensibility of the key early research tools instilled a strong 'open science' ethos in the international Twitter research community which gathered around these tools and methods.

The common focus of many of these emerging tools on enabling, in the first place, the tracking of set keywords and – especially – hashtags also resulted in the emergence of an increasingly dominant subset of Twitter analytics which is best summarized under the title of 'hashtag studies': research initiatives which sought to capture a comprehensive set of tweets containing prominent hashtags relating to specific themes and events, from natural disasters (e.g. #terremotochile; Mendoza et al., 2010) to national elections (e.g. #ausvotes; Bruns and Burgess, 2011a). Such hashtag studies built on the tendency of Twitter users to self-select some of their tweets as relevant to specific topics by including a topical hashtag in the tweet text, and these generated considerable new insights into the self-organizing nature of ad hoc communities on Twitter (Bruns and Burgess, 2011b). However, they also captured only a very specific range of user practices taking place especially around acute events, while being unable to meaningfully investigate the arguably more commonplace practices of non-hashtagged everyday and phatic communication on Twitter. Following the distinctions proposed in Bruns and Moe (2014), such hashtag studies focus largely on the macro level of Twitter communication which builds on hashtags, while ignoring the meso level (everyday interaction with one's followers) and the micro level (public conversations using @replies).

The early popularity of hashtag studies also resulted from the fact that the availability of tools such as TwapperKeeper in the form of a web-based service enabled even researchers with minimal technical skills to track and gather sizeable datasets of all tweets containing specified hashtags (and keywords), limited only by the API restrictions imposed by Twitter Inc. TwapperKeeper simply required researchers to enter their keywords and provided a web interface to download the resultant datasets in user-friendly Excel or comma-separated values formats. Further, such datasets – once gathered – were made available to all users of the site, and TwapperKeeper.com therefore became a de facto clearinghouse for Twitter archives.

However, as TwapperKeeper's popularity and use increased, Twitter Inc. gradually developed the view that its web-based service – and especially its provision of public archives of hashtag and keyword datasets – contravened the Terms of Service of the Twitter API, which prohibited the public sharing of API-derived data in programmatic form. In early 2011, Twitter Inc. ordered TwapperKeeper.com to cease its public service (O'Brien, 2011); subsequently, some of TwapperKeeper's archival functionality was incorporated into third-party client application Hootsuite, while the source code for a DIY version of TwapperKeeper, yourTwapperKeeper, was made available publicly by developer John O'Brien III under an open-source licence. Arguably, this moment is emblematic for a more fundamental and significant shift in Twitter Inc.'s relationship with the developer and researcher community and ecosystem which had developed around its platform, and this marks the beginning of a second, considerably more precarious phase for innovation in Twitter analytics.

Phase two: Precarious access as demand for 'big data' grows

Twitter Inc.'s increasingly restrictive interpretation of the APIs Terms of Service, its attendant discontinuation of whitelisting practices and overall changes to API functionality and access limitations since 2011 constituted a disruption of the established equilibrium between platform provider and third-party developers and researchers that, while undermining many existing research methods and approaches for Twitter analytics, also resulted in considerable new innovation and development. During the first phase of methodological innovation around Twitter, developers and researchers had relied at least implicitly on Twitter Inc.'s continued good will and support towards them, and even – as in the case of TwapperKeeper and the wider whitelisting regime – on a willingness on part of the platform provider to bend its own rules and overlook what could be considered to be breaches of its API rules. As Twitter Inc. began to withdraw its support for the third-party ecosystem which had played a substantial role in bringing Twitter to a position of global prominence, developers scrambled to revise their methods and tools in a way that either would not – or at least not obviously – put them in conflict with the company's new, stricter rules, or would devolve responsibility for any transgressions from the developers to the end-users of their data gathering and processing tools.

This shift can be observed in the transition from TwapperKeeper to yourTwapperKeeper. While the former offered data-gathering functionality as a web-based service, the latter simply provided an open-source version of TwapperKeeper functionality as a package which interested and sufficiently skilled researchers could install on their own servers and could use and even modify as required for their specific purposes. Unless steps are taken to specifically prevent such access, yourTwapperKeeper installations continue to make their archives of gathered data available for download to anybody – not just to the researchers who entered the search terms to be tracked. This breach of the API's Terms of Service is a matter for the administrators of each individual yourTwapperKeeper server instance, not for YTK's developers, and Twitter Inc. would need to pursue these administrators individually if it aimed to comprehensively shut down any unauthorized sharing of API-derived Twitter datasets; to date, it has not attempted to do so. At the same time, the TwapperKeeper experience and the implicit threat of cease-and-desist requests from Twitter Inc. have generally led researchers and institutions operating yourTwapperKeeper instances and similar tools to refrain from publicly advertising such services and sharing their datasets: Twitter Inc.'s very public shutdown of TwapperKeeper.com in March 2011 can be said to have had a notable chilling effect on the sharing of data in the international social media researchers' community.

Conversely, the TwapperKeeper shutdown has led that community to increase its efforts to develop better tools for tracking, gathering, processing and analysing social media data at large scale. In addition to yourTwapperKeeper and its derivatives, such tools also include projects such as the Twitter Capture and Analysis Toolset (TCAT), developed by the University of Amsterdam's Digital Methods Initiative (DMI, 2014), which similarly requires users to install their own TCAT instance on a server they administer. Advancing beyond the mere tweet archiving functionality provided by YTK, TCAT also offers a range of built-in analytics functions which provide first quality control and quantitative insights into the data being gathered. Such new advances in the development of more powerful and complex, yet still Terms of Service-compatible, Twitter research tools also create new divides within the established social media researchers' community, however. They separate researchers and teams who possess the necessary technical expertise to install and operate server-side solutions for data gathering and analysis (now crucially including computer science and related skills) from those who were able to work with the datasets provided by the previous generation of web-based data-gathering services but find themselves unable to operate their own servers. As the capabilities and also the complexity of server-side tools grow, this presents a very tangible risk of dividing researchers into 'big data' haves and have-nots.

Such divisions are also emerging, on a much larger scale, between unfunded and publicly funded scientific research initiatives using open-source tools connecting to the standard Twitter API on the one hand and commercial research projects and companies buying social media data at more substantial volumes from third-party suppliers on the other. Twitter Inc.'s agenda in tightening open access restrictions to the public API from 2011 onwards was evidently also aiming to push those API clients who could afford it to make use of available third-party services such as Gnip and DataSift, which had been accredited by Twitter Inc. as commercial data resellers. (Gnip itself has since become a wholly owned subsidiary of Twitter Inc. itself.) Using such services, it is possible to buy access to tweets in high-volume keyword feeds or from large user populations, or even to comprehensive global Twitter feeds up to and including the full 'firehose' of all tweets, without the limitations in the depth or speed of access imposed by the public API – however, this will commonly generate costs in the tens of thousands of dollars for large one-off data purchases and even higher cumulative costs for longer-term data subscriptions. Additionally, DataSift provides access to historical data, which is not available from the API. However, the volume prices quoted by resellers such as Gnip and DataSift render such services unaffordable for researchers without considerable corporate, institutional or grant funding. To date, only a small number of scientific research initiatives are known to have bought data from these providers, which otherwise mainly service commercial market research services. The vast majority of researchers at public research institutions continue to draw on the public API service and thus remain at the mercy of Twitter Inc.'s decisions about API functionality, access limitations and Terms of Service.

Several statements by Twitter Inc. that acknowledge the importance of Twitter data as an unprecedented record of public communication activities, as well as of independent scientific research as shedding new light on the user practices contained in such data, may be seen as seeking to address this troubling divide between data-rich commercial marketing research and data-poor publicly funded research. In 2010, the company gifted a complete and continuously updated archive of all tweets ever sent to the US Library of Congress, which the Library has subsequently sought to make available to selected researchers. In 2013, it instituted a competition for 'Twitter Data Grants' which are set to provide direct access to Twitter data at high volume. However, neither of these initiatives have so far been able to meaningfully address the lack of affordable large-scale access to Twitter data for publicly funded scientific research. Access to the Library of Congress's comprehensive dataset has been stalled both by the technical challenges of making searchable an archive of billions of individual messages and by difficult negotiations with Twitter Inc. over the conditions of access to the archive, and only in 2013 has the Library finally offered access to its Twitter archive to the three winners of its annual Kluge Fellowship in Digital Studies (Library of Congress, n.d.). Similarly, in 2014 Twitter Inc. selected only six winners from more than 1,300 applicants in the inaugural round of its Data Grants competition (Kirkorian, 2014). Even taken together, these nine grants cannot but fail to address the lack of access to 'big data' on Twitter activities now experienced by scientific social media research.

It must be noted at this point that scientific research into social media uses and practices is not always automatically enhanced and improved by access to larger datasets; as boyd and Crawford (2012) have shown, 'big data' does not always mean 'better data', and important social media research is being done by using comparatively small but rich datasets on social media activities which were gathered through means other than by requesting data from the APIs of Twitter itself or of third-party data resellers. However, for the purposes of this chapter we are concerned specifically with social media analytics as a subset of a wider and more diverse range of social media research methodologies, and this area of social media research is defined largely by its predominantly quantitative approach to working with social media data. Such quantitative analytics also remain possible for smaller datasets, of course – but to put even such analyses of smaller datasets into context (e.g. to benchmark Twitter activities around acute events against longer-term baselines), 'big data' on social media usage patterns across larger user populations and long-term timeframes are indispensable. The development of social media analytics as a serious scientific field crucially depends on researchers' access to 'big data' on the use of social media platforms such as Twitter.

Phase three: Crash or crash through?

In the absence of affordable, or even of available, options for accessing 'big data' on public communication using social media platforms such as Twitter, there is anecdotal evidence that a growing number of researchers are prepared to explore the very limits of the Twitter API, and in doing so also of Twitter Inc.'s interest in strictly enforcing its Terms of Service. We have already seen that even during the earlier, comparatively permissive phases of the development of social media analytics using Twitter data, researchers were frequently sharing their datasets with each other – even if to do so was likely to constitute a breach of the Terms of Service under which API data were provided. In this context, Twitter Inc.'s rules for data provision come into direct conflict with standard scientific practice: first, the open publication of raw datasets is generally encouraged as such datasets are often indispensable for an independent verification of a researcher's findings by their peers; second, public funding bodies such as the Australian Research Council or the UK Arts and Humanities Research Council are increasingly requiring the data and results generated by the projects they fund to be made available publicly under open access models. While exceptions to such rules are commonly made for datasets which are commercial in confidence or otherwise restricted from publication, an argument for such restrictions is difficult to sustain in the case of Twitter datasets retrieved from a public API and containing public messages which – by Twitter Inc.'s own Terms of Service (Twitter Inc., 2012) – remain copyrighted to their original senders. At least in principle then, the further distribution among researchers of datasets containing tweets should put those researches in potential conflict mainly with those Twitter users, not with Twitter Inc.

While such arguments, as well as the overall applicability and force of Twitter's Terms of Service (both for Twitter overall and for the API in particular) in relation to user and researcher rights and obligations, has yet to be tested in full and across various national jurisdictions, it is therefore at least understandable that many researchers appear prepared to bend the API Terms of Service by sharing datasets at least privately, in order to meet their obligations to their scientific peers and public funding bodies. Especially for Twitter researchers working in project teams (e.g. in the context of formal, funded research projects) rather than as sole operators, such sharing is ultimately inevitable, as they must necessarily develop a shared repository of the data gathered in pursuit of the team's research agenda. Even such intra-team sharing – for example, by establishing a yourTwapperKeeper or TCAT server utilized by members of the research team – may already be seen as contravening the API Terms of Service's prohibitions against 'exporting Twitter content to a datastore as a service or other cloud based service' (Twitter Inc., 2013).

It is unlikely that Twitter Inc. would seek to enforce such a narrow interpretation of its rules, but this in turn creates further confusion for researchers. If intra-team sharing of datasets is permissible at least implicitly, then – given the vagaries of what constitutes a research team – where are the limits to such sharing? If, for instance, a small project team funded for a brief period of time is allowed to operate a TCAT server and share its datasets among the team members, could that permission be extended to the members of a larger, indefinitely continuing research group, centre, or institute, or even to an entire university? If multiple universities formed a consortium collaborating on joint social media research projects, could their datasets be shared across all member institutions? In the absence of clear guidance from Twitter Inc. on such matters, as well as of independent legal advice on the validity of such guidance within their home jurisdiction, it is likely that many researchers will continue to be prepared to push the envelope further, at least until Twitter Inc. reprimands them for their actions.

Similar 'crash or crash through' approaches may emerge at a more purely technical level. At present, Twitter's public API is throttled in a number of aspects, as we have already noted. In addition to the fundamental restriction that no client connecting to the streaming API (which provides real-time Twitter activity data) is able to retrieve more than 1 per cent of the total current volume of Twitter activity, other API calls (e.g. to the search API, which delivers recent tweets matching specific criteria, or to the user API, which provides information on public user profiles) are throttled by accepting only a limited number of calls from the same client in each 15-minute window, as well as by delivering large results lists in a paged format that requires multiple API calls. Such limits do not entirely disable, but certainly significantly slow the retrieval of large datasets through such API calls – and it is again likely that such throttling is designed to promote the use of commercial data reselling services instead of the public API.

Provided that sufficient development expertise is available, it is obvious that such per-client access limits can be circumvented comparatively easily by substantially parallelizing API calls. Under this model, as soon as one API client reaches the access limit for the current 15-minute window, another takes over until the next window begins. Here, too, it appears that the extent to which such parallelization is in explicit breach of the API Terms of Service has yet to be tested, especially as few researchers exploring such approaches are likely to publicly advertise this fact. Twitter Inc.'s adjustments to and variable enforcement of its Terms of Service over recent years have created substantial levels of mistrust between the company itself and the social media research community that investigates how its platform is being used for public communication. This has resulted in a chilling effect which has led some cutting-edge methodological innovation to operate with considerable

secrecy and under precarious conditions. This perceived need to operate more clandestinely has also severely undermined the earlier 'open
science' ethos of the Twitter research community, of course – detailed
discussions of such advanced methods are unlikely to take place in
public now, for fear of reprisals from Twitter Inc.

Conclusion: Beyond precarity

The current trajectory of social media analytics – and of Twitter analytics
in particular – as we have described it here, is largely untenable. Twitter
Inc.'s interventions in the developer ecosystem, made largely by adjust-
ing its API Terms of Service and their enforcement, as well as by
throttling the functionality of the public API, have resulted in a divide
between private market research institutions able to afford the commercial data access fees charged by third-party resellers and public,
scientific research initiatives forced to make do with the public Twitter
API. Internally, this latter group is further divided according to scientific researchers' ability to use existing or develop new server-side
data-gathering and analysis tools, as well as their preparedness to bend
the API rules and limitations in order to access the large datasets required
to develop more comprehensive social media analytics.

  Faced with such challenges, it is tempting to suggest that researchers
would be better advised to divert their energy to a more fertile object
of investigation than Twitter has now become, but – while some
researchers may have indeed done so – this too is an unsatisfactory
option. First, the widespread adoption of Twitter as a tool for public communication and debate across a range of fields (from political
debate through crisis communication to everyday sociality) means that
it is now an important medium whose role across these fields must
be researched in detail. In the field of crisis communication alone, for
example, it is crucial that researchers investigate how Twitter is used
to disseminate information during acute events and how emergency
management organizations may engage with and enhance such processes. Second, given that importance, the conduct of such research
cannot be left to commercial market research institutions alone, most of
which would pursue only a very limited range of research questions that
are likely to generate an immediate commercial return on investment.
Rather, what is needed in addition to such instrumental and applied
research is the pursuit of the much more fundamental methodological
and research agendas which will ultimately come to inform such applied
research.

If it is important that fundamental scientific research in the field of social media analytics be conducted, and that such research include Twitter as an especially important platform for public communication, the current precarity of scientific research into Twitter and its uses must be addressed as a matter of priority. This is likely to require several concurrent initiatives: first, researchers' home institutions and funding bodies must be prepared to redress the balance between Twitter Inc.'s commercial agenda on the one hand and the requirements of rigorous scientific engagement with Twitter as a space for public communication on the other. Where necessary, this may have to include a testing of the applicability and legality of the API Terms of Service within relevant jurisdictions. Second, there is a need to articulate more clearly and forcefully to Twitter Inc. the value of the scientific research into the uses of its platform which has been and is being conducted. While such research has been and must be undertaken without predetermining an outcome, it is evident that most of the findings to date have demonstrated the substantial public value of Twitter as a new and largely open-access medium, and such findings have contributed significantly to shifting public perceptions of the platform from being for solipsistic 'what I had for lunch' statements to supporting meaningful engagement across many contexts at a personal as well as professional level: as Rogers (2014) has demonstrated, scientific research has contributed to and even substantially led the 'debanalization' of Twitter. Third, there is a clear and urgent need to develop transparent and mutually beneficial collaborations between scientific and commercial researchers and their home institutions in order to facilitate a continuous conversation about research methodologies, ethics and results, to enable effective and accountable processes of researcher training and knowledge transfer and to ensure the rigorous validation of commercially funded and supported research against scientific criteria. To date, there are a small number of corporate-hosted research labs (including Microsoft Research and Intel Labs) which conduct social media research at scientific standards, and partner with universities and other recognized scientific organizations, without pursuing an inherent corporate agenda. Such industry support for genuine scientific research must be broadened further, especially at a time of limited public funding for scholarly research.

In future, by contrast, if meaningful scientific enquiry into the uses of Twitter is further marginalized in favour of commercially motivated studies by Twitter Inc.'s policies of data access, there is a real risk that the platform may be rebanalized by commercial studies that amount to little more than counts of which celebrity has attracted the most followers or which brands have generated the greatest number of retweets. Similarly, if the capability to conduct 'big data' social media research at scientific levels of accountability and rigour is concentrated in only a handful of corporate-sponsored research labs, there is a significant danger that this concentration and contraction of scholarly social media research threatens the equity of access to research methods and limits the breadth and depth of scientific enquiry and methodological innovation in this important emerging field of research. Such developments are no more in the interests of Twitter Inc. itself than they are in the interest of the scientific research community which has established and continues to develop the fledgling field of social media analytics. The research community itself can fight to avert such developments, but only Twitter Inc. is able to stop them, by reconsidering the frameworks which govern how it provides large-scale data access to scientific researchers.

References

boyd, d. and Crawford, K. (2012) 'Critical questions for big data: Provocations for a cultural, technological, and scholarly phenomenon', *Information, Communication & Society*, 15(5), 662–79.

Bruns, A. and Burgess, J. (2011a) '#ausvotes: How Twitter covered the 2010 Australian federal election', *Communication, Politics & Culture*, 44(2), 37–56.

Bruns, A. and Burgess, J. (2011b) 'The use of Twitter hashtags in the formation of ad hoc publics', paper presented at the European Consortium for Political Research Conference, Reykjavík, 25–27 August 2011, http://eprints.qut.edu.au /46515/, date accessed 1 September 2014.

Bruns, A. and Burgess, J. (2011c) 'Gawk scripts for Twitter processing', *Mapping Online Publics*, http://mappingonlinepublics.net/resources/, date accessed 30 January 2015.

Bruns, A. and Moe, H. (2014) 'Structural layers of communication on Twitter', in K. Weller, A. Bruns, J. Burgess, M. Mahrt and C. Puschmann (eds.) *Twitter and Society*. New York: Peter Lang, pp.15–28.

Bruns, A. and Stieglitz, S. (2013) 'Towards more systematic Twitter analysis: Metrics for tweeting activities', *International Journal of Social Research Methodology*, 16(2), 91–108.

Bucher, T. (2013) 'Objects of intense feeling: The case of the Twitter APIs', *Computational Culture*, 3, http://computationalculture.net/article/objects-of-intense -feeling-the-case-of-the-twitter-api, date accessed 1 September 2014.

Burgess, J. (2014) 'From "broadcast yourself" to "follow your interests": Making over social media', *International Journal of Cultural Studies*, http:// ics.sagepub.com/content/early/2014/01/13/1367877913513684.abstract, date accessed 1 September 2014.

Digital Methods Initiative (DMI) (2014) 'Twitter capture and analysis toolset (DMI-TCAT)', https://wiki.digitalmethods.net/Dmi/ToolDmiTcatm, date accessed 1 September 2014.

Gaffney, D. and Puschmann, C. (2014) 'Data collection on Twitter', in K. Weller, A. Bruns, J. Burgess, M. Mahrt and C. Puschmann (eds.) *Twitter and Society.* New York: Peter Lang, pp.55–68.

Highfield, T., Harrington, S. and Bruns, A. (2013) 'Twitter as a technology for audiencing and fandom: The #Eurovision phenomenon', *Information, Communication & Society*, 16(3), 315–39.

Kirkorian, R. (2014) 'Twitter #datagrants selections', *Twitter Engineering Blog*, https://blog.twitter.com/2014/twitter-datagrants-selections, date accessed 1 September 2014.

Kramer, A.D.I., Guillory, J.E. and Hancock, J.T. (2014) 'Experimental evidence of massive-scale emotional contagion through social networks', *Proceedings of the National Academy of Sciences*, 111(24), 8788–90, http://www.pnas.org/content/early/2014/05/29/1320040111.full.pdf, date accessed 1 September 2014.

Library of Congress (n.d.) 'Kluge fellowship in digital studies description', http://www.loc.gov/loc/kluge/fellowships/kluge-digital.html?loclr=blogsig, date accessed 1 September 2014.

Lomborg S. and Bechmann, A. (2014) 'Using APIs for data collection on social media', *The Information Society*, 30(4), 256–65.

Mendoza, M., Poblete, B. and Castillo, C. (2010) 'Twitter under crisis: Can we trust what we RT?', in *Proceedings of the First Workshop on Social Media Analytics* (SOMA '10), 71–9, http://snap.stanford.edu/soma2010/papers/soma2010_11.pdf, date accessed 13 April 2014.

O'Brien, J. (2011) 'Removal of export and download/API capabilities', *Archive of TwapperKeeper Blog*, http://twapperkeeper.wordpress.com/2011/02/22/removal-of-export-and-download-api-capabilities/, date accessed 1 September 2014.

PR Newswire (2014) 'Facebook reports fourth quarter and full year 2013 results', http://www.prnewswire.com/news-releases/facebook-reports-fourth-quarter-and-full-year-2013-results-242637731.html, date accessed 1 September 2014.

Puschmann, C. and Burgess, J. (2014) 'The politics of Twitter data', in K. Weller, A. Bruns, J. Burgess, M. Mahrt and C. Puschmann (eds.) *Twitter and Society*. New York: Peter Lang, pp.43–54.

Rogers, R. (2014) 'Foreword: Debanalising Twitter: The transformation of an object of study', in K. Weller, A. Bruns, J. Burgess, M. Mahrt and C. Puschmann (eds.) *Twitter and Society*. New York: Peter Lang, pp.ix–xxvi.

Twitter Inc. (2012) 'Terms of Service', https://twitter.com/tos, date accessed 1 September 2014.

Twitter Inc. (2013) 'Rules of the road', https://dev.twitter.com/terms/api-terms, date accessed 1 September 2014.

Twitter Inc. (2014) 'About', https://about.twitter.com/company, date accessed 1 September 2014.

3

Have We Even Solved the First 'Big Data Challenge?' Practical Issues Concerning Data Collection and Visual Representation for Social Media Analytics

Phillip Brooker, Julie Barnett, Timothy Cribbin and Sanjay Sharma

Introduction

Thanks to an influx of data collection and analytic software, harvesting and visualizing 'big' social media data[1] is becoming increasingly feasible as a method for social science researchers. Yet while there is an emerging body of work utilizing social media as a data resource, there are a number of computational issues affecting data collection. These issues may problematize any conclusions we draw from our research work, yet for the large part, they remain hidden from the researcher's view. We contribute towards the burgeoning literature which critically addresses various fundamental concerns with big data (see boyd and Crawford, 2012; Murthy, 2013; Rogers, 2013). However, rather than focusing on epistemological, political or theoretical issues – these areas are very ably accounted for by the authors listed above, and others – we engage with a different concern: how technical aspects of computational tools for capturing and handling social media data may impact our readings of it. This chapter outlines and explores two such technical issues as they occur for data taken from Twitter.

Throughout the chapter, we demonstrate a perspective consistent with the view of Procter et al. (2013) that social researchers wishing to make sense of 'big' social media data should have sufficient knowledge of the underlying concepts of the computational methods and tools they are using, so as to be able to decide when and where to appropriately apply them. Furthermore, we take heed of boyd and Crawford's suggestion that 'when researchers approach a dataset, they need to understand – and publicly account for – not only the limits of the dataset, but also the limits of which questions they can ask of a dataset and what interpretations are appropriate' (2012, pp.669–70). To this end, we highlight how certain technical characteristics and constraints pertaining to the collection and processing of Twitter data can impact on research and how an understanding of these factors might lead to more robust accounts of such data.

Our aim is to demonstrate the mainstream relevance of a commonplace methodological procedure in the social sciences, namely the self-critical reflexive analyses of our methods in terms of their impact on our accounts of the subjects we study. Our goal here is to show the importance of understanding the effects that technical processes may have on our readings of data for all social scientists, not just for those with a background in computer science. Without this understanding it is impossible to make sense of the data at hand. Hence, we promote the idea of thinking of the investigative process as an 'assemblage' (Langlois, 2011; Sharma, 2013) that draws together various social and technical (and other) factors into a unified research process. Here, we refer to the ways in which the research process comes to feature not only conceptual theoretical knowledge and inductive empirical findings, but also how technical issues (such as API rate limiting and spatial mapping algorithms) contribute towards the production of knowledge in multifarious complex ways. How such an assemblage might operate will become clearer as we present our selected two technical issues, and in the discussion that follows.

Reviewing the field

The state of social media analytics

With the field of social media analytics still in relative infancy, there are few methodological practices taken as standard. The tendency thus far has been to fit digital data to existing 'offline' ways of working. As O'Connor et al. note:

> Often the online researcher has little in the way of research precedent to use as a guide to practice online research and, as a result, online researchers frequently turn to established offline practices.
>
> (O'Connor et al., 2008, p.276)

Working from this position, several authors characterize social media data as a special kind of 'offline' social science data. For example, Hine (2006) argues that a key concern of social media analytics is to avoid a loss of quality in data. 'Face-to-face interaction here becomes the gold standard against which the performance of computer-mediated interaction is judged' (Hine, 2006, p.4). This quality problem of social media data is a concern shared by many, with comments being levelled at 'the lack of uniformity in how users fill in forms, fields, boxes and other text entry spaces' (Rogers, 2013, p.205); the representativeness and validity of the data more generally (Tufekci, 2014); and the fact that the production of data is not controlled and led by researchers but appears untamed 'in the wild' (Kitchin, 2014). Kitchin notes:

> The challenge of analysing big data is coping with abundance, exhaustivity and variety, timeliness and dynamism, messiness and uncertainty, high relationality, and the fact that much of what is generated has no specific question in mind or is a by-product of another activity.
>
> (Kitchin, 2014, p.2)

Given the uncertain relationship between digital and 'offline' methods, it becomes important to explore possible ways of rendering visible the characteristics of digital methods to see how and where they fit into existing methodological practices. Our proposed treatment of such data embraces the 'digitality' of researching in this area by advocating a greater working familiarity with computational tools and methods. Emphatically, this is not to say that the work of social media analytics can be reduced to the rote operating of software (see Keegan, 2013). Kitchin summarizes this tension:

> For many...the digital humanities is fostering weak, surface analysis, rather than deep, penetrating insight. It is overly reductionist and crude in its techniques, sacrificing complexity, specificity, context, depth and critique for scale, breadth, automation, descriptive patterns and the impression that interpretation does not require deep contextual knowledge.
>
> (Kitchin, 2014, p.8)

Yet we do not believe this is *necessarily* how social media analytics has to operate. On the contrary, we advocate a mode of reading data which allows computational methods to pick out areas of potential interest which then might be explored more intimately through closer readings.

To do this requires an understanding of how social media data can be affected by technical processes as part of a wider assemblage. As Lewis et al. note, 'As scholars increasingly take up such datasets, they may be better served by interweaving computational and manual approaches throughout the overall process in order to maximize the precision of algorithms and the context-sensitive evaluations of human coders' (2013, p.49). By outlining how this kind of research process works 'on the shop floor', we hope to foster a way of thinking about such technical issues which might facilitate the mainstream usage of digital research methods generally.

We take steps towards respecifying 'big' social media work in this way by concentrating on two issues. First, we demonstrate the effects of a data collection issue – the rate limiting of Twitter's Application Programming Interfaces (APIs), which is a built-in restriction on the flow of Twitter data that may interfere with analyses in significant ways. Second, we remark upon the ways in which computational models (and the visualizations that represent them) might shape our analytic readings of data. Those already working in the field are well aware of these concerns, yet they do not routinely feature in published accounts of relevant work. Consequently, such issues may stand as a barrier to entry by steepening an already steep learning curve. Hence, we openly discuss two such issues, not necessarily as problematic to social media analytics but as presenting an opportunity to make better use of new and powerful data resources.

Addressing the first 'Big Data Challenge'

Before doing so it is useful to describe what we are referring to in the title as the first 'Big Data Challenge'. One much vaunted promise of 'big data' is that we all now have the means to access data from sources like Twitter and to engage in analytic work on large data corpora through processing that data into easily digestible visualizations. Moreover, this work does not necessarily require any special skill with computer science or programming – there is a wealth of freely available third-party software tools to do the 'behind the scenes' technical work for us.[2] In this sense, the first 'Big Data Challenge' refers to (a) having easy access to big data and (b) the availability of tools that facilitate its analysis. Our question in the title – whether or not we are yet in a position to close the book on this first challenge – demonstrates our intention to probe such matters further: can we tap vast data resources unfiltered? Is it really as simple as employing visual models to show us the results? Such concerns are worked out through the process of doing social media analytics and acquiring necessary relevant skills along the way. Our approach here is to more accountably explore this process of doing social media analytics to help figure out what might count as appropriate methods and methodologies.

But why is it important to render transparent what might be argued to be mundane computational issues? Doing social media analytics with Twitter data necessitates an interfacing with the mechanisms governing how users access Twitter data: the Twitter APIs. These APIs allow users to request to access certain slices of Twitter data, according to various search strategies (i.e. by keyword, by bibliographic/demographic information, by random selection and so on). Moreover, once investigators have personal copies of these data, they may then subject them to further algorithmic processes to make their 'big data' analysable, for example in the rendering of statistical information or in the production of visualizations and so on. In this way, computational processes come to feature as essential elements in the production and construction of our data and analyses. As Marres notes, this bringing together of different disciplinary ideas can be equally productive and constricting:

> [Digital] social research is *noticeably* marked by informational practices and devices not of its own making, from the analytic measures built into online platforms (e.g. the number of links, number of mentionings, follower counts), to the visual forms embedded in visualization modules (the tag cloud). Online social research is visibly a distributed accomplishment.
>
> (Marres, 2012, p.160)

This intertwining of technical issues and research methods is foregrounded for the social sciences by Fielding and Lee, who argue that 'Social science has demonstrated how technology both shapes and is shaped by social action. Research methods are no exception' (2008, p.505). As such, since there are computational processes governing data collection and analysis, we may find ourselves better-armed to undertake research in the area if we understand some of the finer points about how these tools and processes work. How exactly do they restrict the data we can harvest? And how exactly do they shape the statistics and visualizations and other analytic outputs which we use to understand that data?

To this end, we now turn to a more pointed examination of two such issues – the possible effects of API rate limiting on data collected through Twitter, and the possible effects of spatial mapping algorithms on data visualizations – as they occur through the usage of a bespoke social media analytics software suite, Chorus.[3] This serves to demonstrate the kinds of issues investigators may find themselves contending with, as well as helping figure out ways of handling them methodologically. Our reflexive focus on the research process itself is very much a mainstream methodological practice of social scientists[4] – we seek to take a self-critical view on the (opaque) process of undertaking research involving data collection through the Twitter APIs and data visualization using spatial mapping algorithms. However, our approach sees such limitations not as *obstacles* to research to be overcome. Rather, we discuss these issues as an exercise in learning the tools of the trade of social media analytics and understanding how they construct the data we analyse, so as to be better able to deal with them as part of our work.

Two practical issues

API rate limiting in Twitter data collection

Twitter data collection is a process mediated through Twitter's various APIs. For the purposes of social media analytics, the APIs are the tools by which users can make requests for specific types of data. This process of using Twitter's APIs to access data necessitates that users write requests as a RESTful statement to return responses in a data interchange format called JSON,[5] or that users take advantage of a third-party client which facilitates the task for non-coders. However, though comprehensive collections of data are available for purchase through data archiving services such as Gnip or DataSift, the Twitter APIs are not completely openly available to users and developers. In fact, several restrictions on their usage are in place; ostensibly this is to prevent misuse of the service by individual users. One such restriction is Twitter's 'rate limiting' of an individual account's API usage, or the rate at which a user can poll the API with requests for data matching a search query. Each API has different rate limits and different software tools will handle those limits in different ways.[6] Providing concrete and quantifiable definitions of these limits is, however, a hopeless task. The 'Search API' (that our example below draws upon) is fairly well documented in terms of its limits, as we go on to discuss. However, the usage restrictions of all Twitter APIs are variably dependent on contextual information: chiefly the volume of data any queries will yield. Hence, for APIs other than Search, Twitter does not provide information as to the exact limits they will impose. All of this makes understanding and navigating through the Twitter APIs a labyrinthine process. We use data collected via the Search API – which handles data based on keywords appearing in tweets and is the most commonly used Twitter API – to demonstrate how the API itself inevitably comes to feature in a burgeoning assemblage built up by the research as it is undertaken.

At the time of writing, Twitter's Search API allows Chorus' data collection program, TweetCatcher Desktop (TCD), to make 450 requests every 15 minutes. Each such request has the potential to capture a maximum of 100 tweets. The Search API allows users to retrieve historical data up to seven days prior to the initial request. On 23 July 2014, using TCD we ran a very general search query for all usages of the term 'black', as a way of exploring the topics and sub-topics of racialized tweet content. To capture the data, we refreshed the query at various points over an approximately four-hour period so as to ensure as comprehensive a dataset as the API would allow. This resulted in a dataset of 28,317 tweets featuring the term 'black'. Plotting the data over time in half-hour intervals within Chorus' visual analytic program TweetVis, it was clear that there were gaps in the chronology of the conversation:

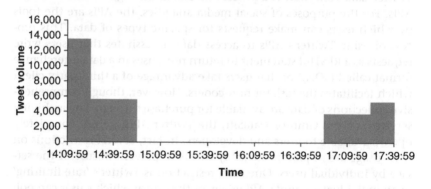

Figure 3.1   Chart to show volume of tweets mentioning 'black' across time (half-hour intervals)

What we see in Figure 3.1 is a striking reminder that Twitter's APIs are restricted and that this may have significant effects on the data we wish to capture through them. For high-volume queries, it is easy to come up against Twitter's API rate limits, such as during searches for general terms like 'black', as well as for trending terms (e.g. 'Obama' in the run-up to the 2012 US presidential election). In this example, we were simply unable to keep up with the pace of peoples' tweets; we were able to capture an average 118 tweets per minute over the four-hour period, whereas the actual conversation skipped along between 450 and 550 tweets per minute. Naturally, this left a sizeable chunk of data missing from our dataset (see Figure 3.1). However, what is less immediately obvious in this rendering of the data are the presence of other breaks in the flow of the conversation we captured, which become more apparent when viewing at a finer level of granularity.

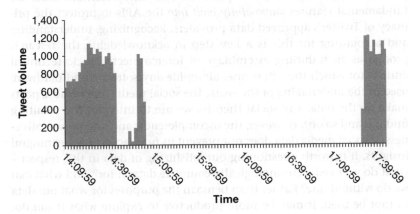

Figure 3.2 Chart to show volume of tweets mentioning 'black' across time (two-minute intervals)

In Figure 3.2, we see the same data grouped into intervals of two minutes. Here we can identify not only the same gap in the data as in Figure 3.1, but also an earlier gap which was previously obscured when viewed with our earlier half-hour intervals. Hence, we now can detect a probable disruption to the flow of data between 14:44:59 and 14:58:59 where only a consistent chronology was visible (or at least presumed) before. It may simply be that people tweeted fewer times during these minutes, though it is equally possible that it is at this point we were reaching the limits of what the API would allow us to see. It is in fact impossible to figure out what has happened from the data or visualizations themselves.

What does this ambiguity mean for social media analytics and social research involving Twitter data? A key insight to draw from this demonstration is that comprehensive collections of Twitter data are not freely available to researchers. Even where we may assume we are capturing the entirety of a conversation, drilling down into finer levels of granularity may show us otherwise. Furthermore, failing to recognize when these rate-limiting issues have occurred may be detrimental to the analyses we draw from our data. Without due care and attention, we may find ourselves using falsely derived conceptualizations of data as chronologically consistent.[7]

It is important here to acknowledge that access to social media data is a highly politicized issue largely driven by commercial concerns (boyd and Crawford, 2012; Rogers, 2013). In this sense, it is a fallacy to believe that any data which is collected through Twitter's APIs (rather than purchased) is complete: incompleteness and unrepresentativeness are fundamental features *purposefully built into* the APIs to protect the primacy of Twitter's approved data providers. Recognizing, understanding and accounting for this is a key step in acknowledging the research process as an unfurling assemblage of interconnected socio-technical entities (of which the API is one, alongside any software and hardware used in the undertaking of the work, the social media users whose posts make up the data, any social theories we use to interpret the resulting findings and so on). However, the incompleteness and unrepresentativeness of social media data does not prevent us from accessing meaningful insights. It is worth questioning our fetishizing of data in this respect – what do we need a chronologically complete dataset for? And what can we do without one? Rather than bemoan the purposes for what our data cannot be used, it may be more productive to explore what it *can* do. Though the methodological and analytic possibilities are impossible to encapsulate fully in the present chapter (in that they will depend largely on the questions being addressed), one such approach is advanced in the following section. However, the salient point remains that perhaps the best way to make sense of data is to attain a deep understanding of how a dataset has been constructed and use that understanding as a resource for designing appropriate analytic approaches with which it may be dealt.

Spatial mapping algorithms in Twitter data visualization

Clearly, there are issues concerning data collection of which researchers in social media analytics would do well to be aware. However, our endeavours in the field have also revealed similar technical issues in data visualization, where collected data is given an analytic relevance through algorithmic processing. There are already multitudinous tools for visualizing social media data – Gephi, NodeXL and Chorus, for instance. Some of these utilize spatial mapping algorithms – computational processes through which entities such as individual words or connected arrays of tweeters (or indeed any other kind of 'node') are located on a 2D visual plane in relation to each other. Though each software package operates uniquely, a unifying feature of these algorithms is their use of mathematical reasoning as a way of representing distinctions between nodes. For example, the Chorus visual analytic suite – TweetVis – features (among other visualizations) a topical 'cluster map' which uses a spatial mapping algorithm to plot individual words contained within tweets, in regard to the frequency of co-occurrences words have with other words in the dataset. In this map, words which commonly co-occur in tweets cluster together, thereby forming distinct topical clusters through which users can navigate and explore. Here, the algorithm is what constructs and constrains the map, and for users trying to read the visualization, the constructions and constraints of the map become an integral part of the resulting analysis. We demonstrate the possible effects of this algorithmic constructing and constraining on analyses, showing how an understanding of the technical goings-on of data visualization is a necessary requirement for those wishing to view it sensibly through the lens of an assemblage.

To exemplify what the effects of a spatial mapping algorithm might look like in the undertaking of a social media analytics project, we draw on previous work[8] on 'racialized hashtags' (in particular, the hashtag *#notracist*). With a dataset collecting all usages of the term *#notracist* over an eight-month period (resulting in 24,853 tweets), we plotted a cluster map of hashtags, to see which hashtags featured together more commonly (Figure 3.3).

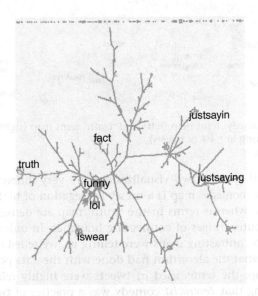

Figure 3.3 Hashtag map of #notracist (labels given to hashtags featuring in ≥1% of tweets)

What this map showed us is that there are two distinct types of hashtag being used across the *#notracist* dataset: first, a collection of 'comedy' hashtags (including *#funny* and *#lol* and others) located in a tightly organized cluster near the centre of the map; and second, an array of 'truth' hashtags (including *#justsayin*, *#justsaying*, *#iswear*, *#truth*, *#fact* and others) appearing on the fringes of topical branches around the outskirts of the visualization.[9] Given that these different themes are located in different areas of the map – 'comedy' in a tight central cluster and 'truth' out towards the fringes of branches – we developed an interest in finding out what exactly this difference might be. To drill into the data further, we filtered the master *#notracist* dataset into two sub-sets: one containing 'comedy' hashtags and one containing 'truth' hashtags. We then plotted cluster maps for all terms contained within either dataset (Figure 3.4).

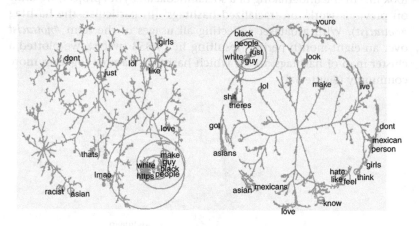

Figure 3.4   'Comedy' term map (left) and 'truth' term map (right) (labels given to terms featuring in ≥4% of tweets)

It is clear that these two visualizations are very different from one another – the 'comedy' map is a messy aggregation of highly interconnected terms, whereas terms in the 'truth' map are densely populated around the outer fringes of connecting branches. In order to interpret what the two contrasting maps were telling us, we relied on an understanding of what the algorithm had done with the data points. For the 'comedy' map, the terms used in tweets were highly related to each other showing that *#notracist* comedy was a practice of tweeting done with lots of different terms and hashtags being used in similar ways (i.e. there are a number of 'stock' formats through which tweeters could accountably claim to be 'doing a joke'). However, for the 'truth' map, our understanding of what we could see in the visualization relied upon an understanding of the functions of Chorus' spatial mapping algorithms. In this map, terms are chiefly located on the outer edges, as far apart from each other as the algorithm will allow. This is demonstrated by the tree-like appearances of topical branches, with virtually no connecting terms in the centre but a high density of terms pushed out towards the edges of the 2D plane. This visible pushing of the boundaries of the algorithm tells us a lot about the data we were working with. The terms used in the 'truth' tweets we identified are typically disconnected from each other and not used together, and we can begin to characterize #notracist 'truth' tweets as evidence of a topic that is not implicitly agreed upon and which reflects a diverse array of strategies for justifying a #notracist claim as a statement.

Again, we ask: What does this mean for social media analytics? Visualizations such as those discussed here are designed to fit data into a model which serves to constrain our data and analytic materials as well as give them visible structure.[10] Hence, our aim in describing the processes through which such models construct and constrain analyses is to set out a requirement for social media analytics that it explicitly *account for* these processes. For example, in the #notracist data described above, it was fundamental to our understanding of the data that we could recognize that 'truth' terms were pushing the Chorus cluster map algorithm to its limits and consequently use that information as a way of figuring out what the 'truth' conversation was about. Crucially, the fact of our data being processed through the algorithm in a certain way is precisely what helped us get to grips with what lay at the heart of that data. Without this we would have been lost. Consequently, we reiterate that these intrusions of computational, technical and mathematical processes into our analyses is not something to be resisted. Rather, they are necessary and productive elements of social media analytics without which we would be unable to characterize the assemblage through which the analysis had been shaped, and ultimately, unable to make adequate sense of the data at hand.

Conclusion

In this chapter, we have outlined how social media analytics incorporates data collection and analytic work in ways which are thoroughly reliant on computational and technical processes. Despite the provocative nature in which the question in the title of this piece was posed, we believe investigators in the field *are* in a position to sensibly account for their work in terms of these processes. Yet these issues are not something we have seen discussed explicitly in the accounts produced thus far. Hence, though our points may be frustratingly mundane to our peers (who may question why researchers would want to write about the inner workings of APIs and algorithms) we nonetheless think it valuable to discuss such things transparently as a means of promoting healthy and robust methodologies for the emerging field.

To that end, rather than depicting software tools in general and in abstract, we have exemplified our ideas with reference to two specific issues arising out of the use of just one software package. This, we hope, gives a flavour of *the kinds of* issues of which researchers must be aware when working with digital data and associated software tools. It is our hope that our accounts of two specific examples can demonstrate just how these kinds of issues intersect with research work in a very direct way. Working in this way, we have shown how technical and computational processes become a 'necessary evil' of the work. Only there is nothing 'evil' about them. Rather, these same processes can be used as resources for conducting (and figuring out how to conduct) analytic work in appropriate ways. However, the use of these processes as analytic resources relies on our having a deep understanding of what they are doing with our data, else we risk wrong-footing our analyses before we even begin. As Manovich notes:

> [Y]ou must have the right background to make use of this data. The [analytic] software itself is free and readily available... but you need the right training... and prior practical experience to get meaningful results.
>
> (Manovich, 2012, p.472)

It is clear that it now becomes our job as researchers to equip ourselves with these understandings of the technical processes on which our work relies; however, much this may take us outside of typical disciplinary boundaries.

All of this may make the analysis of social media data an infinitely more complex issue, in that we are no longer really analysing *only* the data, but an assemblage (Langlois, 2011; Sharma, 2013) of technical and social processes which coalesce to form the datasets and visualizations we find before us. Concerning data collection, we have used the idea of an assemblage to outline how the technical aspects of API rate limiting become built into social media analytics research from the very beginning of the research process. Concerning data visualization and analysis, our described assemblage relied upon our conceptualization of computational processes as having (by necessity) a commitment to numerical 'understandings' of data and how those 'understandings' are translated into images to be read by human researchers. We have no doubt that Chorus' way of doing things is only one among many, and other such issues will invariably arise in a multitude of different ways when doing social media analytics with other tools. As with any software tool, Chorus is not 'just a tool' – it engenders a particular way of thinking about social media data which constructs and constrains analyses in equal amounts. As such, the modest goal of this chapter has been to encourage readers to consider their research work not only in terms of the results and findings to be drawn, but in relation to the myriad processes through which those findings are mediated throughout the endeavour. We advocate *thinking in assemblages* as a requirement for social media analytics generally. Furthermore, we have shown the relevance of assemblages for mainstream purposes, and how the specific properties of an assemblage might be uncovered through the deployment of a key methodological principle – reflexivity – which has informed the present chapter from start to finish. In using the idea of assemblages as a frame for undertaking investigative work, analytic findings would be explicitly situated alongside deconstructions of the processes by which tools are governed by big data and the processes by which those same tools govern the generation of empirical findings. In this sense, we may find ourselves in the business of handling *data processes* rather than data, and of reading *visualization processes* rather than visualizations. The final result of these processes – the compiled dataset or the visual representation – are not objects in and of themselves, but are better thought of as a way of demonstrating how an unfolding combination of human and computational research processes has resulted in a selection of valid and defensible findings.

Notes

1. We take 'big' social media data to refer to volumes of data too large to handle without computational processing and which are derived from peoples' everyday usages of social media platforms such as Twitter.
2. The idea that social media analytics requires no specific skill in its practitioners is contestable – for instance, Keegan (2013) notes that the information technology industry believes itself to be suffering from a lack of trained data

scientists. However, the point remains that there are lots of freely available social media analytics tools with which investigators from any discipline can explore data, and it is no longer a steadfast requirement for practitioners to have any significant skills in programming, data mining, data visualization and so on.

3. Chorus (for further details, see www.chorusanalytics.co.uk) is a free-to-download data collection and visual analytic software suite dealing with Twitter data for social media analytics. Chorus was developed at Brunel University by a team including several of the authors of the present chapter (Dr Tim Cribbin, Dr Phillip Brooker and Prof. Julie Barnett). The development of Chorus was supported in part through the MATCH Programme (UK Engineering and Physical Sciences Research Council grants numbers GR/S29874/01, EP/F063822/1 and EP/G012393/1).

4. Lynch (2000), however, questions the utility of sociology's concern with self-analysis, arguing that it only need to be applied when something particularly interesting will result (as is the case with his own reflexive approach to reflexivity, and we hope, the present chapter).

5. A RESTful statement is one which is written in adherence to REST (or Representational State Transfer) principles, REST being the ubiquitous architectural style that standardizes and underlies the World Wide Web. In regard specifically to handling the Twitter APIs, RESTful statements are the commands by which API users can speak to Twitter's servers to request specific slices of data, which are returned in JSON format. Readers wishing to find out more about using the Twitter APIs and writing API requests should manually start with Twitter's own developer documentation (Twitter 2014a).

6. See Twitter (2014b) for a more detailed account of the rate limiting Twitter applies to its APIs.

7. Other APIs may provide something more like a chronologically complete timeline – for instance, the Twitter Streaming API pushes 'real-time' data matching a query's criteria. However, the Streaming API only provides a percentage sample of tweets requested, where the actual percentage is unknowable and dependent on the volume of tweets requested by the query and concurrent Twitter traffic. Hence, the only way to ensure comprehensiveness of a dataset without running into sampling issues is to purchase Twitter 'Firehose' data – this alone politicizes access to data to the extent that few can afford to ever see a comprehensive dataset.

8. See Sharma and Brooker (2014) for an informal account of this project.

9. Though this chapter is not intended as an empirical study of these tweets, interested readers might wish to note that the 'comedy' hashtags we identified were tweets designed by tweeters to be humorous, whereas 'truth' hashtags were designed to enforce a point that a tweet was 'just a fact' or 'just an observation' and so on. Our analytic work explored the different practices through which users attempted to justify their claims that a tweet was not racist by virtue of it being a joke or a statement of fact.

10. This might be likened to filling a glass with water. As with water taking the shape of the glass it is poured into, the process of collecting and

visualizing social media data serves to furnish amorphous data with a structure. However, as much as these technical processes *construct* data such that they become amenable to analysis, it can be said that the same processes *constrain* data into singular readings – a circular glass gives only a circular shape to the water, but what if other shapes would prove more interesting?

References

boyd, d. and Crawford, K. (2012) 'Critical questions for big data', *Information, Communication & Society*, 15(5), 662–79.

Fielding, N. and Lee, R. (2008) 'Qualitative e-social science cyber-research', in N. Fielding, R. Lee, and G. Blank (eds.) *The Sage Handbook of Online Research Methods*. London: Sage, pp.491–506.

Hine, C. (2006) 'Virtual methods and the sociology of cyber-social-scientific knowledge', in C. Hine (ed.) *Virtual Methods: Issues in Social Research on the Internet*. Oxford: Berg, pp.1–13.

Keegan, B. (2013) 'C-level executives cry out for data scientists', *ComputerWeekly.com*, http://www.computerweekly.com/news /2240205984/C -level-executives-cry-out-for-data-scientists, date accessed 13 November 2014.

Langlois, G. (2011) 'Meaning, semiotechnologies and participatory media', *Culture Machine*, 12, 1–27.

Lewis, S.C., Zamith, R. and Hermida, A. (2013) 'Content analysis in an era of big data: A hybrid approach to computational and manual methods', *Journal of Broadcasting & Electronic Media*, 57(1), 34–52.

Lynch, M. (2000) 'Against reflexivity as an academic virtue and source of privileged knowledge', *Theory, Culture & Society*, 17(3), 26–54.

Kitchin, R. (2014) 'Big data, new epistemologies and paradigm shifts', *Big Data and Society*, 1, 1–12.

Manovich, L. (2012) 'Trending: The promises and challenges of big social data', in M.K. Gold (ed.) *Debates in the Digital Humanities*. London: University of Minnesota Press, pp.460–75.

Marres, N. (2012) 'The redistribution of methods: On intervention in digital social research, broadly conceived', *The Sociological Review*, 60(S1), 139–65.

Murthy, D. (2013) *Twitter*. Cambridge: Polity Press.

O'Connor, H. Madge, C. Shaw, R. and Wellens, J. (2008) 'Internet-based interviewing', in N. Fielding, R. Lee and G. Blank (eds.) *The Sage Handbook of Online Research Methods*. London: Sage, pp.271–89.

Procter, R. Vis, F. and Voss, A. (2013) 'Reading the riots on Twitter: Methodological innovation for the analysis of big data', *International Journal of Social Science Research Methodology*, 16(3), 197–214.

Rogers, R. (2013) *Digital Methods*. London: The MIT Press.

Sharma, S. (2013) 'Black Twitter? Racial hashtags, networks and contagion', *New Formations*, 78, 46–64.

Sharma, S. and Brooker, P. (2014) '#notracist: Multi-hashtags and ambient race-talk on Twitter', *Dark Matter Wiki*, http://www.darkmatter101.org/wiki /notracist_twitter, date accessed 21 January 2015.

Tufekci, Z. (2014) 'Big questions for social media big data: Representativeness, validity and other methodological pitfalls', *Proceedings of the Eighth International AAAI Conference on Weblogs and Social Media*, AAAI Publications, pp.505–14.

Twitter (2014a), *Documentation*, https://dev.twitter.com/docs, date accessed 29 July 2014.

Twitter (2014b) *API Rate Limits*, https://dev.twitter.com/rest/public/rate-limiting, date accessed 17 November 2014.

4
'I'm Always on Facebook!': Exploring Facebook as a Mainstream Research Tool and Ethnographic Site

Eve Stirling

Introduction to the research

This chapter discusses a research project which explored the everyday use of the social network site (SNS) Facebook by first-year undergraduate students in their transition to university. It not only explores the opportunities and challenges of using Facebook as a research site and how this digital approach may differ from a 'mainstream' ethnography, but also argues for this approach to be viewed as 'mainstream' due to the mediated nature of contemporary social life.

The chapter begins with an overview of the research undertaken, introducing the context, study design and study ethics. A discussion of debates in digital ethnography then follows, highlighting some key positions and terms in the field of digital ethnography. Next, the terms 'field site', 'participant observation' and 'field notes' are discussed as digital methods, and some of the issues and ethical tensions of using these are explored using examples from the study. After a reflexive discussion of my experiences in the field, in which I consider my own shifting position in an already 'fuzzy' environment, the chapter concludes with a case for considering such approaches as part of the mainstream ethnographer's toolkit.

The data discussed in this chapter are taken from an empirical study undertaken in 2010 on how first-year undergraduate students in the United Kingdom use Facebook (Stirling, 2014). The study used ethnographic methods to observe student Facebook use and then looked at whether Facebook helped or hindered the students' transition into university life. It explored the cultural practices of the students' use of this SNS in the context of their university experience. The students, their habits and their rituals were of interest, along with their interplay with technology. Facebook is both a pathway and a destination, one that the students used on a daily basis as part of their everyday lives. This site was (and still is) ubiquitous in a great many of the lives of young (18–21-year-old) undergraduate students in the United Kingdom (Ipsos MORI, 2008; CLEX, 2009), with research findings (at the time of the study) showing that 91 per cent of undergraduate students describe themselves as using SNS 'regularly' or 'sometimes' (Ipsos MORI, 2008, p.10). Research in this area suggests that Facebook is a key tool used for social support and supporting academic study (Madge et al., 2009; Selwyn, 2009). It is acknowledged that students do use other SNS and that not all students use Facebook, but this particular site is embedded in everyday student life, and it was the nature of this 'embeddedness' that was the focus of the research.

My Facebook friends

The study consisted of two stages of data collection. Stage one was an online survey questionnaire of the full population of new undergraduate students (approx. 4,700 students). Stage two was a 'connective ethnography', which spans both the virtual and physical spaces of a small volunteer sample of these respondents ($n = 6$). The six ethnographic cases were narrowed down through a series of correspondence and discussions about the detail of the study which resulted in six participants wishing to take part. These were called my Facebook Friends (FbFs). The reasons for this longitudinal approach was that much of the research into students' use of SNS prior to this study was either quantitative and experimental (Vie, 2008; Kirschner and Karpinski, 2010) or based on short-term qualitative analysis using interviews (Selwyn, 2009). There was a lack of longitudinal ethnographic studies that looked in depth at Facebook use over time. At the time of the study, there was much that was unknown (and it could be argued there still is), not least the cultural developments in digital life. A range of authors (Beer and Burrows, 2007; boyd, 2008; Selwyn and Grant, 2009) called for a development of *thick descriptive* ethnographic accounts of the present day use of SNSs *in situ* as opposed to offering research into the potentials of these applications. This idea of writing thick descriptions of how students were using Facebook was a driving factor in the research design. To enable this, a longitudinal 'connective' ethnographic approach was taken lasting the whole of the academic year 2010–2011. The focus was the experiences of students in their transition year and so following them through to its completion was important.

Debates in digital ethnographic practice

Ethnographies and ethnographic practice draw on a wide range of sources of information collected over a period of time from the participant's everyday life to make sense of the world (Hammersley and Atkinson, 1983). Historically, the term 'ethnography' has been intrinsically linked to (and is at the core of) Western anthropology but over time it has been appropriated by a variety of disciplines and this has led to fuzzy boundaries around the use of the term (Hammersley and Atkinson, 2007). Hammersley and Atkinson propose that 'ethnography plays a complex and shifting role in the dynamic tapestry' (2007, p.2) of the social sciences in the twenty-first century. Seminal authors such as Clifford Geertz (1973) and Margaret Wolf (1992) undertook the anthropological study of 'other' cultures and this took place overseas in a land very different from the homeland inhabited by the ethnographer.

More recently the 'other' culture studied may be technologically mediated. Some of the ways researchers have chosen to describe ethnographies, which have some element of digital or Internet within the field site or as a data collection method, include 'connective ethnography' (Leander and McKim, 2003); 'cyberethnography' (Robinson and Schulz, 2009); 'digital ethnography' (Murthy, 2008); 'Internet ethnography' (Sade-Beck, 2004); 'online/offline ethnography' (Markham, 2005); 'netography' (Kozinets, 2010); and 'virtual ethnography' (Hine, 2000, 2005). The last 20 years have seen a growth in exploration and ethnographic understanding of life online through many 'new digital phenomena'. Robinson and Schulz (2009, p.692) suggest the continual evolution of the Internet 'necessitates continual reassessment of fieldwork methods'. It has been a time of flux and methodological terms to describe ethnographies of the Internet have jostled to gain credence. The focus of this chapter is on the use of Facebook as an example of a digital ethnographic site and digital method for undertaking an ethnography. The term *digital* is chosen over 'online', 'virtual' or 'Internet' as I believe it best describes the use of digital devices, spaces and interactions and moves the focus away from a binary description which has historically been used. To foreground this discussion, attention is given in this section to three of these terms: 'virtual ethnography', 'netnography' and 'connective ethnography'. These were chosen for their differing approaches to high-light how ethnographic practice has been viewed in relation to digital lives and how they influenced the present Facebook case study.

Virtual Ethnography (Hine, 2000) draws upon a case study of a media event to explore computer-mediated communication on and about the Internet. This seminal text suggests that the Internet is both a cultural artefact as well as a site for cultural practice. Hine began by trying to understand whether the 'virtual' was different from the 'real' and by approaching Internet use this way, drew a divide between online and offline interactions. She proposes that a virtual ethnography is 'not quite like the real thing' (2000, p.10) in that by only observing the virtual the researcher did not see all of real life. The terms 'online' and 'offline' are not helpful when describing social practices which take place in the digital and/or physical environment. Consequently, it is not helpful to segment the ethnographic practices to digital and physical.

Kozinets (2010) advocates a differing approach when studying online and offline communities. He argues that the two ought to be treated differently and contends the importance of 'the physical component that is always attached to human social behaviour' (Kozinets, 2010, p.63) while maintaining that a separation between the online and offline is possible. In *Netnography* (2010), Kozinets makes the distinction between researching 'online communities' – those that are communities, having elements that cross into the physical – and 'communities online' – those that are solely based in the digital, and that different approaches can be taken to explore each. Netnography supposes that this line can be drawn but this is problematic as the layered nature of digital life is more nuanced.

In contrast, the term *connective ethnography* has been used by Hine (2007) and Leander and McKim (2003) to describe ethnographic studies in which the field sites span both digital and physical spaces. Leander and McKim propose participants are 'in and travel across more than one space at one time' (2003, p.238) and so therefore we as researchers should pay attention to these multiplicities by tracing the flows of their movement between and across the physical and the digital environments and the intersections therein (Leander and McKim, 2003). A connective ethnography describes the use of two or more field sites and describes the connection found between them. The everyday uses of the Internet are more nuanced than the simplicity of one physical site and one digital site. There are layers of digital a person may be involved in, which may include a Facebook Page,[1] a Twitter stream,[2] a 'WhatsApp' group chat[3] and a 'Snapchat' message.[4] The ethnographer needs to be able to move where the participant travels and therefore being 'connected' across the spaces was most appropriate in engaging students' digital practices.

Facebook in everyday life

The Facebook project took a multi-sited connective ethnographic approach to researching both the digital and the physical environments of the undergraduate students. This built upon a previous study that took a solely digital approach to studying Facebook use (Stirling, 2009) which found that to view the digital only was missing many of the social practices which included face-to-face interactions. When studying something that can be transient and fluid, across the digital and the physical, the concept of a field site becomes fuzzy and less rigid. The importance of being embedded in the practices of the participants in order to have an insider view was paramount in understanding this. One of the findings from this study was that students used Facebook Group Chat within lectures. Being an insider Group member was key to viewing these practices and digital methods facilitated this. The next section explores the methods that can be used when undertaking such digital research and how these spaces can complicate our understanding of 'mainstream' ethnographic concepts and practices.

Undertaking an ethnography in digital spaces; field site, participant observation and field notes

This section moves the discussion to key terms that can be used when undertaking an ethnography and explores some nuances between mainstream ethnography and those ethnographies that include digital spaces. I explore the concepts of *field site*, *participant observation* and *field notes* and draw upon practice from the connective ethnographic study of students' Facebook use.

What is the field site?

Bailey (2007, p.2) describes field research as 'the systematic study, primarily through long-term, face-to-face interactions and observations, of everyday life'. These observations of everyday life, in 'everyday contexts' (Hammersley and Atkinson, 2007, p.3) are 'increasingly technologically mediated' (Murthy, 2008, p.849), thus meaning that our understanding of the 'field site' can be problematic. What was once viewed as involving face-to-face contact with participants has, over the last 20 years, broadened to include relationships that are mediated by technology and digital in nature. These digitally mediated interactions take place alongside and within the physical environment which, I argue, cannot be viewed as separate from the digital spaces and interactions. The concept of a field site has broadened to include virtual worlds, gaming environments, SNSs and smartphone apps. In all of these examples, the ethnographer is ideally as far as is possible embedded within the digital technologies and the field site, for example, a Second Life character (Boellstorff, 2008), a World of Warcraft player (Taylor, 2006), an FbF (Raynes-Goldie, 2010) or a user of an app (Crooks, 2013).

Gaining access to the field

One of the field sites in this study was the participants' Facebook Profile. The participants added me as a Friend on Facebook to take part in the study. Prior to this a face-to-face discussion regarding the study took place and informed consent was sought and granted. Buchanan proposes that online and offline are now so interconnected that we should view them as 'a fluid sphere' (2011, p.89) but she contends that this then 'blurs the research boundaries' and the ethical issues relating to this are also blurred. To counter this, participant and researcher expectations and behaviours were discussed to ensure all were happy with the approach. The choice of the participant to add me as an FbF was so that the participants had agency over taking part in the study. They did not have to add me if they decided not to take part and they could delete me from their Friend list whenever they wished. I was not controlling the access to their Profile.

The boundary of the field site

When undertaking an ethnography it is sensible to define the parameters of the study from the outset but to allow for a level of flexibility to follow the movement of the participants. Facebook and the Profiles[5] of the six participants' were the main focus of the study to explore the broader relationship between students, Facebook and the university context. The movements of the participants were followed across the digital and physical spaces through the students collecting photographs of their spaces (wherever they used Facebook – student bedroom, outside a lecture theatre, and walking into university were a few examples). I took screenshots and downloads of their Profiles and undertook face-to-face interviews. The field sites were where the student interactions took place within the digital and physical university environments, including the library, a lecture theatre, their laptop and Profiles. Connections between the field sites were explored by asking the questions, not only 'What is Facebook?' but also 'When?', 'Where?' and 'How is Facebook?' (Hine, 2000). When is Facebook used by the students? Where are the environments in which Facebook is used? How does Facebook fit within the university experience? Facebook has many different sections within the architecture of the website. The original intention was to stick to my participants' personal Profiles as the boundary of the digital field site. This was driven by an ethical decision to focus the research on those people who had given informed consent. Observations were focused only within this space for the majority of the participants. One participant invited me to join a private Facebook Group,[6] which was set up by his classmates to discuss issues relating to the course they were studying. Information on the study and a request for participation in the study were communicated to the Group members via a Wall post. Informed consent was gained from all the group members before I was added to the Group space. Joining the Group offered a set of different interactions and Facebook practices to explore. This meant that the Facebook Group then became a field site in addition to the personal Profiles I was already studying. This is an example of the expanded 'fuzzy' boundary of the field site. This was only possible due to the digital nature of the ethnography which afforded access to the Facebook Group.

Participant observation

Participant observation is a key method of ethnographic research, which differentiates it from other qualitative practices (Delamont, 2004; Hammersley and Atkinson, 2007; Boellstorff et al., 2012), such as interviews or observation (without participating). Observation of the participants is undertaken in the everyday setting of the field site (as discussed in the previous section) and the aim is to understand the cultural practices of those being studied by living alongside them, taking part when appropriate and talking to them about their lives and actions (Delamont, 2004). Boellstorff et al. (2012, p.66) suggest that participant observation 'entails a particular kind of joining in and a particular way of looking at things that depends on the research question, field site, and practical constraints'. Accessing the everyday life of Facebook involved sitting in front of my computer and observing and taking part in the day-to-day activities of my FbFs (the participants on Facebook). As Boellstorff et al. (2012) suggest, it was necessary to prepare myself both technologically and physically before entering the field. A researcher must have the appropriate equipment to be able to access the field site. If a researcher does not have good Internet access and an understanding of how the site works, studying it is challenging. I used a laptop computer and based myself in my own home and also used my smartphone to access Facebook when out and about as the study progressed. I also moved to locations beyond my own home with both my laptop and smartphone. This meant that my observations were not routed in a static location. I visited the physical spaces my participants visited: the student's union, their halls of residence cafe and the university library, and visited Facebook in these locations too. For me I was experiencing the spatialized practices of Facebook use that I saw my FbF doing. The connective ethnographic approach afforded me the opportunity to view the blending and layering of Facebook use across the digital and physical environments.

Field notes

As noted by others, field notes are a key element of recording ethnographic observations (Sanjek, 1990; Wolf, 1992; Hammersley and Atkinson, 2007). The focus in this section is to describe the practice of writing field notes when in the field site of Facebook.

Facebook operates both synchronously (at the same time) and asynchronously (not at the same time). As a result, depending on the practice the researcher is involved in, field notes can be written when observing and experiencing the cultural practice as a notebook can sit alongside the laptop and note taking would not be seen as a distraction to the participants. This is something that is not so easily undertaken in the physical world due to the disconnection from the activity being observed (Boellstorff et al., 2012). The use of digital screenshots to record what was seen was helpful and supplemented traditional hand written field notes. The types of digital screenshots taken included a participant's comment on a Status update or Photo, or those that typified a cultural practice, such as 'Tagging' (highlighting their face and/or name) a Friend in a post or 'Checking in' (highlighting on a digital map) to a particular physical space within the university. The ethics of capturing visual data needed attention (due to the privacy of a participant's identity in photographs) and I ensured I had consent from all my FbF to capture visual data to be used for academic purposes. The visual nature of these notes offers a richer view of the practice than written notes alone. These shots can also be used at a later time to work up to fuller written notes. Boellstorff et al. (2012) compare these to 'scratch notes' (Sanjek, 1990), but these are also key pieces of visual data, which can be used (with the permission of the FbF) as part of the presentation of the study as illustration. This digital nature of recording my field notes was used alongside the more traditional note taking on paper particularly when away from the main computer using a smartphone. My involvement and experience of participant observation, and the field notes that I took of these experiences, culminate together to create the ethnographic texts. In this manner the digital methods supplemented the more traditional ethnographic practices. This mix of digital, multimodal and analogue note taking mirrored the practices I was viewing and offered me a rich array of insights into these practices.

'I am a Facebook addict': Field experiences

The focus of this chapter has been to discuss the use of Facebook as a mainstream ethnographic site and research tool. Thus far, I have drawn on understandings from connective ethnography to present differences in the terms 'field site', 'participant observation' and 'field notes' in digital spaces. In order to bring to life how these differences are experienced and the associated challenges negotiated in traditional, face-to-face ethnographic practice, this section presents a reflexive excerpt from my research journal.

Fieldwork

The time I spent in the 'field' of Facebook was an intense weekly occurrence. I would look at what each of the participants had posted and I would take screenshots of their Profiles. I would take field notes of what I was seeing and being involved in, for example when my participants posted on my Facebook Wall; when my participants were involved with a specific Facebook practice; and uploading and tagging photos from a night out. Although I intended to only check the participants' Profiles once per week, I ended up viewing posts on a daily basis as the participants' Status updates[7] would be visible in my News Feed[8] alongside my other Friends posts. This made the separation of my personal Facebook interactions and my professional, research interactions fairly difficult. At times, it felt like I could not leave the field as my personal interactions were taking place alongside my research interactions. This context collapse (Vitak et al., 2012) meant that gaining separation from the field at the time of data analysis was difficult.

'I'm deactivating my account': My time off Facebook 5 July 2011–5 September 2011

The year-long ethnography came to an end with a self-imposed temporal boundary on 10 June 2011. I decided at the start of the study to limit my interaction with the students to the academic year 2010–2011. Throughout my year of study, I watched the students' updates appearing in my News Feed and had become accustomed to the ebbs and flows of their lives. Watching their experiences of university life and academic life roll out, punctuated with assignment and exam crises, excitement about Christmas or a flatmate's birthday or a funny joke a Friend had posted. As June went on and my detailed analysis of the Profiles was beginning, I found it increasingly hard to stop reading the participants' Facebook updates. I completed the final round of face-to-face interviews and made the decision to hide the participants from my News Feed. I did not want to 'Unfriend' the participants on Facebook, as this was my main form of contact with them and my data source, but I felt I needed some space from the field. At this point, I decided to do something I had been toying with for a while. I decided to deactivate my Facebook account for a month.

This action may seem inconsequential; some readers may think 'so what? Why is she making a big deal out of this? Does she really *need* to deactivate her account? Can't she just turn it off? Leave it alone?' I thought that would be possible, but it was not. My life had revolved in and around Facebook for the last two years and as I admitted at the beginning of my MA dissertation, 'I am a Facebook addict' (Stirling, 2009). I was beginning to feel that I could not gain the distance for an analytical view of the site or my participants' use of it. This ethnography had been immersive. Madden proposes an ethnographer who is immersed in a society or culture they are studying as being 'at one' 'with the sociality of their participant group' and that this can lead to the ethnographer being 'lost' in the field, and that it is important to be able to step back (2010, p.78). There were concerns that the boundaries were blurred between 'participant-as-observer and observer-as-participant' (Hammersley and Atkinson, 1983, p.102) and this made analysis of the field lack rigour or a level of higher thinking. I felt too close and comfortable to be critical. Hammersley and Atkinson suggest that the ethnographer should be wary of feeling 'at home' in the field:

> There must always remain some part held back, some social and intellectual distance. For it is in the space created by this distance that the analytical work of the ethnographer gets done... the ethnography can be little more than the autobiographical account of a personal conversation.
>
> (Hammersley and Atkinson, 1983, p.102)

At this point I needed some space to consider the data away from the field. I had mixed emotions about leaving Facebook. For the first time in this study, I was experiencing what I imagine other ethnographers feel when they have to leave the community they are part of. The difference in researching Facebook is that I had had unlimited access to my FbF Profiles for the last year. The access I had been afforded through the digital field site, it could be said, could not be expected when observing Facebook practices using traditional ethnographic methods. The digital approach meant I could view the Facebook Profiles 24 hours a day, should I have wished. I had to manage the blurring of my personal and professional identities which were both a part of my many interactions on Facebook. I believe this was similar to the experiences of my participants' and I shared the challenges they experienced. My aim was to be authentic within and about the culture being studied. I was making sense of Facebook practices through my own use of Facebook, both personally and as a research tool. This duality of Facebook use, both personal and professional, research site and research tool was complex to manage.

Advancing debates in digital ethnography

In viewing Facebook as a field site there exists some tensions relating to the dichotomy of the online versus offline. Online and offline are not separate entities; they often co-exist in the same space. boyd proposes 'the Internet is increasingly entwined in peoples' lives; it is both an imagined space and an architectural place' (2008, p.26). This 'imagined' space is becoming a central focus of many peoples' lives and 'a real' place as our online or digital lives are a ubiquitous part of day-to-day life. The dichotomy of the terms *online* and *offline* create is problematic when used alongside ethnography and particularly when used in relation to Facebook. In the study of university students, the site was most often used as part of the face-to-face cultures and practices of the participants. In studying students' Facebook use, I have observed that they very rarely operate in a single domain, space, or site, digital or physical. They access Facebook from their smartphone on the way to lectures or they chat to classmates on Facebook Chat on their laptops while sitting next to them in a lecture. This duality of spatial use is a common and an important theme when exploring Facebook use in HE. By paying attention ethnographically to the wider sphere, beyond the digital space, the multiplicity of the cultural practices taking place can be explored. In this project, a multi-sited, connective, ethnographic approach allowed for observation both on Facebook and face-to-face, and it enabled me to explore the complex relationship of the embedded and ubiquitous nature of Facebook. In a connective ethnography there is a blurring of the boundaries of digital and physical spaces.

There are many other methods available to study Facebook, which were not used in this study but could have tracked this blurring of boundaries. For example, the use of a video screen-cast[9] of the user's computer screen would allow the researcher to view the participant's movements within and outside of Facebook. Which order did they navigate the site? What is the relationship between Facebook and the other websites and computer programs they are running? This would help to answer the question: 'in which tasks is Facebook embedded?'

This is a fluid and somewhat changeable landscape. Ellison and boyd (2013, p.169) suggest researchers of social media do not 'become too enamored with these new systems', by being critical and taking time to understand the social practices and the technology. A key approach is to be true to the social practices at the time of study. This study took place in 2010 when the Facebook interface was very different from the 'Timeline' we see today, including separate tabs and images hidden in the photo tab. People threw sheep[10] at each other and 'Pokes'[11] were a daily occurrence. By keeping immersed in the 2010 data I tried to be true to my documentation of Facebook practices in 2010 and not to be influenced by the newer interfaces, communication and interaction practices, such as the 'Timeline' and video streaming which developed over the three years of analysis and writing up the data. Moreover, a researcher needs to aware of the power structures that exist between the website and the wider audience of users. Facebook, the company, protects its assets. There are now very strict guidelines regarding the use of the Facebook logo and the 'brand assets' (Facebook, 2013). In the early days of the website these did not exist, social practices were new and developing (arguably they are still in this process). Now the company has very clear definitions of what 'Like', 'Tag' or 'Comment' mean. Social norms are beginning to develop and it seems from these brand asset definitions that there are expectations from Facebook that users will behave and use these 'tools' in a certain manner. Although these behaviours are also negotiated among Friends, (see also the work of Davies, 2012), I see this as challenging the use of Facebook as a research site in that there are powerful structures controlling and shaping social behaviours.

The digital is now interwoven, in many of our lives, increasingly through the use of portable devices such as smartphones and tablets. This mainstream use of the digital (for most, but not all of us) must be an influence on those researchers who are studying peoples' social lives, whether that be within a digital research site or not.

Conclusion

The approaches detailed in this chapter offer a reflexive view of the use of Facebook in a connective ethnography of students in higher education in the United Kingdom. The cultural practices of students' Facebook use across digital and physical environments were studied, and Facebook was used as one of the field sites and one of the methods of data collection. I propose the culture being studied should be the starting point in influencing the choice of ethnographic methods and that to study the practices of the participants is the important focus whether that is through a digital and/or face-to-face approach. The increasing use of digital devices and digital environments (in this case, by university students) follows that the ethnographer's focus should be responsive to the field, and therefore studying these practices moves to digital methods and to multi-sited approaches. In this example, the cultures of Higher Education and Facebook use in the United Kingdom were explored using a preferred method of a 'connective ethnography' (Hine, 2007). The traditional definitions of field sites when studying students are perhaps the lecture theatre, seminar room or student halls of residence. The digital field site was Facebook, and this is a layer over the physical, traditional sites. This is not divided from, but an extension of, the traditional field site and should be viewed as 'mainstream'. This project provided scope for thinking about 'fuzzy' boundaries in a research project. The use of the digital is not always tangible. My duality of Facebook use, both professionally and personally, meant that my own role was fuzzy. This could be viewed as a tension for other researchers approaching similar projects and wondering whether to use their own SNS account. Given the insights this insider position generated, I propose this was not a negative. A focus for the future is to pay attention to the socially constructed nature of space and the way in which people's practices flow between the digital and physical and the professional and personal spheres.

Notes

1. A Profile for public figures, businesses and organizations. Users can connect with these Pages by becoming a fan and liking them to receive their updates in their News Feed.
2. The stream of tweets (140-character text messages) a Twitter user would see in their Home space.

3. An instant messaging application (app) for smartphones.
4. A time-limited photo messaging app where users send text and/or photo and video messages which are then deleted after a pre-set amount of time (10 seconds).
5. Profile with a capital P here forward is used to describe a Facebook Profile.
6. A Profile for small group communication and for people to share their common interests and express their opinion. It is aimed at non-commercial use.
7. Status update allows users to inform their Friends of current thoughts.
8. The News Feed highlights what a users' Friends post.
9. A screen-cast is a digital recording of computer screen output, also known as a video screen capture.
10. A digital practice, whereby a cartoon 'sheep' is thrown at another user by clicking a button which then shows the sheep on the other users' Wall.
11. A Poke is a way to interact with your Friends on Facebook. It allows one user to digitally poke another, through a 'Poke' message on their Profile.

References

Bailey, C. (2007) *A Guide to Qualitative Field Research*. California: Pine Forge Press.
Beer, D. and Burrows, R. (2007) 'Sociology and, of and in Web 2.0: some initial considerations', *Sociological Research Online*, 12(5), http://www.socresonline.org.uk/12/5/17/html, date accessed 20 March 2009.
Boellstorff, T. (2008) *Coming of Age in Second Life: An Anthropologist Explores the Virtually Human*. Princeton: Princeton University Press.
Boellstorff, T., Nardi, B., Pearce, C. and Taylor, T.L. (2012) *Ethnography and Virtual Worlds: A Handbook of Method*. Princeton: Princeton University Press.
boyd, d. (2008) 'How an qualitative Internet researchers define the boundaries of their projects: A response to Christine Hine', in A. Markham and N. Baym (eds.) *Internet Inquiry: Conversations About Method*. London: Sage, pp.26–32.
Buchanan, E.A. (2011) 'Internet research ethics: Past, present, and future', *The Handbook of Internet Studies*, Chichester: Wiley-Blackwell, pp.83–108.
CLEX (2009). *Higher Education in a Web 2.0 World. Report of an Independent Committee of Inquiry into the Impact on Higher Education of Students' Widespread use of Web 2.0 Technologies*, http://www.clex.org.uk, date accessed 12 May 2009.
Crooks, R.N. (2013) 'The Rainbow Flag and the Green Carnation: Grindr in The Gay Village', *First Monday*, 18(11), http://firstmonday.org/ojs/index.php/fm/article/view/4958/3790.
Davies, J. (2012) 'Facework on Facebook as a new literacy practice', *Computers and Education*, 59(1), 19–29.
Delamont, S. (2004) 'Ethnography and participant observation', in C. Seale, G. Gobo and J. Gubrium (eds.) *Qualitative Research Practices*, London: Sage, pp.217–29.
Ellison, N. B. and boyd, d. (2013) 'Sociality through Social Network Sites', in W. H. Dutton (ed.) *The Oxford Handbook of Internet Studies*. Oxford: Oxford University Press, pp.151–72.
Facebook (2013) *Asset and Logo Guidelines March 2013 (Lightweight version)*, http://3835642c2693476aa717d4b78efce91b9730bcca725cf9bb0b37.r51.cf1.rackcdn.com/FB_MarketGuide_Light.pdf, date accessed 25 October 2013.

Geertz, C. (1973) *The Interpretation of Cultures: Selected Essays*. New York: Basic Books.

Hammersley, M. and Atkinson, P. (1983) *Ethnography: Principles in Practice*, London: Tavistock.

Hammersley, M. and Atkinson, P. (2007) *Ethnography. Principles in Practice* (3rd edition). Abingdon: Routledge.

Ipsos MORI (2008) 'Great expectations of ICT', *JISC*, http://www.jisc.ac.uk/publications/publications/greatexpectations.aspx, date accessed 15 May 2009.

Hine, C. (2000) *Virtual Ethnography*. London: Sage.

Hine, C. (ed.) (2005) *Virtual Methods*. London: Berg Publishers.

Hine, C. (2007) 'Connective ethnography for the exploration of e-Science', *Journal of Computer-Mediated Communication*, 12(2), 618–34.

Kirschner, P.A. and Karpinski, A.C. (2010) 'Facebook®and academic performance', *Computers in Human Behaviour*, 26(6), 1237–45.

Kozinets, R. (2010) *Netnography: Doing Ethnographic Research Online*. London: Sage.

Leander, K.M. and McKim, K.K. (2003) 'Tracing the everyday "sitings" of adolescents on the Internet: A strategic adaptation of ethnography across online and offline spaces', *Education, Communication and Information*, 3(2), 211–40.

Madden, R. (2010) *Being Ethnographic. A Guide to the Theory and Practice of Ethnography*. London: Sage.

Madge, C., Meek, J., Wellens, J. and Hooley, T. (2009) 'Facebook, social integration and informal learning at university: "It is more for socialising and talking to friends about work than for actually doing work"', *Learning, Media and Technology*, 34(2), 141–55.

Markham, A. (2005) 'The methods, politics, and ethics of online ethnography', in N. Denzin and Y. Lincoln (eds.) *The Sage Handbook of Qualitative Research* (3rd edition). London: Sage, pp.247–84.

Murthy, D. (2008) 'Digital ethnography: An examination of the use of new technologies for social research', *Sociology*, 42(5), 837–55.

Raynes-Goldie, K. (2010) 'Aliases, creeping, and wall cleaning: Understanding privacy in the age of Facebook', *First Monday*, 15(1), http://journals.uic.edu/ojs/index.php/fm/article/view/2775/2432.

Robinson, L. and Schulz, J. (2009) 'New avenues for sociological inquiry: Evolving forms of ethnographic practice', *Sociology*, 43(4), 685–98.

Sade-Beck, L. (2004) 'Internet ethnography: Online and offline', *International Journal of Qualitative Methods*, 3(2), 45–51.

Sanjek, R. (1990) *Fieldnotes: The Makings of Anthropology*. London: Cornell University.

Selwyn, N. (2009) 'Faceworking: exploring students' education-related use of Facebook', *Learning, Media and Technology*, 34(2), 157–74.

Selwyn, N. and Grant, L. (2009) 'Researching the realities of social software use – an introduction', *Learning, Media and Technology*, 34(2), 1–9.

Stirling, E. (2009) *We all communicate on Facebook. A case of undergraduates' use and non-use of the Facebook group*, MA Dissertation, University of Sheffield.

Stirling, E. (2014) *Why waste your time on Facebook?: A temporal analysis of first-year undergraduate students and transition in UK Higher Education*, PhD Thesis, University of Sheffield.

Taylor, T.L. (2006) 'Does WoW change everything? How a PvP server, multinational player base, and surveillance mod scene caused me pause', *Games and Culture*, 1(4), 318–37.

Vie, S. (2008) 'Digital Divide 2.0: "Generation M" and online social networking sites in the composition classroom', *Computers and Composition*, 25(1), 9–23.

Vitak, J., Lampe, C., Gray, R. and Ellison, N.B. (2012) 'Why won't you be my Facebook friend?: Strategies for managing context collapse in the workplace', in *Proceedings of the 2012 iConference*, ACM, pp.555–7.

Wolf, M. (1992) *A Thrice-Told Tale: Feminism, Postmodernism and Ethnographic Responsibility*. Stanford: Stanford University Press.

Part II
Combining and Comparing Methods

Introduction to Part II

The problem: What do digital methods add?

Digital media, and data derived from online interactions, potentially offer a hugely valuable addition to the methodological repertoire of social researchers. Cost savings, convenience, the ability to reach hidden populations and the capacity to explore sensitive topics in new ways all contribute to the appeal of digital methods. Such advantages are, however, too often simply taken for granted, reflecting the widespread culture of expectations around the potential of digital technologies. For social scientists, it is important not only to take a more measured approach, evaluating the advantages that digital methods may bring, but also to alert to new biases and omissions that may emerge. Systematic and ongoing comparison of the potential of new methods against their established counterparts is an important part of the mainstreaming of digital methods.

Such comparisons are not necessarily confined to clearly separable pairs of analogue and digital, old and new sets of methods. As digital technologies become embedded in our everyday lives, many of the social situations in which we wish to conduct research combine different media. People do not operate on single platforms at a time, but instead move creatively between them. Social researchers attempting to make sense of these multi-modal lives need research approaches which span different platforms and explore connections between them, rather than confining themselves to exploration of a single medium. Researchers need to be able not just to compare what different methods add, but also to move in an agile fashion between them, building multi-faceted perspectives on multi-modal phenomena. These twin issues, of comparing data derived from different modes and combining such data in exploration of complex, hybrid social situations, form the focus of Part II. The chapters span as follows: interview and survey-based research conducted in a variety of modes; comparison of data derived from social media with the conventional public opinion survey; and combination of data from concurrent online and offline activities to explore the emergence of new literacy practices.

Case studies comparing and combining methods

Given the cheapness and convenience of the online survey and the allure of born-digital data, it has become difficult to resist the pressure that dictates large-scale social research should be taken online. Concerns persist, however, about the extent to which online surveys can substitute for their paper-based counterparts as truly robust social science measures, given that social inequality in access to and use of the Internet persists. Even as the pressures to conduct cost-efficient social research build, it is important to explore the extent to which online modes of research build in various forms of inequality and bias. Online interviews, too, have the capacity to extend the reach of social research, allowing for participants unable or unwilling to meet the demands of a face-to-face interview to have their say. In both cases, however, the concern of the social researcher focuses on understanding what is distinctive about the various modes of research, both in terms of the participants they reach and the capacity of data they provide to meet the needs of our research questions.

This comparison of different research modes forms the topic of Jo Hope's chapter, describing research aimed at understanding the use of online support by parents of people with a rare condition, Rett syndrome. Without an overarching sampling frame to define her population, Hope focused on combining methods to allow her to reach as large, and as diverse a sample of the population as possible. This chapter provides an exemplar of an approach to exploring sample and data biases across online and offline modes of administering surveys and interviews and gives advice on issues to be wary of when combining data from different modes in the same research project.

Javier Sajuria and Jorge Fábrega continue this theme of comparing different modes of data collection with their exploration of Twitter data. Their case study focuses on discussions surrounding the Chilean presidential election of 2013. Sajuria and Fábrega summarize the problematic status of Twitter as an apparent barometer of public opinion against the surveys more conventionally used to explore the issue. Through an inventive means of assigning political affiliation to Twitter users, and analysis of sentiments towards both candidates and policy issues, Sajuria and Fábrega show that what appears to be a matter of political opinion on Twitter is a complex phenomenon that should not be expected to map straightforwardly onto measures of opinion derived in other ways, nor to be taken as predictive of voting intentions. Twitter data, however, proves to offer access to new forms of research question, allowing for exploration of complex issues surrounding the circumstances which promote the expression of specific political opinions and shades of political sentiment. The relationship between the online method and its conventional counterpart is not one of straightforward substitution. Each has its own affordances, and each contributes its own qualities to the research repertoire.

In the final chapter in Part II, Roberto de Roock, Ibrar Bhatt, and Jonathon Adams explore a complex, multi-modal setting which requires them not just to compare different forms of data, but to work across them and explore the ways in which their participants do the same. The situation which they focus upon is the physical learning environment (classroom or lecture room), but this is a learning environment in which the students also work in online spaces, both those which form the official topic of the class and others which the students visited on their own initiative. The ethnography, which de Roock, Bhatt and Adams describe, combines a present observer taking field notes, a camera recording activity within the classroom, semi-structured interviews with participants, recording of students' faces and voices via laptop webcams and logging of on-screen activities. The authors share their experiences of capturing and analysing the multi-modal practices and events that occurred within the classrooms and the online spaces with which they connected. This chapter contains rich advice on the technical and practical aspects of conducting multi-modal research which combines different forms of data, and illustrates the benefits to be derived from making the efforts to do so, in terms of the ability to explore in depth the complex ecologies of interaction which increasingly prevail in our contemporary existence.

Cautions for combining and comparing

Taken collectively, the chapters in Part II contain some useful pointers for researchers who seek to add digital methods and online modes of research into their repertoire:

- Be systematic, but also imaginative, when comparing one research approach with another. Both the identity of participants and the kind of data that emerges may be affected by a shift to a different mode. Combining different modes in a single research project may be a route to maximizing participation: but the researcher needs to be careful to establish that the data from different modes is truly comparable.

- Be aware that 'found data' from social networking sites may provide a new way to explore enduring concerns such as the nature of 'public opinion'. However, the public constituted through social networking sites is not the same as the public constituted through other means, and the nature of opinion itself varies between settings. Social networking sites provide interesting data in their own right, but this does not map neatly onto other ways of understanding the public.

- Where social situations span different media, be prepared to collect data which traverses those media and allows the researcher to align them and explore the connections between them. This kind of research can be technically challenging as tools to facilitate it are in their infancy. As these tools develop, they promise to allow exploration of new forms of social experience and to free researchers from the constraints placed on the scope of our research questions by methods that focus on one medium at a time.

5
Mixing Modes to Widen Research Participation

Jo Hope

In this chapter, I discuss mixing online and offline modes as a means to diversify participation in social research. While Orgad (2009) has discussed adding offline to online modes, I focus on adding digital methods to an offline methodology. I argue that traditional modes of research can make it difficult for some people to participate, leading to potential sample biases.

I use a case study from my own research to illustrate key considerations when using mixed modes. These are reflected in the organization of the chapter, which explores mixed mode recruitment, preparing to use mixed modes and assessing the impact of mixing modes. I argue that if comparability of data is planned into the design, differences between modes can be minimized and the quality of data can be enriched through wider participation. I conclude the chapter with a set of recommendations for how other researchers might fruitfully use a mixed mode approach.

Background

There are debates about the nature, quality and comparability of data collected across different modes. Survey researchers have tended to take a pragmatic approach to combining web and mail surveys (Dillman, Christian and Smyth, 2009), while the legitimacy of online interviews can be contentious. There are concerns that email interview responses, which can be edited before sending, mask the hesitation and repairs evident in verbal interviews (Kazmer and Xie, 2008). Others argue that a lack of embodied cues can make it harder to interpret email communication (e.g. Markham, 2004). Possible limitations of Voice over Internet Protocol (VoIP) interviews include 'drop outs' of video and audio, relatively higher attrition (Deakin and Wakefield, 2014) and a need for interviewer and interviewee to have relevant technical skills and feel comfortable on camera (Hay-Gibson, 2009). If such issues are common they could impact on the quality of online interview data in terms of a greater social desirability bias, lower levels of rapport, poorer in-interview interpretation and recruitment biases, which would affect its comparability with offline data.

The case study presented in this chapter aimed to increase the diversity of participation by avoiding the inadvertent exclusion of some groups through the exclusive use of offline modes of data collection and recruitment. A brief outline of the research aims and design is given below to provide a context for the rest of the chapter.

Research aims and design

The case study presented here is my research into the role of online peer support in the caring practices of parents of people with a rare syndrome, Rett syndrome. Rett syndrome is associated with disability and severe and unpredictable health problems (Smeets, Pelc and Dan, 2011). It is thought to affect about 2,500 females in the United Kingdom (Neurological Alliance, 2003) with a much lower prevalence among males (Kerr, 2002). I was interested in whether online peer-support use was socially differentiated, if it was used for inequitable gains, and how it connected with everyday caring practices. As I aimed to explore both social patterning and individual experiences, a mixed methods approach was used. The first stage involved completion of a choice of paper or online survey by parents of people with Rett syndrome living in the United Kingdom. This focused on use of and attitudes towards the Internet and online support and key demographic information. The second stage included mixed mode, semi-structured interviews with parents of people with Rett syndrome who had used online support within the last three years. A choice was given between face-to-face, telephone and VoIP interviews, with email interviews offered if other modes were unsuitable. Eligible interviewees were recruited through the survey (and later through the online channels described below). The interview focused on the role of online peer support in wider information-seeking and caring practices.

Mixed mode recruitment

Like many other social researchers, I was interested in recruiting a diverse sample from a hidden population with no comprehensive sampling frame. For the survey stage, I aimed to recruit parents from a range of social backgrounds, with differing experiences of the Internet and online peer support. As the survey provided screening for the interviews, it was important to recruit current users of online peer support. In this section, I describe how online recruitment has aided me in reaching a more diverse group of eligible parents.

At the time of my research, there were three charities with different focuses: Rett UK, which aimed to provide support to carers (established in 1985); the Rett Syndrome Research Trust, which focused on genetic therapy and treatment research (established in 2009); and Cure Rett (established in 2012), which aimed to provide support and to fund research. Rett UK's membership database was the largest, most up-to-date list of relatives of people with Rett syndrome available in the United Kingdom ($n = 619$; 555 of whom were identifiable as parent members). Contacts at the Rett Syndrome Research Trust and Cure Rett advised me that the best way to recruit parents interested in their work was through their Facebook Pages. However, as diversity of sample was crucial, I also used recruitment channels.

It has been argued that online support and discussion groups can provide (in this case, widened) access to hidden groups, particularly those sharing a narrowly defined interest, such as a specific illness (Hesse-Biber and Griffin, 2012). Through online searches and consultation with Rett UK members, I discovered a range of Rett syndrome-specific and broader carers' support sites, groups and email lists. However, these sites and groups did not collect or provide enough information to allow me to create a larger sampling frame based on my eligibility criteria. It was therefore not possible to estimate how many parents would see research requests (especially on public pages) or to avoid some parents receiving multiple invitations to participate. This, along with the relatively small Rett UK sample, meant I could not carry out a randomized sample, so instead sampled for diversity. I used this data as a background to relate qualitative findings to social patterning in the survey population without claiming generalizability to the whole population.

I sent personalized letters to all parents and unidentified family members in the Rett UK database in November 2012. These included a paper survey and provided a link to the online survey, so members could choose their preferred response mode. An invitation to participate was also included in Rett UK's paper newsletter, which was sent to all members (including parents, other family members, professionals and others with an interest in Rett syndrome).

I opened research-specific accounts on Facebook, Twitter and Carers UK's online forum to allow me to communicate with others on these sites. I also created a website,[1] allowing me to overcome the limits of recruiting on sites requiring brevity (such as Twitter). This site included a link to my University of Surrey web page and my email address so parents could authenticate my identity. Relevant online gatekeepers were approached to gain permission for me to post recruitment notices directly or (if they preferred), for them to post on my behalf. I posted on online forums at different times of day to gain a wide audience but concentrated on Friday evenings, so my post was displayed at a popular time when more people would see it (Saturday morning).

A follow-up letter was sent to family members on the Rett UK database in early 2013 with a link to the online survey and a form for requesting a new survey or providing information about non-response. A final reminder was also included in Rett UK's paper newsletter. Reminder posts were shared through all online channels used previously, along with requests for interviewees. The two interviewees recruited through online channels also completed surveys before completing the interviews.

Preparing to use mixed modes

This section explores my methodological reasons for choosing mixed modes and how they can be designed to foster comparability. As outlined above, my aim was to encourage participation by a diverse group of parents. By providing a choice of ways to participate, I hoped to avoid inadvertently, excluding participants who were unable to participate in a particular mode. As access to and use of the Internet remains socially differentiated (Dutton and Blank, 2013), the exclusive use of online methods will exclude some people. However, as argued below, the exclusive use of offline methods may exclude other people.

Mixed mode surveys

For people who can touch-type and have access to the Internet in a number of contexts, an online survey may be quicker and easier to complete than a paper version. However, online and offline survey modes can differ, causing mode effects, which can be somewhat ameliorated by standardizing question format and presentation across modes (Dillman, Christian and Smyth, 2009). I therefore created my survey in SurveyMonkey (an online web survey site) and downloaded a PDF version to use as my paper survey. However, some factors led to unavoidable differences between modes, outlined below.

In all paper surveys posted to Rett UK members, I excluded a question about channel of recruitment that was included in the online survey, to avoid disengaging respondents. Similarly, I excluded a question from the web survey about current Internet access as completing a web survey demonstrated access.

There were also some unavoidable experiential differences between modes. First, although I tried to ensure parity between pages by mode, they would format differently on different web devices. Second, respondents were redirected automatically online at key decision questions, but given directions to skip questions in the paper survey. This increased the reading burden on paper survey respondents as well as allowed the completion of irrelevant questions on the paper but not the online survey. As it transpired, however, the 'correct' decision in paper surveys was clear from subsequent answers, which made this less problematic. Finally, I avoided the online survey 'forcing' people to respond to questions before completing a page so they could skip questions as freely as on the paper survey. However, I could not do this for key decision questions without losing the automatic redirection function.

Mixed mode interviews

I chose mixed mode interviews because I was concerned that a synchronous face-to-face interview may be inappropriate for some potential participants. Like many other researchers, my group of interest included people with unpredictable schedules, who worked long hours and had competing demands on their time. I was keen to avoid excluding parents of children with the most severe health problems and full-time workers whose children lived at home. I also wished to avoid geographical mode effects, specifically a bias towards face-to-face interviews in my local region. Finally, I hoped that having a choice would prompt interviewees to choose the most convenient and comfortable mode, which might aid rapport and disclosure.

To support the comparability of interview modes, each was based on the same semi-structured schedule. I tried to make the email interview as like other modes as possible by preserving a conversational element, presenting a few questions at a time and responding flexibly depending upon responses where possible. Fifty eligible parents indicated an interest in participating. At initial research contacts (by email with follow-up by phone), parents were advised that interviews were expected to take between one and a half to two hours. A choice was given between three synchronous modes: face-to-face, VoIP interviews and telephone interviews, with email interviews offered as an alternative if none were suitable. However, I stressed that the content of email interviews would be the same as in synchronous interviews.

Assessing the impact of mixing modes on participation

I carried out a series of tests on demographic mode differences to assess the impact on participation. This section describes my results and can be used as a worked example of how impact could be assessed by other researchers. Although my sample was not randomly selected and not generalizable, I used statistical tests because they are less subjective than judgments based on descriptive statistics (Sapsford, 2007). These results thus demonstrate the strength rather than the generalizability of my findings.

Recruitment from different modes

A total of 190 surveys were received from eligible parents. Given the lack of a comprehensive sampling frame, overall response rate was difficult to assess. There was a 26 per cent response rate ($n = 158$) from the letter recruitment frame. However, a probable overestimation of eligibility means the response rate may have been higher. For instance, some parents contacted me to say their child had had their diagnosis changed by health professionals and there was limited information about 64 relatives on the mailing list, who may not have been parents.

I discovered later that providing people with a choice of mode when their preference is not known can reduce response rate by around 1–9 per cent (see Dillman, Christian and Smyth, 2009 for a summary). I was not aware of this finding at the time of recruitment so it is possible my approach may have slightly reduced the response rate.

To assess the impact of recruitment mode on participation, I compared respondents recruited solely through online sources with those reached through at least one offline channel (sometimes in addition to online channels). This meant I could compare respondents only reached online with all others. Overall, 22 respondents – 12 per cent of my sample – were recruited solely through an online source. The online-only recruits had a younger mean age (41 years old, ranging from 23 to 60 years old) than the other group (52 years old, ranging from 29 to 89 years old). A chi-square comparison of age groups was significant, $\chi(4) = 28.30$, $p \le .001$, with a significant and moderate association between age and recruitment mode (Cramer's V score of .393, $p < .001$). The significance derived mostly from the much higher percentage of the 23–34-year-old age group ($p < .001$) that were reached only online. About 34 per cent of this group were recruited solely online compared to the sample average of 8 per cent. The use of online recruitment more than doubled the number in this age group from 7 to 15. There were no statistically significant differences found in chi-square tests comparing household income and education levels between these groups. However, an error introduced during the printing process meant the bottom three household income groups could not be differentiated in paper surveys, so had to be coded together as 'below £30,000'. This may have masked any differences associated with the lowest household income values.

Factors connected to survey mode choice

I carried out similar comparisons to explore survey mode choice. No significant differences were found in terms of educational level, household income (but see above) and use of mobile Internet devices. Instead mode choice was partly connected to mode of recruitment and to age. Seventy-three per cent of those recruited by letter returned a paper survey while none of the respondents recruited through online channels requested one.

Those who chose an online survey were significantly younger on average than those choosing a paper survey.[2] This partly reflects the overlap between data collection mode and recruitment mode because when letter-recruited parents were tested, the median age of web survey respondents increased to 48.3 years old while the median age of paper survey respondents remained the same. This difference remained significant, although its strength reduced.[3] This supports the suggestion that including an online mode increased uptake among younger parents. However these findings also raise the possibility that mode effects may be confounded with age differences, which is examined in a later section.

Self-rated ability to use the Internet may also have played a part in mode choice. The single person who rated their ability to use the Internet as 'bad' and two of the three who rated it as 'poor' completed a paper survey. Of those who rated their ability to use the Internet as 'good' or 'excellent', 53.9 per cent chose to complete a paper survey. This suggests that once a certain level of online competence is achieved, mode convenience is important but below that there may not be genuine 'choice' between modes.

Table 5.1   Interviewee demographic and socio-economic details by mode

	Face-to-face (*n* = 9)	Telephone (*n* = 5)	VoIP (*n* = 3)	Email (*n* = 3)
Gender				
Female	8	5	2	1
Male	1	0	1	2
Age				
23–34	0	1	0	0
35–44	4	1	1	3
45–54	1	3	2	0
55–64	3	0	0	0
Region resident				
North West	0	3	0	1
South West	2	0	0	0
South East	3	1	1	2
London	2	0	0	0
East of England	0	1	0	0
Yorkshire and the Humber	2	0	1	0
(United Arab Emirates)	0	0	1	0
Occupational status				
Working full time	1	4	2	1
Working part time	3	0	1	1
Unemployed	0	0	0	1
Doing housework, looking after children or other persons	4	1	0	0
Occupation groups of working interviewees				
Managers, directors and senior officials	0	2	2	1
Professional occupations	3	1	0	1
Associate professional and technical occupations	2	1	0	0
Caring, leisure and other service occupations	0	0	1	0

Factors connected to interview mode choice

Just under half of interviews (*n* = 9, including a joint interview with a couple) were undertaken face-to-face, with the rest carried out over the phone (*n* = 5), VoIP call (*n* = 3) and email (*n* = 3).

Table 5.1 presents key demographic characteristics of interviewees. Age was again an important factor, with all interviewees aged over 54 choosing a face-to-face interview over other modes. As hoped, there was not a strong geographical mode bias. Interviews in my region (the

South East) were carried out in all modes and over half of my interviews were with parents living outside my region. However none of the interviews in the North West were carried out in person. In part this was due to parents' concerns about my travelling a long way to interview them, which was sometimes compounded by their doubts about the relevance of their experience. This was particularly true for parents who saw themselves as not using online support 'enough'. I tried to counteract this by reassuring all interviewees of the importance of their account and, where possible, combining travel to interviews with some other research activity. Confidence in ability to contribute to research is therefore a potential bias that could affect recruitment to single mode face-to-face interviews, even when the interviewer is able to travel widely. One man from the United Arab Emirates participated in an interview. Basic screening did not pick this up earlier as he had previously lived in the United Kingdom for one year as a Masters student. However, I agreed to interview him as it added interesting data about the use of UK online support by a foreign national.

Occupation status also appeared to play a part in participation in interviews, but household income alone did not seem to have an impact (but see earlier problems with this measure). All but one of the full-time carers chose face-to-face interviews (one carer from the East of England chose a telephone interview). All, except one parent who worked full time (who was a freelancer), chose modes of interview that were not face-to-face. No interviewees working at the most senior level participated in a face-to-face interview. This could reflect the additional time burden of a face-to-face interview, which requires a longer 'lead-in' time (finding a suitable room, setting up equipment and offering a cup of tea) than more time-bounded Skype or telephone interviews or asynchronous email interviews.

None of the four men who participated chose a face-to-face interview on their own. One man took part in an interview alongside his wife and three others choose online-mediated modes. One male interviewee chose email because it fitted into his working day while an (unemployed) male interviewee cited a communication preference: 'I personally feel that I write better than I speak/converse'. Google Hangouts (a VoIP) was used by one male interviewee in a way that suggested a cultural element to what Hanna (2012) calls the 'neutral yet personal' space of a Skype interview, which offers comfort without intrusion:

I am an Arab, I am a Muslim [...] in fact the reason that I delayed my interview with you two weeks ago if you remember... [was] in fact to have interview with my, with my family around me ... because I don't feel comfortable when I talk [...] to a woman while I am alone.

Here the presence of his family on one side of the screen (in a different room) with the interviewee on the other allowed him to feel comfortable participating in a one-to-one interview with a female interviewer.

Table 5.2 shows how mode choice differed by online competence and use of the Internet at work. All those who chose a VoIP interview rated their ability to use the Internet as 'excellent' and used it at work. This did not hold for email interviews, which may be due to the ubiquitous diffusion of email use in the United Kingdom (97 per cent), compared with 45 per cent use of VoIP software (Dutton and Blank, 2013). Conversely, almost all interviewees who rated themselves as 'good' rather than 'excellent' users of the Internet chose an offline form of interview, while among more confident and experienced Internet users a range of modes were used. Length of time using the Internet may also have been important, with the person using the Internet for the least time (six years) choosing an offline mode. Overall, this echoes the survey finding that a certain level of competence appears necessary to allow a genuine 'choice' between modes.

In summary, adding online recruitment and online data collection modes led to a greater inclusion of younger parents, working parents, geographically distant parents and men, but VoIP use may have been limited to the most confident Internet users.

Table 5.2 Internet expertise and confidence by mode of interview

	Face-to-face (*n* = 9)	Telephone (*n* = 5)	VoIP (*n* = 3)	Email (*n* = 3)
Years using Internet				
0–5 years	0	1	0	0
6–10 years	3	4	1	1
11–15 years	5	0	2	1
16–20 years	0	0	0	1
Self-rated ability to use the Internet				
Good	3	2	0	1
Excellent	5	3	3	2
Uses the Internet at work				
Yes	3	4	3	2
No	5	1	0	1

Assessing the impact of mixing modes

This section demonstrates how mixed mode data can be examined to test cross-mode comparability.

Assessing mode effects in survey responses

In mixed mode survey research a key concern is measurement error: differences in how questions are answered by mode. It is difficult to disentangle mode effects from subgroup effects (Dillman, Christian and Smyth, 2009) when certain subgroups are overrepresented in a particular mode, as here. However, some recent research comparing mode effects between mail and web surveys found no significant differences in terms of the choice of more extreme categories on rating scales or on missing item counts (Dillman et al., 2009b; Börkan, 2010). Börkan (2010) argues that where web and mail mode effects have been found, these were in studies not specifically designed to compare mode effects.

My own data supported these findings as there was no evidence of one group scoring more strongly on both ends of the scale on a common attitude question (about confidence in health professionals) and the mean response was very similar (paper was 4.0 and online was 3.8). I also split the data by age groups to compare differences in the same question by mode and found no evidence of extreme responses at both ends. Similarly, there was no significant difference between the mean percentage of missing data in paper surveys (3.3 per cent) and online surveys (4.3 per cent). This suggests there were no mode effects masked by subgroup differences in age. This was however difficult to interpret as in higher age groups there were smaller numbers of respondents, so percentages could be misleading.

It has been suggested that open response boxes are used differently online, with digits used instead of alphanumeric numbers, affecting character count (Fuchs, 2009). Written text can vary in size while text typed into survey software does not. I therefore tested for mode effects in the completion of the further comments box at the end of the survey. The proportion of respondents completing this box was similar and not significantly different (26.7 per cent on the paper and 23 per cent on the web survey). The mean number of words used was virtually identical (12.2 for paper, 12.5 for online) and characters (without spaces) were very close, 55.7 on paper and 56.5 online. Neither comparison was significantly different. However, ten respondents used margins in the paper survey to embellish answers to closed questions, which was not possible in the web survey, although similar clarifications were included in the further comments box.

In summary, there were no significant differences between modes in terms of measurement error as tested here. This suggests that web and paper survey data were similar in terms of responses, meaning this data could be combined without serious concerns about comparability.

Assessing mode effects in online interviews

To assess the mode effects in online interviews, I focused on addressing concerns in the literature related to research process, technical problems, establishing rapport and the expression and interpretation of emotion.

The attrition in email interviews differed from other modes. Three parents did not initially respond to the first interview email after giving consent (one parent did not respond to follow-up contacts, one withdrew due to time commitments and the third withdrew because her daughter was in intensive care). However, when other parents changed their minds about participating in other modes of interviews, they always informed me first. This may reflect differences in expectations between synchronous and asynchronous modes of communication, where a response to an email can be postponed or, at times of difficulty, ignored.

Two of the three email interviews were completed. Following a long email silence I managed to re-establish contact with the other interviewee who told me they had experienced a mental breakdown, that an email interview was too pressured and they wanted to change to a face-to-face or telephone interview. We agreed to terminate the interview altogether after a mutually agreed delay and they agreed to allow me to use their existing data.

These experiences highlight the difficulties of using email interviews with people with unpredictable schedules, whose situations may change either before or during the interview. It also highlights that for some members of this group, an email interview, though episodic, may represent a greater felt commitment of time.

Skype presented particular, but not usually insurmountable, technical challenges. After problems with unclear audio, one Skype interview had to be transferred to a telephone interview. In both other cases, connections on both sides of the interview were good enough for it to go ahead. Audio glitches during these interviews were infrequent. When they did occur they were dealt with during the interview, with questions or answers repeated on request.

The other element of Skype that made it different from a face-to-face interview was eye contact. I developed a technique to mimic eye contact by moving the video window of the interviewee to just below my webcam, but it was disconcerting not to have a similar experience of eye contact from the interviewee. However, like Deakin and Wakefield (2014), I did not experience any difficulties developing rapport when interviewing over VoIP.

Humour was important across all modes of interviews, both in terms of reducing tension and increasing rapport. This was expressed in terms of laughter in the verbal interviews (including over VoIP) and included jokes made by interviewees in both completed email interviews (indicated by a smiley emoticon: ☺).

Similarly, some parents in each mode discussed sensitive topics relating to their emotional response to their child's diagnosis, with one parent moved to tears during a VoIP interview. In email interviews parents conveyed emotion through the use of exclamation marks (as described by Kazmer and Xie, 2008) but also through descriptions of emotional states and quotation marks.

Two email interviews also felt relatively spontaneous in tone. These were both carried out on work accounts (both parents reassured me they were happy to do so). Both had a conversational quality at odds with the carefully crafted and constructed email responses described by James and Busher (2009), while one carried out on a personal account could be stilted, with short responses, although stronger rapport, with more embellished answers, was eventually established. This may be due to a potentially greater use of email by both working interviewees, who had mobile and work access to the Internet, while the other interviewee did not. The following excerpt from one of the work email interviews demonstrates expression of emotion, while the volume of words and uncorrected spelling mistake towards the end suggest some unselfconscious spontaneity. The text is in response to a question about the interviewee's experience of receiving her daughter's diagnosis.

Catherine: Appalling to say the least. Ellen's community paed refused for a long time to actually voice her opinion on what she thought was wrong with Ellen, kept saying delayed development!!! When me and her Dad refused to leave her office until she told us what she 'thought' it was, she then said that she thought it was Rett Syndrome which of course meant nothing to us. She then said she had sent a blood sample from Ellen to GOSH for testing (no permission from us to do this!) and that in the meantime we should go home and look up RS on the internet!!! [...] [After the diagnosis there was] still no further support, so I then called GOSH who were great and we went there the next day to see a genetist who told us the science bit and hooked us up with a doctor specialising in RS, I also contacted Rett UK, we then had more support. Still makes me very angry today!

Other than the higher dropout rate in email interviews, the only other difficulty was a lack of telling pauses and retractions. These were present in synchronous interviews when parents began to talk about contentious topics such as the role of perceived class differences in befriending other parents. VoIP interviews were very similar to face-to-face interviews except for the occasional technical problem. Overall then online interviews could be equivalent to offline interviews in eliciting detailed accounts, allowing emotional expression, building rapport, aiding disclosure and attaining – for habitual email users at least – some level of spontaneity in email interviews.

Conclusion and recommendations

My aim in using mixed mode recruitment and data collection was to widen participation. Mixed mode recruitment was successful in allowing me to access a wider age range of parents than via a single mode. Similarly, adding online modes encouraged the participation of a wider range of parents, including those who worked full time and geographically distant parents. Significantly, online methods seemed to be more attractive to male participants, who can be underrepresented in survey research (O'Rourke and Lakner, 1989), and research on sensitive topics (e.g. Lloyd, 1996). Attempts to make data collection modes as equivalent as possible may have contributed to the lack of mode effects found in tests on the survey data. It was possible to build rapport in all interview modes, demonstrated by interviewees' ability to express emotion, use humour and disclose about sensitive experiences within each mode. While email interviews could be disrupted by changes in circumstances and could be perceived as a heavier commitment, they enabled some parents to participate who were unwilling or unable to participate in other modes. They could also be spontaneous and unedited, particularly when used by people with greater access to the Internet, although telling pauses and retractions were absent. Similarly, while VoIP interviews could be disrupted by technical problems, they allowed wider participation among the most confident Internet users and shared many aspects of face-to-face interviews.

I conclude this chapter with the following recommendations for researchers considering combining online and offline modes:

- Mixed mode recruitment should be considered when sampling for diversity, but not generalizability, among a hidden population.
- Offline, as well as online, modes of data collection should be offered when carrying out research in a population where not all members are very confident Internet users.
- The use of online data collection should be considered when trying to recruit men to studies, particularly those with sensitive topics.
- When mixing modes, steps should be taken to provide as similar a research experience as possible across modes.
- When combining online and offline surveys:

  - different modes should be offered consecutively – for example, paper surveys sent with a first letter – with a link to the online mode provided at follow-up;
  - mode effects should be investigated before data are combined.

- A choice of interview modes should be offered to avoid geographical biases in interview mode, if feasible.
- Consider offering alternatives to face-to-face interviews for groups with heavy time constraints or unpredictable schedules.
- Differences in the research process across modes that may affect rapport or data quality should be explored and discussed when reporting findings.

Notes

1. See http://rettonlinesupport.wordpress.com/.
2. Online survey respondents had a median age of 45.4 years, while paper survey respondents had a median age of 54.4 years old, a significant difference, $U = 2633$, $z = -3.99$, $p < .001$, $r = -.29$. These results suggest that age difference accounted for about 29 per cent of the differences found in choice between survey modes.
3. $U = 1745.5$, $z = -2.40$, $p < .05$, $r = -.19$. These results suggest that about 20 per cent of differences in survey choice among letter-recruited parents could be explained by age.

References

Börkan, B. (2010) 'The mode effect in mixed-mode surveys: Mail and web surveys', *Social Science Computer Review*, 28(3), 371–80.

Deakin, H. and Wakefield, K. (2014) 'Skype interviewing: Reflections of two PhD researchers', *Qualitative Research*, 14(5), 603–16.

Dillman, D., Christian, L. and Smyth, J. (2009) *Internet, Mail and Mixed-Mode Surveys: The Tailored Design Method* (3rd edition). Hoboken, NJ: Wiley.

Dillman, D., Phelps, G., Tortora, R., Swift, K., Kohrell, J., Berck, J. and Messer, B.L. (2009) 'Response rate and measurement differences in mixed-mode surveys using mail, telephone, interactive voice response (IVR) and the Internet', *Social Science Research*, 38(1), 1–18.

Dutton, W.H. and Blank, G. with Groselj, D. (2013) *Cultures of the Internet: The Internet in Britain. Oxford Internet Survey 2013*, http://oxis.oii.ox.ac.uk.

Fuchs, M. (2009) 'Differences in the visual design language of paper-and-pencil surveys versus web surveys: A field experimental study on the length of response fields in open-ended frequency questions', *Social Science Computer Review*, 27(2), 213–27.

Hanna, P. (2012) 'Using Internet technologies (such as Skype) as a research medium: A research note', *Qualitative Research*, 12(2), 239–42.

Hay-Gibson, N.V. (2009) 'Interviews via VoIP: Benefits and disadvantages within a PhD study of SMEs', *Library and Information Research*, 33(105), 39–50.

Hesse-Biber, S. and Griffin, A.J. (2012) 'Internet-mediated technologies and mixed methods research: Problems and prospects', *Journal of Mixed Methods Research*, 7(1), 43–61.

James, N. and Busher, H. (2009) *Online Interviewing*. London: Sage.

Kazmer, M. and Xie, B. (2008) 'Qualitative interviewing in Internet studies: Playing with the media, playing with the method', *Information, Communication and Society*, 11(2), 257–78.

Kerr, A.M. (2002) 'Annotation: Rett syndrome: Recent progress and implications for research and clinical practice', *Journal of Child Psychology and Psychiatry*, 43(3), 277–87.

Lloyd, M. (1996) 'Condemned to be meaningful: Non-response in studies of men and infertility', *Sociology of Health and Illness*, 18(4), 433–54.

Markham, A.N. (2004) 'The Internet as research context', in C. Seale, G. Gobo, J.F. Gubrium and D. Silverman (eds.) *Qualitative Research Practice*. London: Sage, pp.328–45.

Neurological Alliance (2003). *Neuro Numbers: A Brief Review of the Numbers of People in the UK with a Neurological Condition*. London: Neurological Alliance.

Orgad, S. (2009) 'How can researchers make sense of the issues involved in collecting and interpreting online and offline data?', in A. Markham and N. Baym (eds.) *Internet Inquiry: Conversations About Method*. Thousand Oaks, CA: Sage, pp.33–53.

O'Rourke, D. and Lakner, E. (1989) 'Gender bias: Analysis of factors causing male underrepresentation in surveys', *International Journal of Public Opinion Research*, 1(2), 164–76.

Sapsford, R. (2007) *Survey Research* (2nd edition). London: Sage.

Smeets, E., Pelc, K. and Dan, B. (2011) 'Rett syndrome', *Molecular Syndromology*, 2, 113–27.

6
Do We Need Polls? Why Twitter Will Not Replace Opinion Surveys, but Can Complement Them

Javier Sajuria and Jorge Fábrega

Introduction

Monitoring and using social media to understand – or influence – public opinion is not a new thing. Companies, political parties and organizations alike are keen to observe what their followers say, what people are commenting on their Facebook Pages and what is said in the comments sections of YouTube and Instagram. Moreover, a great deal of work has been done in building social media teams in charge of both engaging and analysing what people exchange through these platforms. To some extent, these phenomena have questioned whether traditional, more expensive, ways to observe public opinion are still required. The regular route for understanding public opinion, both at the consumer and the political levels, relies heavily on surveys. These instruments present their own advantages depending on the scope of the research. Moreover, they enjoy a fair amount of validity among the scientific community as proper instruments to analyse public attitudes.

Twitter, on the other hand, has been widely contested by the academic community as a valid way to analyse public attitudes and behaviour. Different attempts to predict election outcomes from Twitter have failed, and scholars (Gayo-Avello, 2012; DiGrazia et al., 2013) have argued about the usefulness of social media data to understand large-scale political events. The same has been argued in relation to other events, such as the Eurovision Song Contest or popular TV shows (e.g. *The X Factor*). The underlying consensus is that Twitter does not present the conditions required by traditional research approaches to produce accurate forecasts. Hence, some recent attempts have pursued a different route: comparing Twitter data to opinion polls. Some recent efforts (e.g. Beauchamp, 2013) aim to forecast candidates' approval ratings by matching them with Twitter data from the previous period. In that way, the goal is no longer in predicting elections (i.e. left to opinion polls), but to analyse how close are the discussions on Twitter to more valid representations of public opinion.

This chapter aims to expand this line of research by using two different strategies. On the one hand, we use retweet networks to estimate the political position of Twitter users. Second, we take the content of the tweets from those users to compare their views on different topics with data from public opinion surveys. Scholars (Ansolabehere, Rodden and Snyder, 2008; Bartels 2010; Iyengar, Sood and Lelkes, 2012) have already established the presence of a relationship between political positions and attitudes towards public issues, such as equal marriage and the electoral system. We use the estimation from Twitter data to compare the results with opinion polls and provide a more informed picture of when, if possible, social media can substitute or complement them.

We use data from Chile for 2013, focusing in the period before the presidential election. The Twitter data was gathered from 17 September to 17 December 2013 using the Twitter public streaming API. Survey data, on the other hand, comes from a mainstream source in Chile: the seasonal survey from the Centro de Estudios Públicos (CEP), a recognized Chilean think tank. We discuss the validity issues of each source and the strategy to assess their accuracy.

Our results show that, according to the expectations, Twitter data is still not appropriate for substituting opinion polls. However, there is an interesting story to be told in relation to candidate support and tone. In the Chilean case, the supporters of the leading candidate, and later president, Michelle Bachelet, are more likely to express their views on Twitter with a positive tone. Moreover, when the support for Bachelet predicts significantly the support for certain policies (according to survey data), there is a correspondence in the positive tone of the tweets from her Twitter supporters. This is something that does not happen in the case of those who support other candidates. In other cases, we see supporters that tend to be less likely to use a positive tone on their tweets, even when survey data says that, on average, they support the policies that are talking about. This is consistent on our hypothesis that electoral viability is related to higher likelihood of a positive tone in the tweets.

This chapter will go as follows. First, we discuss the literature on opinion formation and the role of political position. Then, we move into the discussion of using social media data to forecast political events and understand public attitudes. This is followed by a discussion of the Chilean case and the elements of electoral viability. We then explain the methods used to estimate political positions and filter the relevant topics. The results are presented to demonstrate how we derive the conclusions stated above. In our discussion, we extrapolate from these results to make a compelling case of how much researchers should rely on these sources and what is the actual potential of new media for valid academic research.

Literature review

Ideology and public opinion

Political ideology is relevant for public opinion. This is a bold statement, but not unjustified. Zaller argued in 1992 in his well-known Receive-Accept-Sample (RAS) model that people who are more politically aware tend to have more stable and defined attitudes. For Zaller, ideology was a product of this awareness. The more aware a person is, the more stable are their ideological positions. Then, people with more defined ideology or systems of belief will look for information from partisan voices. That is, liberals will search for opinions from liberal elites and will reinforce their own liberal views. This will reflect on preferences for public policies (such as redistribution or welfare in the case of liberals) and approval ratings. Conversely, Zaller claims that less aware people have also less stable ideological positions. In turn, this will reduce their 'attitude constraints' creating inconsistency. In short, more ideology leads to more consistent attitudes.

The empirical evidence supports this view. For example, Bartels (2005) studies how views on tax reform in the United States are explained by ideology and levels of education. Converse (1975) makes a similar case in relation with voting behaviour, while Dalton (2000) analyses the role of party identification (usually used as a measure for ideological position) in today's politics. Outside the United States, there is growing body of literature on the topic. López-Sáez and Martínez-Rubio (2005) explain how ideological positions change the level of credibility in governmental information. Based on the case of the 11-M terrorist attacks in Madrid, they found that right-wing people believed that their voting behaviour had been affected more by official information, while left-wing respondents were more influenced by unofficial information.

Estimating people's political position is, then, extremely relevant to understand political attitudes. Traditional measures have relied on survey questions where people can position themselves in 1–10 (or 1–7) scales, indicate their preferences for the existing political parties or self-identify as liberals or conservatives. The validity of each of these measures has been widely discussed (see discussion in Ansolabehere and Hersh, 2012) and is usually dependent on the political system of each country. In multiparty systems, measures of left-right scale might be an over-reduction of the complexity in which people can position politically. Accordingly, countries with two-party systems are more suitable for such scales. In the case of Chile – the case under study – the presence of two big coalitions for the last 20 years allows us to use methods that are similar to two-party systems.

Using social media for forecasting elections and understanding public attitudes

Since Nate Silver's fairly accurate predictions of the last US elections in 2012, forecasting events has become an attractive topic. Nowadays, we can find statistical models to predict the outcome of the FIFA World Cup, the winner of the Eurovision contest or the next armed conflict in the world. With unequal results, the advancements of forecasting models rely heavily on the quality of the information they use to base their predictions. For examples, attempts to produce similar election forecasts in Chile (Bunker, n.d.) have failed, mainly due to the inability of pollsters to estimate turnout. Similar situations can be observed in other Latin American countries, where the low quality of survey data produces bad forecasts.

A similar discussion has been taking place in academic spheres studying social media. Daniel Gayo-Avello's (2012) now-seminal piece on the topic explained, in a very crude way, why most attempts to provide electoral predictions using Twitter have failed. In Gayo-Avello's opinion, there are no real studies predicting elections, but they fit their models against past events (he calls them post-hoc analysis). This practice creates a large number of successful 'predictions', but there are big questions about how these results would actually fit with future events. Another criticism is that there is no clarity on how to equate tweets to votes. In that regard, a recent study (DiGrazia et al., 2013) attempted to correlate the raw count of tweets with the raw count of votes, although this approach has been heavily questioned for its validity. In general, criticisms about prediction attempts are wide and well grounded.

The field has now started to move away from electoral outcomes to compare Twitter data with some indicators from public opinion surveys. The substantive grounds for the move are clear. The same as responses in a survey, tweets can be understood as public expressions of private attitudes. On the other hand, voting is a different kind of action, more complex, which is constituted by a large array of preferences, attitudes and motivations. The relationship between tweets and survey responses, hence, is more justifiable and sensible. Both respond to a process of opinion formation and thus can be compared as units of observation of a similar nature.

On another note, information from Twitter is relevant as much as any other elite source is. As discussed above, Zaller's RAS model relies on the notion that people who don't hold strong views about certain topics will rely on whatever is more salient to them at the moment they need to elicit a response. In that way, priming plays a significant effect. People can be primed by the media, through pundits, news and other means. But they can also use trusted sources of information, usually from elites. Elite discourse is key in the process of opinion formation, as it influences people's opinions by reinforcing their preconceptions and affecting the level of salience of certain information.

Nick Beauchamp (2013) has inaugurated the field by using Twitter data to observe how it can predict the popularity of different candidates in state-level surveys. His results show how can we use Twitter to interpolate the text from the tweets to indicators of candidates' popularity. His preliminary findings have clear implications for cases when accurate polling data is not easily available. Our approach follows from this logic. If we approach tweets as expressions of personal attitudes, we can use them to understand key elements of public opinion. Moreover, there is more in Twitter than tweets. For example, Barberá (2015) has been successful in estimating users' political positions based on who they follow. We take a slightly different approach. As we explain below, instead of using following networks, we prefer retweets. We take advantage of the current research on the level of homophily of these networks (Lietz et al., 2014) to estimate the political position of those who participate in them. Our preference for retweet networks stems from the substantive difference between following someone and retweeting that person. Although both actions can be motivated by ironic or sarcastic motives, one is a one-off, relatively costless and private action (following), while the other exposes the user's timeline to someone else's tweets. The action behind it reflects a more active statement, whatever that is.

Another way to obtain public attitudes from social media is through text analysis. The use of text as data is a growing area of work in political research. From scaling text to obtain political positions (Laver, Benoit, and Garry, 2003; Lowe, 2008, 2013) to the use of topic modelling for understanding representatives' responsiveness on social media, the field has grown significantly in the last decade. We are interested in a particular area, sentiment analysis. The purpose of this approach is to use semi-automated methods to understand the polarity of certain sections of texts. By polarity, we mean the position of the text in terms of positive or negative dimensions. The use of sentiment analysis is also well documented (Godbole, Srinivasaiah and Skiena, 2007; Pang and Lee, 2008), and it has been applied to Twitter.

This chapter takes advantage of this literature and aims to advance it by looking beyond candidates. The field has been mildly obsessed with forecasting candidate support, while much has yet to be said about policy positions.

The case of Chile in the context of electoral viability

The 2013 presidential election in Chile was particularly different from previous opportunities, at least since the end of Pinochet's dictatorship in 1990. First, it was the end of the first democratic right-wing government in over 50 years. President Piñera's administration had won the election in 2009 and was facing a difficult situation in terms of public approval. Moreover, his coalition suffered from the resignation of their candidate due to mental health concerns. A new candidate, Evelyn Matthei, former minister of labour, had to take the role and agreed to compete.

Second, the candidate from the left-wing coalition, Michelle Bachelet, was the front-runner by a large margin. The CEP survey showed a support of 47 per cent, while Ms Matthei, her closest contender, only reached 14 per cent. Ms Bachelet left the presidency in 2010 with arguably the highest approval ratings in Chile's history. While she remained absent from Chilean politics, she was always in the lead of the opinion polls.

Third, each sector had other interesting, yet unlikely-to-win candidates. On the one hand, former socialist Marco Enríquez-Ominami was pursuing the presidency for the second time, after obtaining a respectable 20 per cent in 2009. In 2013, however, his share was half of that. From the right wing, an independent, Franco Parisi, was also gaining strong support, risking Matthei's options. The CEP survey showed a support of 10 per cent, which is close to his final share in the election.

Fourth, there was a group of five other candidates, which raised the number to nine, the highest in Chile's recent history. Nevertheless, none of them got more than 5 per cent of the vote share.

We understand electoral viability as the perceived capability of a candidate of winning an election, and this is an attribute that only Michelle

Bachelet had. According to the survey data from CEP, 78.2 per cent of the respondents believed that Ms Bachelet would become the next president, while only 5.2 per cent believed that Ms Matthei had a chance. None of the remaining seven candidates got more than 1 per cent of the mentions. In a scenario like this, the low level of competition should be reflected in the discussions among supporters of each candidate. That is, supporters of Michelle Bachelet should be more confident, and eventually more positive, when engaging in political discussions in the time prior to the election. There are no motives for them to engage in negativity.

Hypotheses

Based on the theory discussed above, we aim to test the following three hypotheses.

> *Hypothesis 1*: Consistent with the expectations of the literature, the share of supporters of each candidate on Twitter will not be useful to predict the actual share on the survey.

The main argument in support of this hypothesis lays in the lack of probabilistic sampling of Twitter data. Although the information obtained through Twitter's public streaming API is a sample of 1 per cent of the total, research (Morstatter et al., 2013) has shown that it does not consist in a probabilistic random sample. Any result we get from our estimation is likely to differ from the results of the opinion survey.

> *Hypothesis 2*: Michelle Bachelet's Twitter supporters are more likely to use a positive tone when tweeting about political issues.

This hypothesis stems from the electoral viability argument. Supporters of Bachelet are in no need to engage in violent, negative discussions on Twitter. They are the most likely winners of the forthcoming election, and even the supporters of the other candidates recognize that.

> *Hypothesis 3*: Where there is a statistically significant relationship in the survey data between supporting a candidate and supporting a given policy, that relationship is reflected in a higher probability of a positive tone on Twitter.

This hypothesis consists on the idea that support for a policy can influence the way in which users who support the same candidate talk about the policy issue. We do not expect a significant difference among candidates, as the same argument should run for all of them.

Data and methods

Data sources

Our data comes from Twitter's public Streaming API according with two criteria. On one hand, during the second half of October 2013 (two weeks before the election), we collected Twitter accounts who explicitly declared their intention to vote for a particular presidential candidate using hashtags with the following structure #yovotoZZZ (meaning 'I will vote for ZZZ') where ZZZ represents the name or last name of one of the four main candidates: Michelle Bachelet, Evelyn Matthei, Marco Enriquez and Franco Parisi. Each tweet contained all the relevant metadata, such as location, URLs, date of creation and the users who tweeted them. This filter allowed us to identify the political preferences of 4,111 accounts.

On the other hand, we collected tweets that were posted between the months of September to December 2013 in Chile using any of the following concepts that were relevant during the presidential campaign. Each of them were topics in which candidates showed polarized positions: equal marriage ('matrimonio igualitario', '#avp'), changes to the electoral system ('binominal'), abortion ('aborto'), copper ('codelco', 'nacionalizaci.n del cobre') and constitutional changes ('asambleaconstituyente*', '#ac'). To validate the method, we also included a search on a topic for which we do not expect polarized opinions based on political preferences: tweets about the Chilean national football team manager ('sampaoli').

To guarantee that tweets were written in Chile, we filtered the collected data by its location (either self-reported location or geographical coordinates when they were available). By means of these filters, we obtained 152,240 messages including tweets and their retweets. Finally, from the above collection we selected all the users' accounts who retweeted messages from any of the politically identified users. This allowed us to expand the original dataset from 4,111 to 5,603 accounts. The steps followed to assign political preference to those retweeters are explained in the next subsection.

The survey data comes from the quarterly survey from the CEP. The survey was conducted between 13 September and 14 October 2013. This is a nationally representative survey with a sample of 1,437 respondents.

The margin of error is 3 per cent. All calculations were conducted using the weighting instructions from CEP.

We have chosen five different topics that were asked in the CEP survey as dependent variables: constitutional reform, equal marriage, electoral reform, abortion and the ownership structure of the copper mines. Constitutional reform relates to a campaign started in 2013 to establish a constitutional assembly in the country. In the case of electoral reform, this refers mostly to the different attempts to change the way in which the members of Congress are elected. Equal marriage was a hot topic during the campaign, with most candidates supporting some sort of legal protection for same-sex couples. The case of abortion is particular, as Chile is one of the few countries in the world that does not allow abortion under any circumstances. As such, some of the candidates, including Bachelet, showed their support for allowing abortion under certain circumstances. Finally, Chile's copper mines create the greatest income of the country. Prior to the dictatorship, all the operation of the mines was under the state-owned company Codelco. There are some political actors (and some of the candidates) who promoted that the state should regain control of the mines.

Estimating political positions from retweet networks

Let S represents a set of individuals who explicitly declared their intention to vote for some candidate in the set C. Such that S_c represents the subset of individuals in S, supporting a given candidate $c \in C$.

Let M be the set of tweets written by individuals in S and M_c be the subset of messages written by each individual $s \in S_c$, supporting the candidate $c \in C$.

Let R represent another set of individuals who have retweeted at least one message written by individuals in S. Then, for each individual $r \in R$,

$$r_c = \text{count}(M_c)$$

and

$$r_{\text{total}} = \Sigma c r_c.$$

Then,

$$r_{\text{wc}} = \frac{r_c}{r_{\text{total}}}$$

is the weight of individuals in S_c within the set of individual r's retweets.

Finally, we defined r_p as individual r's political position as,

$$r_p = \max{(r_{wc})}|r_p > 0.5$$

Figure 6.1 shows the results for $c = $ *Bachelet, Matthei, Parisi, Enriquez* and the data specified in the previous subsection. As shown, for all candidates and controversial issues retweeters predominantly retweet messages from individuals with political affinity giving support for the claim that retweeting on political issues is mostly a homophily-like behaviour.

Calculating the sentiment behind the tweets

For the purpose of this exercise, we rely on an unsupervised method to calculate sentiment analysis. Unsupervised methods use several ways to

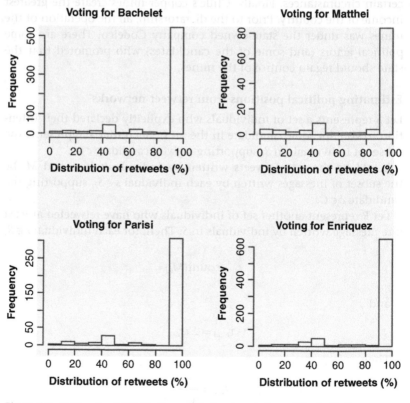

Figure 6.1   Retweeters' distribution of their retweets by political affinity
Note: The x-axis shows that there is a high homophily level on each of the retweet networks.

compare the text with some baseline lexicons or dictionaries and assigns scores to the different units of observations.

In this case, we have used our own Spanish translation from the lexicon created by Wilson et al. (2005) and the sentiment R packages (Jurka, 2012; Sajuria, 2014). The original English lexicon uses a trained naive Bayes algorithm to classify the polarity of the words between negative and positive. Since this is a preliminary exercise, instead of re-training the algorithm, we use the voter algorithm. Each tweet is deconstructed into single words, and they are compared to the lexicon. The algorithm then counts the number of positives and negative words in each tweet. Whenever the majority of words are positive, the whole tweet is classified as such. The same procedure operates for words classified as negative. When the words that do not have a pre-set polarity are a majority, the algorithm classifies tweet as neutral. Subsequently, we created a dummy variable called 'positive' for each tweet, with value of one if the classification of that tweet is such, and zero otherwise.

Modelling support for candidates on tone and support for policies

As Barberá (2015) explains, electoral support should be orthogonal to support on Twitter for a given candidate. However, we are departing from that discussion in two ways. First, we are looking at support for policies, which are not subject to a vote. Moreover, we aim to compare if the support for a candidate can be used as predictor for both support for a given policy and the sentiment of those talking about that policy. Therefore, we need to estimate different models for each dataset.

For the Twitter data, we model the positive tone of tweets about a given policy (*positive*), expressed as a dummy variable, as a function of the support for a given candidate (*candidate*), the sex of the respondent (*sex*) and whether the respondent lives in Santiago or somewhere else in Chile (*santiago*). The last two variables are traditional controls that can be used when understanding political support. We developed our own algorithm to detect the sex of the Twitter user and its location (when not geotagged). The link function is a logistic regression, and can be expressed as follows:

$$p(positive = 1) =.$$

In the case of the survey data, the dependent variable changes for support (*support*) for a policy. The independent variables remain the same and the model has a similar expression,

$$p(support = 1) =.$$

In the case of each datasets, we estimated five models, one for each of the policies. The 'candidates' variable only considers four contenders, although the last Chilean election had nine. We are focusing on those who got the highest share on the first round: Michelle Bachelet (who went onto the run-off election and became finally elected), Evelyn Matthei (the other candidate that went onto the run-off election), Marco Enríquez-Ominami and Franco Parisi. Bachelet and Enríquez-Ominami are considered centre-left/left wing candidates, while the other two are centre-right/right. Together, these four candidates obtained 92.82 per cent of the votes during the first round of the presidentialelection.

Results

In relation to the share of supporters for each candidate, our estimation on Twitter should be independent to the support shown on the survey. Table 6.1 shows the identification or support for all the candidates included in our models per dataset. The results provide support for Hypothesis 1, as we can see no evident connection between the share of those who support any given candidate on the survey and those who we estimate on Twitter.

Table 6.2 shows the estimation results using the CEP survey dataset. In essence, we can observe that the support for certain candidates can act as a predictor of the support for certain reforms. In particular, the support for candidates (any) seems to be positively related with support for some of the policies. Women, on the other hand, tend to be more supportive of equal marriage than men and less supportive of electoral reform. People living in Santiago are also more supportive of equal marriage, but have a negative likelihood to support abortion law, and transferring the ownership of the copper mines back to the state.

Table 6.1 Support for candidates

	Twitter (%)	CEP survey (%)
Bachelet	39	47
Matthei	4	14
Enríquez-Ominami	32	7
Parisi	17	10

Table 6.2   Logistic regression using CEP survey data

	Dependent variable				
	Constitutional change (1)	Equal marriage (2)	Electoral reform (3)	Abortion (4)	Copper ownership (5)
Other	2.056***	2.130***	1.866***	1.459**	3.392***
candidates	(0.441)	(0.424)	(0.485)	(0.623)	(1.028)
Evelyn	0.310	0.206	0.884***	0.582**	0.403
Matthei	(0.269)	(0.296)	(0.277)	(0.287)	(0.331)
Franco Parisi	0.596*	0.516	0.734*	1.045***	0.979**
	(0.355)	(0.326)	(0.386)	(0.361)	(0.402)
Marco	0.776**	1.293***	0.849***	1.404***	1.564***
Enríquez-Ominami	(0.215)	(0.342)	(0.328)	(0.366)	(0.498)
Michelle	0.311	0.259	0.553**	0.366*	0.748***
Bachelet	(0.215)	(0.223)	(0.224)	(0.218)	(0.263)
Sex (women)	−0.297*	0.531***	0.302*	0.239	0.102
	(0.162)	(0.170)	(0.167)	(0.175)	(0.208)
Location	0.212	0.353**	0.190	−0.242	0.412**
(Santiago)	(0.162)	(0.167)	(0.164)	(0.179)	(0.208)
Constant	0.516**	1.381***	−0.474**	0.490**	1.053***
	(0.216)	(0.230)	(0.233)	(0.226)	(0.283)
Observations	1,437	1,437	1,437	1, 437	1,437
Log likelihood	−918,345	−856,686	−919,870	−765,994	−594,736
Akaike Information Criterion	1,852.689	1,729.371	1,855.741	1,547.987	1,205.473

Note: $*p < .1$; $**p < .05$; $***p < .01$.

In the case of the Twitter data, the picture looks a bit different. As explained above, our data does not come from a probabilistic sample. As such, the relevance of statistical significance is lower. Without a random sample, we cannot assume that our estimations will reflect the larger population of users on Twitter. Hence, we focus more on the direction of the coefficients and less on the standard errors. The results shown in Table 6.3 express the coefficients from the logistic regression on the probability of a tweet having a positive tone.

As predicted, supporters of Michelle Bachelet are more likely to tweet with a positive tone on almost all the models. The only exception consists on the model about equal marriage. In the case of supporters for the other candidates, the tones differ across the models. Women are less likely to use a positive tone on every one of the topics than men, while people tweeting from Santiago are more likely to use a positive one.

Table 6.3 Logistic regression using Twitter data

	Dependent variable				
	Constitutional change (1)	Equal marriage (2)	Electoral reform (3)	Abortion (4)	Copper ownership (5)
Michelle Bachelet	0.395 (0.307)	−0.381 (0.554)	0.447 (1.066)	0.069 (0.325)	16.128 (1,348.160)
Evelyn Matthei	0.970** (0.446)	−0.118 (0.794)	−14.537 (1,135.237)	0.386 (0.467)	18.038 (1,348.160)
Marco Enríquez-Ominami	0.018 (0.316)	−0.252 (0.561)	−0.215 (1.112)	−0.053 (0.363)	14.826 (1,348.160)
Franco Parisi	−0.559 (0.436)	−0.147 (0.975)	0.230 (1.213)	0.323 (0.460)	15.062 (1,348.160)
Sex (women)	−0.232 (0.157)	−0.232 (0.290)	−0.466 (0.572)	−0.330 (0.247)	−1.015 (0.944)
Location (Santiago)	0.204 (0.150)	0.328 (0.266)	0.373 (0.435)	−0.198 (0.248)	0.858 (0.627)
Constant	−2.409*** (0.305)	−1.106** (0.554)	−3.162*** (1.044)	−1.647*** (0.319)	−18.017 (1,348.160)
Observations	2,195	434	478	696	137
Log likelihood	−716.758	−230.063	−98.071	−272.456	−38.025
Akaike Information Criterion	1,447.515	474.126	210.143	562.912	90.051

Note: $*p < .1$; $**p < .05$; $***p < .01$.

Table 6.4 shows no clear support for Hypothesis 3. Only in the case of supporters of Michelle Bachelet there is a consistency between the support for an issue in the survey and the occurrence of a positive tone on Twitter. That is the case for the topics of electoral reform, abortion law and the ownership of the copper mines. Interestingly, supporters of Mr Enríquez-Ominami show some decoupling on this regard. Their tone when discussing equal marriage, electoral reform or abortion is not positive, even when the survey data shows that, in average, they are more likely to support these issues. A similar case takes place among supporters of Matthei and electoral reform and among supporters of Parisi and constitutional reform.

Discussion

This exercise has been an attempt to expand the field of understanding public opinion through social media data. Much of the discussion has

Table 6.4 Comparison between support and positive tone

	Constitution		Equal marriage		Electoral reform		Abortion law		Copper owner	
	Survey	Twitter	Survey	Twitter	Survey	Twitter	Survey	Twitter	Survey	Twitter
Michelle Bachelet					*		*		*	
Evelyn Matthei					*		*			
Marco Enríquez-Ominami	*		*		*		*		*	
Franco Parisi	*				*		*			
Sex (women)	*		*		*					
Location (Santiago)			*						*	

Note: *$p < 0.05$ (only for survey data).
Light grey: increase in probability; dark grey: decrease in probability.

been exploring the notion that Twitter, and other social media, can be a useful – and cheaper – alternative to public opinion surveys. As shown above, there have been some attempts both to analyse Twitter data and compare it to polls. Our approach is an extension of that literature, by incorporating two new elements. On the one hand, we use an innovative way to estimate the political position of Twitter users, by looking at their support for candidates. On the other hand, we depart from the traditional question of relating candidate support on Twitter with similar indicators from surveys. We believe that, given the special nature of this social media platform – such as its non-representative population of users – support for a candidate on Twitter should be orthogonal to similar measures from probabilistic samples. Our results are an initial confirmation of that.

Another contribution of this chapter comes from the notion of electoral viability. We have used that framework to propose that supporters of the leading candidate are more likely to use a positive tone on Twitter. Our results show a preliminary support for this, but they should be taken carefully. There are still some validation tests to perform, in order to provide error measurement to this relationship. However, this is a promising initial attempt.

With regard to the comparison between survey and Twitter data, our results are inconclusive. The supporters of one particular candidate, Enríquez-Ominami, are less likely to use a positive tone on Twitter when discussing topics they support. This is surprising, and this might reflect deeper dynamics of public discussion. An option for future research could be to focus on this particular case and understand what are the drivers of this phenomenon. One option is electoral viability – Enríquez-Ominami suffered throughout the campaign from a lack of momentum, especially compared to his performance in 2009 – as a driver of tone. However, given the impressive advantage that Ms Bachelet had on this regard, it becomes difficult to model this assertion with the data we have available.

A word of caution should be given with regard to our estimation of political positions. As we have discussed before, there are other ways to estimate political positions of Twitter users that use followers–following relationships. We believe that there is something intrinsic in retweet networks that make them more useful in assessing if a given user holds a clear political position. While following another user is a rather cost-less and private act, retweeting is none of the above. However, we also know that revealed preferences are not necessarily the same as the real. As such, we still need to develop a way to test our estimations against well-respected procedures.

Finally, sentiment analysis is not free from criticism. Machine learning processes, or even counting algorithms such as the one we use, are incapable of understanding sarcasm and irony. Furthermore, in the case of our paper, there are not many tools available to produce sentiment analysis in Spanish. Hence, the translation we produced for this chapter relies on the accuracy of the English lexicon. Further developments on this point would consist of training some sort of naive Bayesian classifier using only tweets in a language different than English.

In summary, our goal is to propose new roads for future investigation, based on the notion that social media interactions can produce meaningful, complementary information to opinion polls.

References

Ansolabehere, S. and Hersh, E. (2012) 'Validation: What big data reveal about survey misreporting and the real electorate', *Political Analysis*, 20(4), 437–59.

Ansolabehere, S., Rodden, J. and Snyder, J.M. (2008) 'The strength of issues: Using multiple measures to gauge preference stability, ideological constraint, and issue voting', *American Political Science Review*, 102(2), 215–32.

Barberá, P. (2015) 'Birds of the same feather tweet together: Bayesian ideal point estimation using Twitter data', *Political Analysis*, 23(1), 76–91.

Bartels, L.M. (2005) 'Homer gets a tax cut: Inequality and public policy in the American mind', *Perspectives on Politics*, 3(1), 5–31.

Bartels, L.M. (2010) 'The study of electoral behavior', in J.E. Leighley (ed.) *The Oxford Handbook of American Elections and Political Behavior*. Oxford: Oxford University Press, pp.239–61.

Beauchamp, N. (2013) 'Predicting and interpolating state-level polling using Twitter textual data', *Meeting on Automated Text Analysis*. London: London School of Economics.

Bunker, K. (n.d.) *Tresquintos: Análisis Políticos y Predicciones Electorales*, www.tresquintos.com, date accessed 1 August 2014.

Converse, P.E. (1975) 'Public opinion and voting behavior', in F. Greenstein and N. Polsby (eds.) *Handbook of Political Science (Vol. 4)*. Reading, MA: Addison-Wesley, pp.75–169.

Dalton, R.J. (2000) *The Decline of Party Identification*. Oxford: Oxford University Press.

DiGrazia, J., McKelvey, K., Bollen, J. and Rojas, F. (2013) 'More tweets, more votes: Social media as a quantitative indicator of political behavior', *PLoS One*, 8(11), e79449.

Gayo-Avello, D. (2012) 'I wanted to predict elections with Twitter and all I got was this Lousy paper: A balanced survey on election prediction using Twitter data', *arXiv preprint arXiv*, 1204, 6441.

Godbole, N., Srinivasaiah, M. and Skiena, S. (2007) 'Large-scale sentiment analysis for news and blogs', *International Conference on Weblogs and Social Media*, Boulder, CO, 26–28 March 2007.

Iyengar, S., Sood, G. and Lelkes, Y. (2012) 'Affect, not ideology a social identity perspective on polarization', *Public Opinion Quarterly*, 76(3), 405–31.

Jurka, T.P. (2012) *Sentiment: Tools for Sentiment Analysis*. R package version 0.2, http://CRAN.R-project.org/package=sentiment.

Laver, M., Benoit, K. and Garry, J. (2003) 'Extracting policy positions from political texts using words as data', *American Political Science Review*, 97(2), 311–31.

Lietz, H., Wagner, C., Bleier, A. and Strohmaier, M. (2014). 'When politicians talk: Assessing online conversational practices of political parties on Twitter', *Computing Research Repository*, (CoRR), abs/1405, 6824.

López-Sáez, M. and Martínez-Rubio, J. (2005) '¿Influyeron los procesos de comunicaci'on sobre los sucesos del 11-M en las votaciones del 14-M? La percepción de los jóvenes en función de su ideología política', *Revista de Psicología Social*, 20(3), 351–67.

Lowe, W. (2008) 'Understanding wordscores', *Political Analysis*, 16(4), 356–371.

Lowe, W. (2013) 'There's (basically) only one way to do it', *Social Science Research Network*, http://ssrn.com/abstract=2318543.

Morstatter, F., Pfeffer, J., Liu, H. and Carley, K.M. (2013) 'Is the sample good enough? Comparing data from Twitter's streaming API with Twitter's firehose', *International Conference on Weblogs and Social Media*, Cambridge, MA, 8–11 July 2013.

Pang, B. and Lee, L. (2008) 'Opinion mining and sentiment analysis', *Foundations and Trends in Information Retrieval*, 2(2), 1–135.

104   *Combining and Comparing Methods*

Sajuria, J. (2014) *Sentimiento: Package for Sentiment Analysis in Spanish [beta].* R package version 0.1, available from https://github.com/jsajuria/sentimiento.

Wilson, T., Wiebe, J., and Hoffmann, P. (2005) 'Recognizing contextual polarity in phrase-level sentiment analysis', *Proceedings of the Conference on Human Language Technology and Empirical Methods in Natural Language Processing.* Stroudsburg, PA, USA: Association for Computational Linguistics, pp.347–54.

Zaller, J. (1992) *The Nature and Origins of Mass Opinion.* Cambridge: Cambridge University Press.

7
Video Analysis in Digital Literacy Studies: Exploring Innovative Methods

Roberto de Roock, Ibrar Bhatt and Jonathon Adams

Introduction

Vignette Part A

Marta, an 11-year-old student, watches as Mrs Smith, her experienced language arts teacher, projects an image on the board of the digital poster creation app, Glogster.com. She walks students through the next part of their activity creating posters promoting pet welfare for a local animal shelter contest. As students upright their laptop screens and begin working, Marta dives into her class work with her friend and collaborator, with the app open on her laptop on a project that will eventually win the classroom contest.

Vignette Part B

Simultaneously, Marta clicks back to an open window to resume the massively multiplayer online game she had been playing during lunchtime, Movie Star Planet.[1] Here she continues composing her avatar's profile narrative, interacts with a friend in another classroom through their in-game characters and plays mini-games with dozens of other players among the thousands currently online. Nearly all of them are strangers to each other from all over the world, yet core participants in this online community. Marta quietly discusses what she is doing in the game with her classmate and will continue through private messages in Movie Star Planet during her next class.

The above vignette is taken from a classroom ethnography (de Roock, 2015) examining the 1:1 integration of laptops into the classroom

105

curriculum, exploring how students resist and respond to the 'official' curriculum along with their unofficial, or non-standardized, literacy practices (Barton and Hamilton, 1998), the latter largely exemplified in off-task activities such as social chat and game-play. Fairly 'standard' classroom ethnography methods (Watson-Gegeo, 1997) were used: the researcher took notes while a tripod mounted professional grade camcorder recorded student and teacher talk and movements over a period of eight months, along with semi-structured interviews. From these methods, data emerged which resulted in vignette Part A. These particular data uncover a structured and largely procedural engagement of the project, channelled through the dictates of the official curriculum.

Through software installed on the student laptops to record students' faces via webcams, talk through their laptop mics and a multitude of computer activities including video of their on-screen actions, a profoundly more complex picture of 'what happened' began to emerge, including data that informed vignette Part B. These data reveal Marta's complex and nuanced digital poster construction process along with a rich and varied digital 'underlife' (Goffman, 1961) within the classroom, including consequential engagement (Gresalfi et al., 2009) with literacy tools through digital composition and social interaction within a virtual world. Such salient insights gained about Mrs Smith and Marta were absent in vignette Part A and would have been overlooked in 'standard' ethnography, but were captured in the second layer of data (see Figure 7.1) reassembled in vignette Part B. This is a characteristic example of the kinds of insights we wish to explore and share in this chapter.

As technology rapidly develops, researchers are left with the challenge to adapt their methods and data analysis practices to address new research problems in a different light, and in ways that match the pace of change. As interactions and literacy practices are increasingly played out in digital environments (such as, online, through digital devices and mediated by software and hardware), new ways to examine them need to be explored. The *capture*, *analysis* and *representation* of multi-modal data pose many challenges and remain 'contentious and as yet unresolved' in much multi-modal literacy research (Flewitt, 2011, p.295).

In this chapter, we extend this discussion and address this lack of resolution by drawing together insights gained from three separate, yet methodologically, similar studies. Building on our previous work (e.g. Bhatt and de Roock, 2013; Bhatt et al., 2015), our intention is to bring the practical tools of our data collection, management, ethical issues and broader implications to bear on a much-needed theorization of

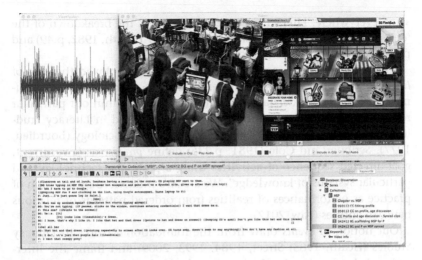

Figure 7.1 Transana's interface

Note: Clockwise from top left: audio waveform; two synced video streams including a screen-in-screen image of Marta's Moviestar Planet gameplay; data management trees; and a unified transcript.

Source: de Roock (2015).

transformative digital methods. We hope – and have found in our own work – that this allows for deeper exploration of emerging digitally mediated practices and their theoretical and disciplinary implications in Literacy Studies and the social sciences more broadly.

Literacy Studies

In this section, we orient the general reader to the field of Literacy Studies to better understand the theory, context and research problems that steer our methodological considerations. Barton (2001) describes Literacy Studies as originating from scholars such as Giroux (1983), Willinsky (1990), Bloome and Green (1991), Gee (2000), Baynham (1995), Scribner and Cole (1981), Heath (1983) and Street (1984) who are united theoretically in using 'an everyday event as a starting point' (Barton, 2007, p.4) for examining literacy and therefore approaches people's practices with texts 'as much a part of learned behaviour as are ways of eating, sitting, playing games and building houses' (Heath, 1982, p.49). This was a significant change in the direction of literacy research from earlier 'autonomous' models of literacy which framed literacy as a 'uniform set of technical skills' (Street, 2001) to be applied the same everywhere. Literacy Studies acknowledges the breakdown of the 'dichotomy between oral and literate traditions' (Heath, 1982, p.49) and places considerable attention on local context.

Following other Literacy Studies research, we employed the lens of *literacy events* and *practices* to understand literacy practices as communities themselves understand them (Street, 2001) within our particular research contexts. The definition of *practice* adopted in Literacy Studies emerges from the broader field of Bourdieusian sociology (Bourdieu, 1977). Scribner and Cole (1981, p.236) define *practice* as 'a recurrent, goal-directed sequence of activities using a particular technology and particular systems of knowledge'. We are also influenced by a notion of practice as performances of realities from ordered patterns of relations between entities (Law, 2012).

Our notion of *events* draw from the foundational works in Literacy Studies (Heath, 1983; Street, 1984, 1993, 2009) and frame the interaction being analysed, which are embedded within broader *literacy practices*. *Digital literacy events* thus are empirical occasions in which digital text is central and is mediated, produced, received, distributed, exchanged and so on via 'digital codification' (Lankshear and Knobel, 2008, p.5). Taken together, our analytical and empirical task of investigating digital literacy practices involves the textual activities, their resultant texts, the patterns of behaviour surrounding their creation, attitudes and values that inform them (through broader ethnographic detail) and the overall material environment. With these sensibilities, an exploration of digital literacy events must incorporate an exploration of the practices being constructed and maintained across multiple modalities and timescales (Lemke, 2000).

Research methods in Literacy Studies

While research on literacy phenomena takes on virtually every imaginable form (Duke and Mallette, 2011) from case studies to experimental designs to aggregate statistical analysis, Literacy Studies has usually taken an ethnographic approach, with methodological approaches that seek out naturalistic data (Heath, 1984, p.252). Heath and Street (2008, p.29) define literacy ethnographies as involving 'detailed systematic observing, recording, and analysing of human behaviour in specifiable spaces and interactions', with a wide variety of data collection methods including 'surveys, formal interviews, focus groups, photography, and activity logs along with spatial maps, video recorders, or audio recorders'. Therefore, much of the toolkit for data collection utilized and theorized about in Literacy Studies involves non-digital materials and a central role of the researcher as an 'instrument' of data collection.

In problematizing ethnographic research in digital environments, we build on Hine's (2004, p.1) notion of *virtual ethnography*, which is 'adaptive... to the conditions in which it finds itself'. Digital literacy events are, in this respect, multi-modal and made up of multiple resources such as video, text, sound and image. The wide range of communicative modes are subsequently united as a complete package and 'made of the same stuff and fabricated on the same plane' (Cope and Kalantzis, 2004, p.215). This is salient, as the kinds of data emerging from their exploration needs to reflect this complexity, in contrast to more traditional ethnographic traditions that rely on text-based transcripts supported by still images.

The tools used to capture such data therefore need to allow a wide range of communicative modes to be analysed together. The methodological shift in recording digitally rich data is reflected in the development of theories exploring communication under the general heading 'multi-modality'. Multi-modal research is where multiple forms of meaning making are considered beyond the spoken text and therefore require richer data than text-only transcripts of spoken data, such as gaze, gesture and proxemic relations of social actors. Through our work with digital literacies, we agree with Norris's (2002) contention that in order for 'adequate' multi-modal analysis, it is a prerequisite to develop multi-modal transcription methods for video data.

Video analysis

With the employment of new technologies, audio and video data collection has become common in the analysis of interaction (Heath et al., 2010; Knoblauch, 2012). The kinds of multi-modal data which emerge and their diversity of form present particular challenges, which require 'descriptive and analytical tools that can both accommodate their variability and reflect their complexity' (Flewitt, 2009, p.40). Knoblauch and Schnettler (2012) argue that video analysis – the sequential analysis of naturalistic interactional video data – requires methodological rigour along with a deep foundation in ethnographic fieldwork.

Video recording

With rapid developments in digital media, a wide range of recording devices have become available to researchers in the form of inexpensive handheld video cameras, video-recording-enabled phones and portable media players, as well as small, wearable video hardware such as GoPro and Swivl. The question of what these additions do to the ethnographic toolkit of literacy research is addressed by Kuipers (2004, p.167), who argues that rather than simply increasing the amount of data, video actually 'forces us to confront ethnographic subjects as actors who are managing information in a multi-modal environment'. This framing of the employment of video highlights the questions we raised when deciding to employ video data and subsequently influenced later choices including what additional instruments we would adopt.

The role of video also needs to be understood in context. As a tool for the collection of data, its impact on the collection of data needs to be thought out. The use of video recording may seem straightforward, but there are many considerations beyond merely framing a lens for recording. According to Silverman's (2013, p.62) guide to qualitative research 'one camera is fine for most purposes', which carries the assumption that 'most purposes' are the same. However, if the focus is on the interactions between gesture, gaze and other communicative modes alongside online textual practices, then multiple cameras and/or another dimension of viewing will be necessary. This is what leads us to adopt screen recording alongside video.

Screen recording with video

Screen recording can be used as a tool to record the processes of on-screen composition (Geisler and Slattery, 2007). This can also be achieved with additional features from qualitative and quantitative dimensions using screen casting or usability-testing software such as TechSmith's Morae (Asselin and Moayeri, 2010). Synchronously capturing learners' complete interactions on- and off-screen was attempted by Bigum and Gilding (1985) some 30 years ago. For them, writing, movements and talk around a task required two monitors, a video mixer, a video tape recorder and a means of splitting the computer video signal. More recent and linguistically oriented studies that involve screen-capture include explorations of news writing production (Catenaccio et al., 2011), discursive analysis of Facebook chats (Meredith and Stokoe, 2014) and its use alongside think-aloud techniques in gauging Internet literacy practices (Asselin and Moayeri, 2010).

Computer Assisted Qualitative Data Analysis Software

Software tools are virtually a necessity to organize and manage data produced by video ethnography and analysis. The use of Computer Assisted

Qualitative Data Analysis Software (CAQDAS) has become standard practice in many forms of qualitative analysis. The affordances of different CAQDAS products to manage and facilitate analysis emerges from the potentially overwhelming complexity of data in terms of files and density of data. For example, the combination of multiple video angles with screen-in-screen format we adopted naturally necessitated the use of the most appropriate CAQDAS tools particularly to aid transcription creation and manipulability.

The software we chose was influenced by the questions we formulated and sought to address (Cohen et al., 2007). We therefore turned to the various forms of 'bleeding edge' (Woods and Dempster, 2011) CAQDAS to aid our researches and prepare and present our transcripts. In our cases, these were ELAN (Wittenburg et al., 2006) and Transana (Woods and Dempster, 2011), which allow for deeper insights into the character of the interactions taking place during classroom activities.

These software enable all files to be viewed in one interface, so specific points in the recordings could be revisited, viewed at multiple speeds with both video angles simultaneously and transcribed on one or more transcripts. ELAN's interface supports a transcriptional system along a horizontal timeline (Bezemer and Mavers, 2011) to represent multiple modalities whereas Transana is designed for more standard, detailed vertical transcriptions in the tradition of Conversation Analysis (Woods and Dempster, 2011).

An important point to remember with CAQDAS is that it organizes and structures data for analysis but does not *do* the analysis. Interpretative work is still necessary, and issues of CAQDAS epistemologies emerge, as researchers are bound by the biases and leanings of software designers in terms of coding and interface representation (Bhatt and de Roock, 2013), which influences the interpretation of data. For example, while Transana is biased towards more traditional Jeffersonian vertical transcripts (as shown in Figure 7.1), ELAN allows the representation of multi-modal data in 'modal stacks'.

Digital tools for digital literacies

In our own efforts to capture ongoing naturalistic interactions between social actors and mediating tools (computers, whiteboards, peers, teachers and so on), we utilize a range of software, hardware and theoretical resources to capture and analyse gesture, spoken language, textual practices and interactions with digital actors. What follows is a combined reflection of three separate yet methodologically similar research projects conducted in uniquely different classroom contexts: a UK Further Education college (Bhatt, 2012), a Japanese university (Adams, 2013) and a US sixth-grade primary Mexican-American classroom (de Roock, 2015).

Capturing digital literacy events

Our methodological setups were designed to capture and explore the construction of meanings and choreography of digitally mediated practices. We analysed 'social action' (Scollon, 2009, p.6) in the digital literacy events, which involved meaning making with mediating digital texts and the communicative resources available to the actors such as gesture, gaze and spoken language. Influenced by approaches to ethnomethodological video analysis (Koschmann et al., 2007; Heath et al., 2010), the focus was on the step-by-step construction of meanings through the microanalysis of communicative modes during the unfolding of student 'work' (the official classroom literacy practices) and 'play' (the unofficial literacy practices highlighted in vignette Part B) in the classrooms.

The screen-in-screen format (with synchronized audio) was captured using Blueberry Flashback Recorder on student laptops along with video and audio from an HD tripod mounted camera. Recordings were captured from students sitting in groups and later synchronized. Combined with researcher field notes, this generated a detailed data stream of ongoing interaction with, through and around the student laptops on multiple computers simultaneously with a wider shot to capture higher-quality audio and gestures, as well as facilitating ease of syncing. The ability to view and transcribe multiple video of on-screen and off-screen activity simultaneously was essential to explore the emergent digital literacy events and practices.

Video cameras were used to capture both the interactions of the participants with the computer screen (such as tracing the goal of deictic finger gestures) and to capture facial expressions and other activity between the students in front of the computer and, if necessary, the teachers. Screen recording software was incorporated into setups in order to capture all screen activity and audio using the computer microphone, which proved less physically intrusive than an external microphone. Due to their tight framing, built-in webcams did not prove particularly useful for analysis beyond data management and identification of speaker, but external USB webcams functioned much as camcorders with the advantage of being integrated into the screen-in-screen image by Flashback.

Management and analysis

Data management when conducting video analysis includes a number of additional layers of decision-making than other methods. The video files were large and the Flashback files were in proprietary format, so had to be converted and reduced in size. This was a time-consuming process, but the resulting video resolution was clear enough for detailed analysis, and high-quality audio targeting interaction near the laptop was preserved. Supporting ethnographic field notes were also part of the methodologies to contextualize the video during later analysis (Knoblauch and Schnettler, 2012).

Data were managed using Transana to group recordings by session and create common gisting 'transcript' files. These summaries of the data were then coded using a grounded method (Glaser and Strauss, 1968) to focus on phenomena of interest and grouped thematically. Particular clips were then exported to ELAN where they were synced for multi-modal transcription and analysis. The subsequent representational systems that emerged (Figure 7.1, using Transana) integrate the combined modes of actors' activities as digital texts are created.

Multiple views of salient instances provided an opportunity for deep dives into the digital literacy events. CAQDAS tools afforded manipulability (slowing down, segmentation, etc.) and multi-modal conventions (Bezemer and Mavers, 2011) to account for the complex interplay of related of practices we see Marta engaging in (in vignette Part B). These include her gazes and movements, talk around the task and interactions with search engines, *Movie Star Planet* and other websites. Importantly, and as we have seen, these are not always work-related practices, but the subsequent representational system which emerged integrates these yet allows us to parse them out for analytic attention, as her work is being done (e.g. see Figure 7.1).

While this resulted in rich findings, transcripts (whether vertical or horizontal) and still images limit the presentation of the data in academic journals, although possibilities for sharing the multi-modal data online are being explored. Still images lose the richness of data, and detailed transcripts are difficult to understand. One strategy we use in presenting findings in digestible ways is rendering salient segments into vignettes (as we do in the opening of this article) to 'tell a story' of the unfolding of a digital literacy event. This proves useful primarily for written presentation style and ease of reading for analysis purposes.

Findings

Our methods brought careful attention to the ecology of digital practices and interactions. We were able to uncover aspects of the complex and close relationship between the communicative resources employed by social actors and mediating tools in digital literacy activity, the features of the texts being written and the construction of meaning making surrounding it, and the influence of web-based actants (search engines, virtual worlds and so forth). Through video transcripts, high amounts of deictic gesture (both through gaze and hand use) were employed in meaning making and structuring the interactions. The spoken content was also shaped by the text types, with spoken meanings directed to what could be observed in the videos with minimal personal input such as summarizing or expressing feelings.

Added to this, screen recording brought a dimension that forced us to rethink how classroom activities are carried out. We discovered literacies of typically outside-of-classroom origins being mobilized as resources inside of the classroom, such as Marta's creative distribution of attention evident in vignette B, which blurs the distinction between her digital literacy practices construed as either 'work' or 'play' in nature; these are precisely the interactions between the official and unofficial digital literacy practices highlighted in our introduction.

Deep exploration into digital literacy events, each with a particular focus, found the girls' enactments of literacy and identity transformed when laptops facilitated their peer network's entanglement with a pre-existing assemblage of other adolescents, software developers, hardware and software, which they in turn transformed through participation in the online multiplayer world. A mindful combination of theory and video technology allowed a detailed analysis of the network's various 'moving parts' that interfaced with the girls in the emergence of the literacy events.

In one of our research projects (Adams, 2013), ELAN made possible the analyses of hand gestures in combination with the spoken language. As some gestures were under 0.5 seconds long, identifying and analysing these and their relation to particular speech events yielded various insights into multi-modal meaning making, something which would not have been possible through field notes and observation alone. In another of our studies, through the transcriptional system of ELAN a student's use of Google search to guide composition was conceptualized as an interaction (Bhatt and de Roock, 2013).

In the instance of Marta's practices (de Roock, 2015), the Glogster.com digital poster created by her and her partner, while winning the class competition for best design, largely echoed the teacher/classroom discourse while contrasting sharply with both community norms and the relatively complex design of their online profiles and avatars in

Movie Star Planet. From a pedagogical perspective, such practices address broader digital literacies and participation skills (Jenkins et al., 2006) that were generally lacking with in-school and less complex informal practices, indicating the importance of understanding and drawing on the non-curricular digital media practices of students, video games in particular (Gee, 2000, 2004, 2010; Gee and Hayes, 2010).

Expanding the discussion on digital methods

Technologies for digital methods have the potential to 'expand the perceptual capabilities' of researchers, 'enabling them to see or hear... in more detail' (Greeno, 2009, p.814). The insights outlined above demonstrate the complexities and diverse range of issues that need to be considered when employing digital methods in research into communication framed within Literacy Studies. But the implications are potentially much wider than Literacy Studies and can be considered in the broader area of social sciences where human activity is being captured and analysed in a multitude of contexts.

Key lessons learned

As Flewitt (2009) suggests, a critical stance on the impact of new technologies on communication is necessary, and this stance applies to each step in the choice of methods, analysis, data management and preferred representation of data. The following section offers a summary of key lessons learned in our application and reflections on the choices made with our digital methods.

First, in the set-up of screen recording software, installation was carried out either on the researchers' personal computers or on those of the students. When installed on student computers, security and software issues posed some barriers but ultimately allowed recording multiple instances at once and facilitated ease of students starting and stopping recording at will (Asselin and Moayeri, 2010). Using the researchers' computer posed other problems as participants were using different computers to those they were familiar with in their classroom practices. This was reduced by introducing the researchers' computers for a period of time before the data collection sessions. In both setups, issues such as the software crashes or students prematurely shutting down the computer resulted in loss of data for that session. This risk can be reduced but never eliminated by, carrying out several trial runs before the main data collection, perhaps as part of a pilot study, or using multiple redundant data sources for high stakes recordings.

For the capture of audio, boom microphones attached to the cameras and wireless versions were employed for one of our projects. The internal microphones of the computer were also used to capture participants' audio as they worked on their class projects. We recommend high-quality omnidirectional microphones that work via the computers and screen recording software thereby syncing automatically and picking up talk around the task and even the entire class if required.

The number of cameras and angles were decided based on the focus of capture and research interest. Camcorders enabled a wider angle of recording to capture the space around the participants. They are also small, reducing the possible intrusiveness of such equipment for the participants. Positioning the camera at an angle to the participants (instead of directly opposite them) also appeared to make the cameras less intrusive as the recording 'eyes' did not 'stare' directly towards them in their immediate field of vision. These decisions, of course, are influenced by a range of research concerns including the extent to which features such as gaze, paralanguage, interaction with peers and so on are central to the research questions being explored.

Ethics

Ethical practices around video material are less established than with numerical and text-based research (Prosser and Loxley, 2008) and remain fairly undefined and ambiguous in institutional guidelines for ethical approval. With informed consent, for example, permission regarding the collection of data involves not just the site of the recording but the reproduction of the material including the potential altering of images, followed by editing of sequences of video, which could frame the actions of a participant in a different light. In our research, care was taken to avoid any potential problems by using screen recordings and clearly stating the context of the still images as extended sequences of interaction in representing the data in the write-ups. One way of avoiding this was giving the option for participants to have their faces concealed if they were to be used in publications outside of the initial project.

Also, related to screen recording is the issue of 'incidental data' (Asselin and Moayeri, 2010) and the potential invasive nature of detailed and continuous screen recording. With the screen capture software chosen, participants can have the option to pause and restart the recording during the recording process using a pause/restart icon in the taskbar menu. Participants were also able to inform us if there were any sections of the recording that they wanted to delete. In one of our studies, this was achieved by a review of the recording in a follow up interview in which the recording was discussed. Also with such data capture, complete anonymity can be difficult to maintain, as participants' movements and screen activity are of importance for analysis and evidence. To address security concerns, data were kept in encrypted, password-protected folders when stored both offline and in cloud storage.

We suggest that protocols surrounding approval of such digital methods become more clearly defined with the following guiding questions:

- Should data be stored *only* in a secure, encrypted, password-protected digital environment with commercial data security protection, even if not housed at the researcher's institution?
- Should incidental data of non-participants be continually obscured or deleted?
- Should participants be allowed the option to pause and restart recordings, then to review and delete recordings?
- Should participants be allowed the option that their faces be pixelated or blocked out in screenshots?

Conclusion

At a time when social lives, interactions and literacy practices are increasingly played out with mediating digital technology, new methods offer different ways of addressing research questions, stimulate researchers to ask new questions and in so doing generate new forms of data. Our work is grounded in Literacy Studies and its ethnographic commitment to carry out 'descriptions that take into account the perspectives of members of a social group, including the beliefs and values that underlie and organize the activities and utterances' (Schieffelin and Gilmore, 1986, p.viii). With our sites of investigation framed as 'digital literacy events' and located within the broader social and literacy practices such events build and maintain, Literacy Studies presents a theoretical approach to explore a wide range of interaction across a wide range of evolving social practices. As Barton (2007) states, literacy is 'ecological'; it is embedded in other human activity, social life and thought and position in history.

The approach we have detailed builds on other ethnographic traditions committed to better understanding human activity in digital environments. Some examples include online and Internet ethnography (Hine, 2004), 'connective ethnography' (Leander, 2008) and other ethnographic approaches to researching computer mediated communication (e.g. Barnes, 2002; Konijn, 2008). In placing ourselves within such lineage, we stress that, while proficiency with digital research tools are a prerequisite to effectively carry out digital data gathering, management and analysis, it is only one aspect of the research process. Traditional analogue interpretative work by researchers remains at the heart of the process and this is unchanged, if potentially enhanced, with digital methods.

Note

1. A Danish fashion themed free-to-play massively multiplayer online game (MMO), www.moviestarplanet.com.

References

Adams, J. (2013) *Analysing the Construction of Meanings With Mediating Digital Texts in Face-To-Face Interactions.* Unpublished PhD thesis, Lancaster University.

Asselin, M. and Moayeri, M. (2010) 'New tools for new literacies research: An exploration of usability testing software', *International Journal of Research and Method in Education*, 33(1), 41–53.

Barnes, S.B. (2002) *Computer-Mediated Communication: Human-to-Human Communication Across the Internet.* Boston: Allyn and Bacon.

Barton, D. (2001) 'Directions for literacy research: Analysing language and social practices in a textually mediated world', *Language and Education*, 15(2), 92–104.

Barton, D. (2007) *Literacy: An Introduction to the Ecology of Written Language* (2nd edition). Oxford: Blackwell.

Barton, D. and Hamilton, M. (1998) *Local Literacies: Reading and Writing in one Community.* London: Routledge.

Baynham, M. (1995) *Literacy Practices: Investigating Literacy in Social Contexts.* London; New York: Longman.

Bezemer, J. and Mavers, D. (2011) 'Multimodal transcription as academic practice: A social semiotic perspective', *International Journal of Social Research Methodology*, 14(3), 191–206.

Bhatt, I. (2012) 'Digital literacy practices and their layered multiplicity', *Educational Media International*, 49(4), 289–301.

Bhatt, I. and de Roock, R. (2013) 'Capturing the sociomateriality of digital literacy events', *Research in Learning Technology*, 21(4), http://www.researchinlearningtechnology.net/index.php/rlt/article/view/21281.

Bhatt, I., de Roock, R. and Adams, J. (2015) 'Diving deep into digital literacy: emerging methods for research', *Language and Education*, (ahead-of-print), 1–16. DOI: http://dx.doi.org/10.1080/09500782.2015.1041972.

Bigum, C.J. and Gilding, A. (1985) 'A video monitoring technique for investigating computer-based learning programs', *Computers and Education*, 9(2), 95–9.

Bloome, D. and Green, J.L. (1991) 'Educational contexts of literacy', *Annual Review of Applied Linguistics*, 12, 49–70.

Bourdieu, P. (1977) 'Outline of a theory of practice (Esquisse d'une théorie de la pratique)', Transl. by Richard Nice (Repr.). Cambridge: Cambridge University Press.
Catenaccio, P., Cotter, C., De Smedt, M., Garzone, G., Jacobs, G., Macgilchrist, F., Lams, L., Perrin, D., Richardson, J.E., Van Hout, T. and Van Praet, E. (2011) 'Towards a linguistics of news production', *Journal of Pragmatics*, 43(7), 1843–52.
Cohen, L., Manion, L. and Morrison, K. (2007) *Research Methods in Education* (6th edition). London: Routledge.
Cope, B. and Kalantzis, M. (2004) 'Text-made text', *E-Learning and Digital Media*, 1(2), 198–282.
de Roock, R. (2015) *Digital Literacies as Interactional Achievements: A Multimodal Approach to Understanding Learning with New Digital Media* (Unpublished doctoral dissertation). Tucson, AZ: University of Arizona.
Duke, N.K. and Mallette, M.H. (2011) *Literacy Research Methodologies* (2nd edition). London: Guilford.
Flewitt, R. (2009) 'What are multimodal data and transcription?', in C. Jewitt (ed.) *The Routledge Handbook of Multimodal Analysis*. London: Routledge, pp.40–53.
Flewitt, R. (2011) 'Bringing ethnography to a multimodal investigation of early literacy in a digital age', *Qualitative Research*, 11(3), 293–310.
Gee, J.P. (2000) 'The new literacy studies: From "socially situated" to the work of the social', in D. Barton, M. Hamilton and R. Ivanic (eds.) *Situated Literacies: Reading and Writing in Context*. London: Routledge, pp.180–96.
Gee, J.P. (2004) *Situated Language and Learning. A Critique of Traditional Schooling*. London: Routledge.
Gee, J.P. (2010) *New Digital Media and Learning as an Emerging area and 'Worked Examples' as one way Forward*. Cambridge, MA: MIT Press.
Gee, J.P. and Hayes, E. (2010) *Women and Gaming: The Sims and Twenty-first Century Learning*. New York: Palgrave Macmillan.
Geisler, C. and Slattery, S. (2007) 'Capturing the activity of digital writing: Using, analyzing, and supplementing video screen capture', in H.A McKee and D.N.N. DeVoss (eds.) *Digital Writing Research: Technologies, Methodologies, and Ethical Issues*. Cresskill, NJ: Hampton Press, pp.185–200.
Giroux, H.A. (1983) *Theory and Resistance in Education: A Pedagogy for the Opposition*. London: Heinemann Educational.
Glaser, B.G. and Strauss, A.L. (1968) *The Discovery of Grounded Theory. Strategies for Qualitative Research*. London: Weidenfeld and Nicolson.
Goffman, E. (1961) *Asylums. Essays on the Social Situation of Mental Patients and Other Inmates*. Garden City, NY: Doubleday and Co.
Greeno, J.G. (2009) 'Theoretical and practical advances through research on learning', in J.L. Green, G. Camilli and P.B. Elmore (eds.) *Handbook of Complementary Methods in Education Research*. Washington, DC: American Educational Research Association; Mahwah, pp.795–822.
Heath, C., Hindmarsh, J. and Luff, P. (2010) *Video in Qualitative Research: Analysing Social Interaction in Everyday Life*. Los Angeles; London: Sage.
Heath, S.B. (1982) 'What no bedtime story means: Narrative skills at home and school', *Language in Society*, 11(1), 49–76.
Heath, S.B. (1983) *Ways with Words: Language, Life, and Work in Communities and Classrooms*. Cambridge: Cambridge University Press.

Heath, S.B. and Street, B.V. (2008) *On Ethnography: Approaches to Language and Literacy, Research*. London: Routledge.

Hine, C. (2004) 'Social research methods and the Internet: A thematic review', *Sociological Research Online*, 9(2), http://www.socresonline.org.uk/9/2/hine.html.

Jenkins, H., Clinton, K., Purushotma, R., Robison, A. and Weigel, M. (2006) 'Confronting the challenges of participatory culture: Media education for the twenty-first century', http://digitallearning.macfound.org/atf/cf/%7B7E45C7E0-A3E0-4B89-AC9C-E807E1B0AE4E%7D/JENKINS_WHITE_PAPER.PDF.

Knoblauch, H. (2012) 'Introduction to the special issue of qualitative research: Video-analysis and videography', *Qualitative Research*, 12(3), 251–4.

Knoblauch, H, and Schnettler, B. (2012) 'Videography: Analysing video data as a "focused" ethnographic and hermeneutical exercise', *Qualitative Research*, 12(3), 334–56.

Konijn, E. (2008) *Mediated Interpersonal Communication*. London: Routledge.

Koschmann, T., Stahl, G. and Zemel, A. (2007) 'The video analyst's manifesto (or the implications of Garfinkel's policies for studying practice within design-based research)', in R. Goldman, R., Pea, B. Barron and S.J. Derry (eds.) *Video Research in the Learning Sciences*. Mahwah, NJ: Routledge, pp.133–43.

Kuiper, J.L. (2004) ' "Voices" as multimodal constructions in some contexts of religious and clinical authority', in P. LeVine and R. Scollon (eds.) *Discourse and Technology: Multimodal Discourse Analysis*. Washington, DC: Georgetown University Press, pp.167–83.

Lankshear, C. and Knobel, M. (2008) *Digital Literacies: Concepts, Policies and Practice*. Oxford: Peter Lang.

Law, J. (2012) 'Collateral realities', in F.D. Rubio and P. Baert (eds.) *The Politics of Knowledge*. London: Routledge, pp.156–78.

Leander, K. (2008) 'Toward a connective ethnography of online/offline literacy networks', in J. Coiro, M. Knobel, C. Lankshear and D. Leu (eds.) *Handbook of Research on New Literacies*. New York: Lawrence Erlbaum Associates/Taylor and Francis Group, pp.33–65.

Lemke, J.L. (2000) 'Across the scales of time: Artifacts, activities, and meanings in ecosocial systems', *Mind, Culture, and Activity*, 7(4), 273–90.

Meredith, J. and Stokoe, E. (2014) 'Repair: Comparing Facebook "chat" with spoken interaction', *Discourse and Communication*, 8(2), 181–207.

Norris, S. (2002) 'The implication of visual research for discourse analysis: Transcription beyond language', *Visual Communication*, 1(1), 97–121.

Prosser, J. and Loxley, A. (2008) *Introducing Visual Methods, National Centre for Research Methods*, http://eprints.ncrm.ac.uk/420/1/MethodsReviewPaperNCRM-010.pdf, date accessed 20 August 2014.

Schieffelin, B.B. and Gilmore, P. (1986) *The Acquisition of Literacy: Ethnographic Perspectives*. Norwood, NJ: Ablex Public Corporation.

Scollon, R. (2009) 'Action and text: Towards an integrated understanding of the place of text in social (inter)action, mediated discourse analysis and the problem of social action', in R. Wodak and M. Meyer (eds.) *Methods of Critical Discourse Analysis* (2nd edition). London: Sage, pp.139–83.

Scribner, S. and M. Cole (1981) *The Psychology of Literacy*. Cambridge, MA: Harvard University Press.

Silverman, D. (2013) *Doing Qualitative Research: A Practical Handbook* (4th edition). London: Sage.

Steinkuehler, C., Gresalfi, M., Barab, S., Siyahhan, S. and Christensen, T. (2009) 'Virtual worlds, conceptual understanding, and me: Designing for consequential engagement', *On the Horizon*, 17(1), 21–34.

Street, B.V. (1984) *Literacy in Theory and Practice*. Cambridge: Cambridge University Press.

Street, B.V. (1993) *Cross-Cultural Approaches to Literacy*. Cambridge: Cambridge University Press.

Street, B.V. (2001) *Literacy and Development: Ethnographic Perspectives*. London: Routledge.

Street, B.V. (2009) 'The future of "social literacies"', in M. Baynham and M. Prinsloo (eds.) *The Future of Literacy Studies*. Basingstoke: Palgrave Macmillan, pp.21–37.

Watson-Gegeo, K.A. (1997) 'Classroom ethnography', in N.H. Hornberger and D. Corson (eds.) *Encyclopedia of Language and Education*. Dordrecht, The Netherlands: Springer Netherlands, pp.135–44.

Willinsky, J. (1990) *The New Literacy: Redefining Reading and Writing in the Schools*. London: Routledge.

Wittenburg, P., Brugman, H., Russel, A., Klassmann, A., and Sloetjes, H. (2006) 'Elan: Aprofessional framework for multimodality research', *Fifth International Conference on Language Resources and Evaluation*, Genoa, Italy, 24–26 May 2006.

Woods, D.K. and Dempster, P.G. (2011) 'Tales from the bleeding edge: The qualitative analysis of complex video data using transana', *Forum Qualitative Sozialforschung/Forum: Qualitative Social Research*, 12(1), http://www.qualitative-research.net/index.php/fqs/article/view/1516.

Part III

Developing Innovations in Digital Methods

Introduction to Part III

The problem: What is the nature of innovation in digital methods?

The previous chapters have explored different methodological approaches in the use of digital methods (i.e. the use of quantitative and qualitative approaches and corresponding concerns with 'big data' and rich or 'thick data' in Part I), as well as seeking to tease out what digital methods add by comparing and combining these with 'offline' or traditional approaches (as considered in Part II). The next three chapters develop these themes by considering innovation in digital methods. It is tempting to regard digital methods as innovative in-and-of themselves, to take for granted that innovation inheres in the digital, to equate 'digital' with 'new' or 'advanced'. A question underlying the contributions in this section is therefore what do we mean when we say that digital methods are innovative? Are we referring to the use of digital methods per se (as compared with non-digital or 'offline' methods), or are we referring to the use of particular methods and approaches that further contribute to the development of existing digital methods?

The flip side to the question of innovation in digital methods is what gets left out in the rush to discover the innovative? The three chapters that follow both embrace and resist the notion of innovation in digital methods and the social sciences in different ways. They consider the absences of materiality, the body, space and place in their arguments about, and iterations of, innovation in digital methods. At first glance, concerns about materiality and embodiment may resemble the considerations of old; however, in a period of rapid change in the social sciences, where new platforms and modes of data are constantly emerging, the consideration of these questions is arguably more necessary than ever.

Redistributing, repurposing and revisiting social science concepts and methods in digital research

The emergence of new digital technologies, and corresponding possibilities for new research questions and procedures on the one hand, and the persistence of complex issues on the other, mean that a fine balance is necessary when choosing the right methods for the topic under investigation. This balancing act may include a challenge to the accepted boundaries of social science methods (or a redistribution of methods); it may involve a repurposing of existing methods; or it may involve the revisiting and extension of established concepts in the deployment of methods.

Chapter 8, by Adolfo Estalella, starts with a consideration of how social science research methods come into being, taking digital methods themselves as an empirical object of study. Estalella draws on a period of ethnographic observation at Medialab-Prado (MLP) – a collaborative space for the creation of prototypes stemming from experimentation with software, hardware and raw materials. Medialab-Prado brings together academics, technologists, hackers and a range of non-expert participants to work on projects and create prototypes. For example, one such prototype ('Re:farm the City') involved the creation of small urban allotments using materials such as wooden boxes as well as different kinds of hardware and software for measuring temperature, humidity and water levels. The discussion of the practice of prototyping therefore served to highlight several features of digital methods: (a) that there is an overlap between the digital and the material; (b) that digital methods are multiply located rather than disembodied or a-geographical practices solely located in cyberspace; and (c) that they explicitly or implicitly involve the contributions of a range of collaborators, not only experts. Finally, Estalella argues that the conditions necessary for prototyping – in which instability, uncertainty or even failure are legitimate outcomes – are the necessary conditions for the creation of new methods.

In Chapter 9, Emma Hutchinson cautions that we are sometimes too much in a hurry to discover the new rather than identifying how we can extend or transform the existing in our use of digital methods. Hutchinson argues that digital methods have been dogged by the drive to innovation while existing methods and procedures that have much to offer when dealing with particular research aims and questions (e.g.

visual theory and methods) are often not considered in research designs using digital methods The chapter draws on research conducted on the online identity and embodiment of players of the massively multiplayer online role playing game (MMORPG) *Final Fantasy XIV*. This research provides the backdrop to a discussion about the use of photo elicitation interviews in an online context; and specifically to discuss the use of photos and screenshots of gaming avatars in asynchronous online interviews with gamers. The repurposing of existing methods can provide social science researchers with new or extended opportunities to explore data. Hutchinson found that the use of photos and avatar screenshots in the online photo elicitation interviews both reinforced the argument, in visual theory, that identity, appearance and embodiment are highly constructed, while providing an opportunity to discuss this in ways that remained sensitive to the needs of her participants.

In Chapter 10, the final chapter in Part III, Victoria Tedder is also concerned with the reinsertion of the material and physical in digital methods, specifically in relation to the learning and transmission of skills. The chapter considers the different components of skilled activity (e.g. haptic, visual and sensory processes) and highlights a gap in the digital methods literature with regard to how skills are learnt and trans-mitted in digital environments. Drawing on research with crafters and gardeners Tedder considers the varying ways in which different online platforms (e.g. video sharing sites such as YouTube, blogs and micro-blogs, and web forums) and digital technologies (e.g. devices for the uploading of video, images and other content) enable different aspects of skill transference. These platforms and technologies enable the inter-actions that occur between the physical and the material in order to carry out different skills (such as knitting, paper crafts and stitching). As well the above, the chapter discusses a case study involving the repli-cation of the historic Queen Susan Shawl through the collective efforts of a group of knitters. In this way the chapter revisits and extends sociological understandings of skill.

Questioning innovation in digital research

The chapters in this section provide some useful questions for tenta-tively identifying innovation in digital methods, albeit in varying ways that cut across the definitions, descriptions, constructions, and uses of digital methods:

• Who gets to use the method(s)? Are they only perceived as legitimate when used by experts or can others also use them?

- Do the definitions and descriptions of the method acknowledge the existing approaches and methods that have informed them rather than framing them as 'new'?
- Do the definitions and descriptions of the method include a reflection on the material, physical and embodied processes entailed in using them?
- Are the methods 'emplaced' or located in place and space rather than a-geographical?
- Are the methods stable and fixed or under development? Are they closed or open/shared?

8
Prototyping Social Sciences: Emplacing Digital Methods

Adolfo Estalella

Redistribution of methods

Research methods in the social sciences has a history of intense development during the twentieth century. The historical accounts that describe the invention of interview methods, survey techniques, and modern ethnography have demonstrated that social researchers and scholars have exerted great effort in aid of their development. In the twenty-first century, the conditions for the invention of new research methods have been radically transformed with the extension of digital technologies. Many blogs and websites display tag clouds, a technology based upon textual analysis techniques; no less widely spread are the technologies for visualizing hyperlink patterns that draw on the technique of social network analysis. These are but two examples of technologies developed by non-scholars that are based on the application of social science research methods. Noortje Marres (2012) has described this process with the notion of redistribution of methods, highlighting the fact that research methods are now used and even produced anew by people with no formal credentials in the social sciences.

The emergence of new (digital) methods beyond the circumscribed limits of academia challenges scholars to reconsider how the social sciences may reinvent their methods. The process of redistribution offers the opportunity to expand their repertoire drawing inspiration from, or even incorporating, those methods developed by amateurs, non-experts and technology users. This chapter examines one of such method called prototyping, a socio-material device for the production of knowledge. I approach prototyping as an empirical object that forms part of the social worlds I have researched. My discussion is based on an ethnography undertaken in 2010 at the critical centre Medialab-Prado,[1] an institution that works at the intersection of art, science and technology. The activity of Medialab-Prado is organized around the notion and practice of prototyping, which involves tinkering with technologies, recycling materials, and extensively documenting the process.

The chapter is organized as follows. I introduce first the practice of prototyping at Medialab-Prado, and then describe the forms of material engagement in prototyping to suggest that we consider prototyping a process of conceptual exploration and theoretical elaboration. Two distinctive dimensions of prototyping are discussed in the following sections. I describe the effort to make prototypes open to the continuous reconfiguration through practices of documentation and hospitality, but for this to occur certain conditions are necessary, such as the use of space. I propose that we may consider prototyping a digital method that deploys experimental conditions for the production of sociological knowledge. Further, I argue that prototyping as a method is not only instantiated through digital technologies but configured in face-to-face situations through forms of material engagement.

Prototyping

Medialab-Prado (MLP) is a cultural centre, part of Madrid City Council's Area of Culture, which has been populated by hackers, artists, technologists and scholars since it was founded in 2004. In the last ten years the institution has sustained one of the most productive research programmes in Spain on the social and cultural dimension of digital technologies, and has gained recognition throughout Europe.[2] Its activity is organized around workshops, talks and seminars that involve a community of regular local participants; large workshops are also periodically organized in which participants from abroad take part. The centre defines itself as devoted to experimenting with digital technologies in their varied expressions, including digital art, technological design (based on Free Software, open source hardware) and forms of knowledge production (digital humanities, citizen science, and so on).

MLP mobilizes in its everyday practice only free and open source technologies such as the operating system Linux, the programming language Processing, or the web platform MediaWiki. Free Software is a type of technology characterized by a property regime that allows for copying, modifying and redistributing its source code. Programmers of Free Software made public the interior design of technology and release work-in-progress or beta versions so that anybody can take part in their development. In this sense, Free Software has been described as a type of technology, a moral genre, a form of material practice and a mode of knowledge production (Leach et al., 2009; Coleman, 2013). But Free Software is too the social collective that is enacted in this process of technological development; the anthropologist Chris Kelty has conceptualized it with the notion of recursive public: 'a public that is constituted by a shared concern for maintaining the means of association through which they come together as a public' (Kelty, 2008, p.28).

The ethos of Free Software imbues the activity of MLP, invoking openness, collaboration and experimentation as its principles. There is a constant encouragement to make all the knowledge and information generated and shared at MLP publicly available through copyleft-like licenses, which permit copying and modifying information and reproducing MLP-created designs in other places. More importantly, Free Software is integral to prototyping, a cornerstone notion and practice that shapes MLP's everyday activity. MLP's clear preference for this free and open ecology of digital technologies sheds light on the relevance of considering the values inscribed in digital technologies when analysing and developing digital methods. For if digital technologies have different values inscribed on them so could be the methods that are constructed mobilizing those technologies.

'In the Air' and 're:farm the city' (aka re:farm) are two examples of prototypes that were developed at MLP in their early stages; both of them take the city as an object to be researched and acted upon. In the Air, a project developed by Nerea Calvillo and collaborators (2010), has designed tools for measuring and visualizing microscopic agents that populate the air, and tools for exploring how these agents interact with the city.[3] The project has tried to construct sensors (with no success) using modest materials that can eventually be distributed and located in private houses. They have developed a software program that visualizes air components and locates their density over the city. Its first design, produced in a MLP workshop, was a 'diffuse façade', a system that visualized the air's components through a coloured cloud of water on the exterior façade of the centre.[4]

re:farm the city has been working around the city since 2009, creating tools for urban farmers while prototyping urban allotments and building communities around them. The project was originally conceived by Hernani Dias (2010) in Barcelona and travelled that same year to a MLP workshop, where it would return for another one in 2011. Participants in re:farm the city have built visualization software and electronic sensors for measuring temperature, humidity and watering using Arduino and other open source hardware technologies. In addition to hardware and software tools, the set of infrastructures produced includes wooden boxes, composters and mobile cases for allocating small allotments, very often using recycled materials. re:farm the city mobilizes do-it-yourself (DIY) and recycling practices that are intermingled with open software and hardware technologies. Moreover, all the activities of the project are documented and published on the project's website, and almost all the knowledge produced is available under open-access conditions in an easy-to-edit wiki, with enough detailed information for anyone to reproduce and build similar designs.[5] The diverse set of practices that are required in the workshops organized by re:farm gives the opportunity to participate to almost anybody, no particular technological skills are needed.

The prototype is a common concept in technological design contexts where it refers to testing artefacts that precede the final technological design; MLP has however re-elaborated the practice and notion of prototype to signify something else. re:farm the city, for instance, not only produces tools for urban farmers but by helping and teaching people how to grow vegetables it also helps to grow a community around each allotment. re:farm gathers people at the same time as it develops technology and produces the knowledge for doing so; in this process of material tinkering prototyping opens a space for experimenting with digital technologies and forms of sociality. Prototypes are therefore not just fragile objects and unstable technologies but the associated collectives gathered around them. We have seen this kind of configuration over recent years in projects like Free Software and Wikipedia. The online encyclopaedia, Wikipedia, is a work in progress with no stable and definite edition; it is constantly evolving as a result of the collective efforts of hundreds of thousands of contributors.

Prototypes in MLP make of their provisional 'beta' state a virtuous mode of social production and reproduction that recursively enacts its own public. As Alberto Corsín Jiménez (2014) has defined it: the prototype works through its openness and tentativeness as descriptor for both an epistemic object and an epistemic culture; it is a mode of knowledge production enmeshed in its own forms of sociality. Tinkering with materiality, designing objects, hacking software, documenting practices and exploring the properties of materials, prototyping resonates with a recent conversation in the social sciences (e.g. Ratto, 2011) that contends that we could consider forms of material engagement as practices of theoretical production. By material engagement I am referring to practices in which objects do not play the role of simple tools but they are a key part of the research exploration (Marres, 2009), in this case, the qualities and affordances of materials are not given in advance but are the result of the relation that the researcher establishes with them.

Material engagement

Before going on with my description it is important to outline my conceptualization of research methods. Existing social science methods shape our empirical practices by establishing the protocols and rules we must follow in our research. Despite their canonical status, they have an empirical foundation described, for example, in accounts of the development of the survey (Igo, 2007), interviews (Savage, 2010) and field notes (Sanjek, 1990). Recent discussion (Savage, 2013) on the social life of methods has criticized the view of methods as neutral instruments for the production of empirical data. Rather than thinking of them solely as tools I follow the conceptualization put forth by John Law and Evelyn Ruppert (2013), who propose viewing methods as devices. By this term they mean the patterned teleological arrangements that 'assemble and arrange the world in specific social and material patterns' (2013, p.230). This concept highlights the heterogeneous condition of methods: more than a set of rules, they are arrangements of people, infrastructures and knowledge arranged in a precise spatiotemporal pattern.

It is easy to see how the method of interviewing arranges a particular social encounter: two people meet for a period of time during which one poses questions to the other in a conversation, which is recorded and later transcribed. The interview arranges in spatial and temporal terms a situation that is mediated by certain infrastructures and particular social rules for the production of empirical data and whose ultimate objective is the production of social scientific knowledge. Law and Ruppert's (2013) proposal is part of a growing interest in exploring conditions under which the methods of the social sciences are reshaped or even reinvented (Lury and Wakeford, 2012b) and this chapter on digital methods and prototyping seeks to contribute to this literature.

The relation between digital technologies and digital methods is very often instrumental; the most common configuration takes the shape of a tool used for gathering, analysing, or producing visual representations of empirical data. Sometimes they are publicly accessible technologies used by social scientists; Christine Hine (2007), for example, used the commercial software for network analysis, Google TouchGraph technology, to crunch and visualize the hyperlinking patterns of websites. On other occasions, technologies can also be purposely designed for elaborating new research techniques, as illustrated by many of the cases described in this book; in both scenarios, digital methods are articulated through technologies that have been turned into tools. Yet prototyping composes a different relation between methods and material technologies: it neither mobilizes ready-to-use tools for the production of empirical data (Rogers, 2013) nor does it take technologies as evocative objects to think with (Turkle, 2007). The materials, technologies and artefacts that participate in prototyping are part of a process of tentative exploration that enacts a form of conceptual elaboration that demonstrates the material craft of knowledge production.

Prototyping resonates with the recent proposal for critical making, developed by Matt Ratto (2011) and others. Critical making is 'a research program that explores the range of practices and perspectives connecting conceptual critique and material practice' (Ratto, Wylie and Jalbert, 2014, p.86). Drawing inspiration from design practices, critical making displaces the traditional methods of social sciences – instead of observing technology designers or users in an attempt to describe the social dimension of technology, critical making organizes knowledge production through workshops and encounters aimed to produce artefacts through collaborative practices. The objects designed in these encounters are not the ultimate goal, but rather a means for the production of new sociological concepts: it is in the process of technological tinkering and material engagement that new conceptual elaborations are produced. Critical making is therefore a practice and method 'intended to bridge the gap between creative physical and conceptual exploration' (Ratto, 2011, p.252).

Certainly, re:farm the city does more than simply design cheap infrastructures for urban allotments. The project seeks to increase participants' interest in the food they eat by helping them produce it, and it aims to recover local species of vegetables and produce knowledge about them. In so doing re:farm explores the limits of urban life, the distinction between nature and society, the boundaries between the rural and the urban social fabric and the interface between communities and technologies. Working with mundane recycled materials, experimenting with digital technologies and documenting these practices, re:farm the city materially re-farms and conceptually reframes the city. In so doing the project reshapes the urban environment through a sophisticated reflection on the relation of the city with our food and the opportunity to intervene in this process through digital technologies.

There is a twofold displacement in the conventional configuration of digital methods that takes place in prototyping, both in the role of the empirical and in the relationship between the method and material objects. First, the production of new concepts and the construction of theory do not follow the common path of data production, analysis and writing. Prototyping is not a method for producing empirical data; sociological knowledge is elaborated in embodied and face-to-face contexts, through practices of material engagement and in places carefully designed for this kind of work.

Second, the method is not materially inscribed in a tool, as for example is the case when social network analysis is materially inscribed in hyperlink representation technologies. The production of knowledge in prototyping is the result of material tinkering, collective design and collaborative experimentation. The method in this case is a device that emerges in the process of material engagement. In this sense prototypes may be described as socio-technical assemblages that intertwine material construction and conceptual production; they unfold experimental ambiences for conceptual exploration, but in order for this to happen certain conditions are necessary.

Openness

At MLP, prototypes are produced during large workshops in which a few dozen people meet for three weeks to create visualizing software programs, develop electronic artefacts and discuss the social and political aspects of digital technologies. 'Interactivos?' is one of MLP's lines of enquiry that aims to problematize the simple notion of interactivity, which for some people 'was reduced during the 1990s to the idea of pressing a button', according to Marcos García, director of MLP. Months before the annual 'Interactivos?' workshop event, the centre makes an international call for ten projects that will be funded for materials and tools. A second call is later made for selecting three or four dozen collaborators whose travel expenses are paid for. The 2010 'Interactivos?' workshop gathered forty people: a few from Spain, half from the rest of Europe, and some from America. At the workshop, collaborators (as they are called) choose the project they want to collaborate on and during the following days an atmosphere of conviviality pervades the centre. Improvised seminars and small workshops are organized by participants to teach others specialized techniques. The intense work during the day continues till very late and often extends into the night in the bars of the neighbourhood.

The 2010 'Interactivos?' workshop was organized around the topic of 'neighbourhood science' with the objective of reflecting on how MLP and similar centres could be considered citizen laboratories. The motto explicitly invoked the process by which amateurs and aficionados are becoming more relevant in the production of scientific knowledge in our societies; its goal was 'to set up small urban experimental laboratories to foster neighbourhood participation based on experience, on the passion for learning and sharing that is characteristic of amateur and hacker culture' (Medialab-Prado, 2010). One of the projects worked to create a method for urban naturalists, another investigated the relation between urban and virtual environments, and a third was a DIY, easy-to-assemble photobioreactor. Since being held for the first time in Madrid in 2006, 'Interactivos?' has travelled all around the world and the workshop's methodology has been replicated in London, Lima, Mexico, Dublin and Ljubljana.

The workshop's topic strongly resonates with the research programme on the co-production of science developed by Science and Technology Studies (STS) over the last three decades, making evident that research centres and universities are not the only sites in which scientific knowledge is produced (Nowotny, Scott and Gibbons, 2001). These authors contend that science is progressively produced by new agents in completely new sites, and sound knowledge is now created by amateurs and non-experts, associations of patients, civil organizations and activist movements (Jasanoff, 2004).

Workshops are events for production and although some of the creations are exhibited, yet exhibition is not an overall aim for MLP. When I arrived at the centre in 2010 there were a few projects exhibited in its main room: a modified computer made of recycled hardware and cardboard boxes, and a visual intervention that the creator was trying to fix but that would not last long. The prototypes of MLP are unstable and precarious artefacts: very often they don't work, and even if they do, they are so fragile that they never last for long. The workshops are more of an event that prompts the initiation or continuation of prototypes under development than an opportunity to finalize them. Instead of seeking technological closure and the production of stable versions of technological artefacts, prototypes invest in their own openness. This orientation resonates with the inductive practice proper to certain methodologies in the social sciences that call for flexible research designs; however openness refers here to a sociomaterial state: a condition of temporal suspension involving artefacts that are in permanent development and a design that must be flexible to accommodate changes in its material and social composition at any time. In the first stage of workshops the invocation of openness means, for instance, that the initial design proposals must be capable of accommodating the proposals of different collaborators.

There is not any standard protocol for developing prototypes; it is always a tentative exercise full of uncertainty. There is not a specific method for constructing the urban allotments of re:farm the city; its construction has to be worked out in each case. The method, we may say, is elicited in the process of socio-material exploration during prototyping: the method of prototyping turns into a form of prototyping methods – a second displacement in the articulation of digital methods. If we follow Law and Ruppert's (2013) conception that methods are socio-material arrangements, then prototypes can be seen as methodological devices that invest in making social and material assemblages open to continuous reconfiguration over time. The distinctive element when compared with conventional methods is the suspension of temporality: the prototype aims at reproducing over time the epistemic condition of its socio-material arrangement. Being always incomplete, in a precarious and fragile state, the prototype is a method that calls for the participation of others to sustain its productive condition. In this sense openness is a temporal operator that projects the prototype into the future: the prototype as a temporal method of epistemological hoping.

But openness is only possible under the very precise conditions that are unfolded in MLP. Two other practices are oriented to open prototypes: first, the documentation of the process and second, the hospitality that mediates the relationships in MLP. The centre invests great effort in documenting all its events: talks and seminars are streamed online and recordings are uploaded to the Internet. During the workshops participants are prompted to document their activities in a wiki platform and all the information is offered under a copyleft-like licence. re:farm has documented in detail the different projects and technologies developed, and its wiki contains information on farm containers, devices for seeds, watering systems, diverse electronic sensors and software tools. The documentation may be a graphic, for instance depicting the containers, on other occasions it is the design of a workable electronic board for controlling watering while on vacations.[6] To a great extent, MLP is translating the common Free Software practice of documenting code into accounts of the process of prototyping; documentation oriented to allow others to replicate prototypes.

Openness is enacted too in the form of a social practice that permeates the sociability at the centre: hospitality. Cultural mediators (*mediadoras culturales*) are in charge of introducing the centre to any newcomer; while their role could be conceived as that of museum caretaker it is very different. Cultural mediators are responsible for sustaining a convivial atmosphere, taking care of the physical space, documenting the activities and pursuing their own research projects. If the process of documentation tries to open the past by keeping a material memory of events, the practice of hospitality intends to open the present by taking care of the ambience of events. We may say that hospitality is the spatial translation, in a face-to-face context, of the openness that in Free Software is enacted by documentary practices. While it may seem unusual to invoke hospitality as a technique or method for the social sciences, it is no more so than the notion of establishing rapport in ethnographic research. If rapport is intended to build trust and establish a positive relationship with research subjects during empirical work, hospitality is aimed at figuring out an epistemic ambience for the production of knowledge in a collective space.

It is not clear what experimenting with methods might entail or how to turn methods into experimental objects, but this might be an apt description of prototyping. However, for methods to become experimental objects they require specific conditions that in MLP involve mobilizing infrastructures, setting up spaces, practicing hospitality and carrying on activities of documentation; these are the conditions for prototypes to be developed. We may distinguish two different methods that are intertwined during the workshops at MLP: one that is brought into existence in a tentative process in which prototypes are assembled through material engagement; and another that provides the experimental conditions that allow for the first one to be brought into existence. Thinking of method as a twofold distributed arrangement of space and materiality challenges us, first, to rethink how material practices establish the conditions of possibility for conceptual elaboration; and second, to reconsider the conditions for experimenting with research methods in the search for reinvention.

Space

The topic of digital methods may be contextualized into a larger and recent conversation in the social sciences that has called for the reinvention of the repertoire of research methods. It has resulted in a series of proposals that look for inspiration in the arts (Back, 2012), explore new forms of collaboration (Konrad, 2012) and search for new approaches to the empirical (Adkins and Lury, 2009). The contributions of this literature have been enormously rich and diverse, opening the way for completely new inventions of methods (Lury and Wakeford, 2012a).

Little attention has been paid however to the role that space has in the production of new methods: Does the invention and innovation of digital methods need specialized spaces or can it occur in any place? It may seem an unusual question for the social sciences, but the history of experimentation has demonstrated the relevance of space in the production of science. Experiments require specialized sites characterized by specific infrastructures, spaces and social relations like laboratories, museums, botanic gardens and observatories, among others (Galison and Thompson, 1999). We may consider whether, in certain situations, space is necessary for the invention of digital methods and what kinds of specialized spaces may social sciences need for this task. I am thinking in space as the effect of heterogeneous relations (Law and Hetherington, 2000) and place as a particular articulation of those relations (Massey, 1994).

During the celebration of the 2010 'Interactivos?' workshop in MLP a group of five advisors were in charge of assessing the projects. These advisors then met with the coordinators and participants of each project on a regular basis. In one of the advisor's internal meetings they commented that collaboration between the projects was low and suggested changing the distribution of the groups in the large room in order to promote interaction between them; a few days later they reorganized the spatial arrangement of the groups. Taking care of the spatial layout of the workshop was intended to promote collaboration. On another occasion the use of space was a technique for transparency: in 2010 there were only a large room and a small office in MLP so all the management meetings took place in the large public room in a gesture of elected, or forced, transparency.

A participant used to refer to MLP as a 'face-to-face Internet'; on other occasions the centre was understood as an experiment into the 'analogization' of digital culture, a site in which digital culture was translated into the configuration of a face-to-face site. This is not exclusive of MLP, as hackerspaces are sometimes understood as a manifestation in the physical realm of production model of peer-to-peer networks (Kostakis, Niaros and Giotitsas, 2014). Something similar occurs with Burning Man, the famous artistic event annually held in the desert of Nevada. It is portrayed by some participants as a spatial realization of the values of digital culture: 'a mirror of the internet itself' (Turner, 2009, p.83). MLP, like these other places, may be considered a site where certain values attributed to the Internet and digital technologies like openness, horizontality, transparency and collaboration are inscribed in material infrastructures and translated in the organization of space.

Celia Lury and Nina Wakeford (2012b, p.15) have referred to what they call 'inventive' methods as 'devices of auto-spatialization, whose movement [...] is both topological and nomadic: topological in that they bring together what might have seemed distant, and disconnected and nomadic in that they are processual, iterative, emergent and changeable'. The reference to the spatialization of methods provides a clue to the reconsideration of the conditions under which methods may be reinvented. MLP is certainly not an academic institution, however it is a site where non-scholars and people with no conventional credentials experiment with digital technology and produce knowledge, and in this process we may say that they invent new research methods. This process is especially intensified in certain sites that I will call places for redistribution of methods: sites that in their spatial translation of the values attributed to digital technologies provide the conditions for experimentation with and innovation in digital methods.

Emplacing methods

I have described in this chapter the practice of prototyping at MLP as an instance for the production of sociological knowledge. I have argued that we may consider prototypes as instantiations of digital methods that problematize the convention that equates digital methods with digital technologies. Prototypes at MLP shed light on a relevant aspect of methodological invention in the contemporary moment: They show us novel configurations of digital methods that are brought into existence in face-to-face contexts through practices of material engagement. In so doing, they point out to the epistemic dimension of different practices like documentation and hospitality and the relevance of space for constructing epistemic ambiences for the production of sociological knowledge. To sum up and close my argument I now turn to consider the particular conditions under which methodological innovation happens in MLP.

I have designated MLP as a place for the redistribution of methods, a site where new techniques for the production of knowledge are developed by non-scholars. But in order for social scientists to take the work carried out in these places seriously they have to reconsider their approach to methodological invention. Methodological knowledge has traditionally depended on a reflexive gesture by which social scientists scrutinize their own practice, as many of the chapters in this book illustrate. The writing genre that accounts for this exercise usually takes the form of a reflexive report. The sites for redistribution of methods seem to emplace us to operate a twofold displacement in our conceptualization of methods and empirical descriptions that I have tried to perform in the writing style of this chapter. The method in this account is not my own practice but an empirical object, it refers to the arrangements that my counterparts in the field deploy for the production of sociological knowledge. Under these circumstances my writing does not follow the conventional reflexive genre but takes the form of an ethnographic description.

John Law (2004) has called for more risky methods, arguing that we need to be more flexible and generous if we want to renew our repertoire. He has argued that we need 'Multiple method. Modest method. Uncertain method. Diverse method' (2004, p.11). For if new methods are produced by non-scholars in places that allow for the redistribution of methods, the methodological repertoire of the social sciences could be renewed by empirically describing those methods or becoming practically engaged with them. In the first case (describing methods) we can return to our conventional techniques to describe these methods; this chapter is an example. In the second case (engaging practically) social scientists may participate in places for the redistribution of methods, taking part in the process of methodological innovation. In both situations, places for the redistribution of methods are sites full of uncertainty and social science researchers need to inculcate a sense of modesty in their own practices in order to recognize other forms of non-conventional expertise; doing so opens the opportunity to extend the methodological repertoire of the social sciences with multiple and diverse methods.

Mike Savage and Roger Burrows (2007) have warned of a coming crisis of empirical sociology arising from the progressive digitization of our societies and the entry of completely new agents into the production of sociological knowledge. They argue that the social sciences are progressively losing their relevance due to this process. In this chapter, I have tried to show that MLP seems to the reverse this argument: the participation of new agents in the production of sociological knowledge is an opportunity for the social sciences. MLP demonstrates that places for the redistribution of methods seem to challenge us to reconsider not only 'how' but 'where' we reinvent the digital methods for the social sciences.

It is not unusual to point out the experimental conditions of different methods; an expression that highlights the role that method plays in setting up the conditions of possibility for experiments. Less common is the exploration of how to turn methods into experimental objects. Certainly it is not clear what shape this kind of experimentation would take but the prototypes of MLP provide us with some clues. Methodological experimentation points in this case to a displacement of observational practices and a move towards other approaches in which the world is not only investigated but engaged with, too. The method is not in this case a set of procedures or rules for producing empirical data but a methodological device that carefully set up the conditions for tentatively producing social scientific knowledge; in this sense we might think of MLP as a place that experiments with methods in the process of prototyping social science.

Acknowledgements

I want to express my sincerest gratitude to the people of Medialab-Prado. This chapter was only possible thanks to them. I want to mention explicitly Hernani Dias and Nerea Calvillo for sharing with me moments of discussion and an opportunity to understand their epistemic practices. Thanks to Yvette Morey and Steve Roberts for their careful reading and comments during the editorial process. This chapter is part of a long ethnographic project I have carried on in collaboration with my colleague and friend Alberto Corsín Jiménez; it has been enriched by long debates and shared conversations between us.

Notes

1. This ethnographic research was carried out in collaboration with the anthropologist Alberto Corsín Jiménez.
2. In 2010, Medialab-Prado was given an Ars Prix award by the renowned Ars Electronica Festival.
3. This part of the project was developed and led by Susana Tesconi in 'Interactivos? 2009' under the project Glob@s.
4. The software developed by the project is available at its website: http://www.intheair.es/.
5. It is possible to consult this information in the wiki of 're:farm the city': http://refarmthecity.org/wiki/index.php.
6. Some of the designs for 're:farm the city' are available here: http://refarmthecity.org/wiki/index.php.

References

Adkins, L. and Lury, C. (2009) 'Introduction: What is the empirical?', *European Journal of Social Theory*, 12(1), 5–20.
Back, L. (2012) 'Live sociology: Social research and its futures', *The Sociological Review*, 60(S1), 18–39.

Calvillo, N. (2010) 'Infra(proto)types'. Paper presented at the *Prototyping Cultures: Social Experimentation, Do-It-Yourself Science and Beta-Knowledge*, Madrid, Spain, 4–5 November 2010.

Coleman, G. (2013) *Coding Freedom. The Ethics and Aesthetics of Hacking*. Princeton and Oxford: Princeton University Press.

Corsín Jiménez, A. (2014) 'The prototype: More than many and less than one', *Journal of Cultural Economy*, 7(4), 381–98.

Dias, H. (2010) 'Re:farm the city. Connecting food to people', Paper presented at *The Prototyping Cultures: Social Experimentation, Do-It-Yourself Science and Beta-Knowledge*, Madrid, Spain, 4–5 November 2010.

Galison, P. and Thompson, E. (1999) *The Architecture of Science*. Cambridge, MA: The MIT Press.

Hine, C. (2007) 'Connective ethnography for the exploration of e-science', *Journal of Computer-Mediated Communication*, 12(2), 618–34.

Igo, S.E. (2007) *The Averaged American: Surveys, Citizens and the Making of a Mass Public*. Cambridge, MA: Harvard University Press.

Jasanoff, S. (2004) *States of Knowledge: The Co-Production of Science and the Social Order*. London: Routledge.

Kelty, C. (2008) *Two Bits. The Cultural Significance of Free Software*. Durham: Duke University Press.

Konrad, M. (ed.) (2012) *Collaborators Collaborating. Counterparts in Anthropological Knowledge and International Research Relations*. New York and Oxford: Berghahn.

Kostakis, V., Niaros, V. and Giotitsas, C. (2014) 'Production and governance in hackerspaces: A manifestation of commons based peer production in the physical realm?', *International Journal of Cultural Studies*, first published on 13 February 2014 doi:10.1177/1367877913519310.

Law, J. (2004) *After Method. Mess in Social Science Research*. Oxon: Routledge.

Law, J. and Hetherington, K. (2000) 'Materialities, spatialities, globalities', in J. Bryson, P. Daniels, N. Henry and J. Pollard (eds.) *Knowledge, Space, Economy*. London: Routledge, pp.34–49.

Law, J., and Ruppert, E. (2013) 'The social life of methods: Devices', *Journal of Cultural Economy*, 6(3), 229–40.

Leach, J., Nafus, D., and Krieger, B. (2009) 'Freedom imagined: Morality and aesthetics in open source software design', *Ethnos*, 74(1), 51–71.

Lury, C. and Wakeford, N. (eds.) (2012a) *Inventive Methods. The Happening of the Social*. Oxon: Routledge.

Lury, C. and Wakeford, N. (2012b) 'Introduction: A perpetual inventory', in C. Lury and N. Wakeford (eds.) *Inventive Methods. The Happening of the Social*. Oxon: Routledge, pp.1–24.

Marres, N. (2009) 'Testing powers of engagement. Green living experiments, the ontological turn and the undoability of involvement', *European Journal of Social Theory*, 12(1), 117–33.

Marres, N. (2012) 'The redistribution of methods: On intervention in digital social research, broadly conceived', *The Sociological Review*, 60(S1), 139–65.

Massey, D. (1994) *Space, Place and Gender*. Minneapolis: University of Minnesota Press.

Medialab-Prado (2010). *Interactivos?'10: Neighborhood Science Workshop*, http://medialab-prado.es/article/taller-seminario_interactivos10_ciencia_de_barrio, date accessed 4 February 2015.

Nowotny, H., Scott, P. and Gibbons, M. (2001) *Re-Thinking Science: Knowledge and the Public in an Age of Uncertainty*. Oxford: Polity.

Ratto, M. (2011) 'Critical making: Conceptual and material studies in technology and social life', *The Information Society: An International Journal*, 27(4), 252–60.

Ratto, M., Wylie, S.A. and Jalbert, K. (2014) 'Introduction to the special forum on critical making as research program', *The Information Society: An International Journal*, 30(4), 85–95.

Rogers, R. (2013) *Digital Methods*. Cambridge, MA: MIT Press.

Sanjek, R. (ed.) (1990) *Fieldnotes. The Makings of Anthropology*. Ithaca and London: Cornell University Press.

Savage, M. (2010). *Identities and Social Change in Britain since 1940: The Politics of Method*. Oxford: Oxford University Press.

Savage, M. (2013) 'The "social life of methods": A critical introduction', *Theory, Culture and Society*, 30(4), 3–21.

Savage, M. and Burrows, R. (2007) 'The coming crisis of empirical sociology', *Sociology*, 45(5), 885–99.

Turkle, S. (2007) *Evocative Objects. Things We Think With*. Cambridge, MA: MIT Press.

Turner, F. (2009) 'Burning man at Google: A cultural infrastructure for new media production', *New Media and Society*, 11(1&2), 73–94.

9
Digital Methods and Perpetual Reinvention? Asynchronous Interviewing and Photo Elicitation

Emma Hutchinson

Introduction

This chapter considers the ways in which images can be included in online interviewing when researching a group that enjoys the sharing of images to augment their textual communication. At a time when people upload pictures more frequently than ever via social media (Shontell and Yarow, 2014), it is timely and important to extend a visual aspect to digital social research methods, informed by the insights of visual sociology. This approach favours the use of established social research methods online with modest refashioning (Pink, 2012). The development of digital social research methods has been dogged by the idea of innovation as the answer to all social research questions. However, for most people, online social interaction does not necessarily change very quickly (Baym, 2009). The drive for innovation appears misplaced, especially when the 'new' aspects of online interaction are constantly overemphasized to the point where existing social research methods are ignored. Yet, in a study of online spaces, where the nature of information can be either visual or textual, and where different types of recording are possible, this approach may be insufficient (Garcia et al., 2009). The chapter thus argues that extending existing methods to newer digital terrain is useful, but in a way that is sensitive to alternate ways of co-producing data with respondents in online spaces.

This chapter draws on research conducted on the online identity and embodiment of players in the massively multiplayer online role-playing game (MMORPG) Final Fantasy XIV. The game's story posits the player as an adventurer stumbling into a crisis that could cause the end of the world unless the player works with others to prevent it. Such video games feature massive environments populated by players from all over the world and represented as humanoid avatars who can interact with each other to drive their progress through a narrative. Online gamers persistently use specific modes of communication and only incorporate new modes when these complement their existing communication. Gamers use a wide variety of methods to communicate with each other, including forums, social media, YouTube, podcasts, gaming websites and blogs. These modes of interaction are both textual and highly visual, which point towards the possibility of incorporating visual methods in such a study.

The chapter is presented as follows. Initially, there is an overview of photo elicitation and how images play an important part of online self-representation. The next section considers the process of conducting such interviews and the attendant ethical issues. This includes an examination of some of the methodological issues around online interviewing, such as the lack of face-to-face interaction while involving the avatar in the interview encounter. The final section highlights the meaning of the avatar to the player and the repercussions for online interviewing.

An introduction to photo elicitation interviews and online self-representation

Photo elicitation interviews consist of creating an interview schedule linked to photos that are both meaningful to the respondent and relevant to the research topic (Pink, 2007). One frequent example is the life history interview (Hirsch, 1999). The interviewer asks the respondent to show a selection of photos that represent different aspects of their life, and explain to the interviewer what is happening and its significance in their lives. Photos tend to trigger memories for respondents in a way that words do not (Banks, 2001). The main point is that the respondent must have a particular connection to the photo (though the photo need not be their personal one) for the process of photo elicitation to be successful (Harper, 2002). For example, Pink (2007) used photos of bullfighting to discuss the sport with Spanish fans who were invested in the sport as knowledgeable spectators. Her research also points to how photographs can be analysed and interpreted in different ways, ranging from the respondents' meanings to the researcher's interpretations of the same material. For example, Pink (2007) set out a series of bull-fighting photos in chronological order for interview, while her respondents re-arranged them in terms of their content. Their actions were driven by the visual culture associated with bullfighting, where certain ways of presenting photographs of the sport were predominant (Pink, 2007). Photo elicitation thus represents an interesting method that has the potential to be extended online, where images play an important part of self-representation and a group's visual culture. Rose (2013) has argued that the rise of the Internet has coincided with the growth in visual culture, whereby images are increasingly used as 'tools with which communicative work is done' (Rose, 2013, p.27), which can be perceived in image sharing via social media.

Hum et al. (2011) examined different types of Facebook Profile pictures, which serve as the main picture representing the user. They noted how users did not always just use individual pictures – sometimes group photos were used. Photo elicitation could thus involve a wider range of images that potentially represent the respondent than previously used. Considering recent claims that we upload 18 billion images daily to sites such as Facebook, Instagram and Whatsapp (Shontell and Yarow, 2014), there is also much broader scope for using social media and online image sharing in photo elicitation. This chapter argues that the potential for their use in research remains relatively untapped.

Avatars, screenshots and self-representation in gaming environments

For the purposes of my study with gamers, it could be argued that the relationship between the player and the avatar is such that screenshots of the avatar carry the same meaning for the player as if they were presented with a photo of themselves or something they hold as deeply important to them. Video games are broadly premised on the player identifying strongly with the avatar to immerse themselves in the game, which is achieved by interacting with the game space (Giddings, 2007). This can be observed through players' talk about play – most tend to alternate between 'I' and 'him/her'/'he/she' in the course of talking about a game. Giddings' (2007, p.46) study of his sons playing a Lego racing game led one of them to comment 'I'm the one who makes the Lego Racers go'. Rather than identifying as the person driving the car, he recognized himself as the agent acting on the Lego figure behind the wheel to propel them around the track. The shift in speech may thus occur when switching between one's own role in the game, and something attributed to the avatar (Erkenbrack, 2012). In social terms, the avatar is deemed both an extension of the player into the space, and a representative of the player (Taylor, 2003). As such, players often take screenshots and record videos of their avatar while playing, such as recording a fight with a monster, or documenting time with friends (Taylor, 2006). This also points to the potential for incorporating screenshots of the avatar in photo elicitation interviews with the player, which can encourage the player to reflect on their relationship with the avatar and the experience of play.

My personal involvement with the gaming community highlighted the importance of screenshots to players. Part of my research was predicated on my own experiences of gaming since childhood and I sought to counter the perception among respondents that researchers are hostile towards gaming. Many of my respondents talked about popular media perspectives of gaming, particularly gaming's alleged links to anti-social behaviour and violence as emphasized by certain researchers (e.g. Bushman and Anderson, 2009) and the players' consequent desire to co-produce research that would reflect their experiences of gaming. I also drew on my knowledge of gaming and online image sharing in various ways, from groups of players sharing pictures of each other to websites such as deadendthrills.com where players share artistic images taken in video games.

Screenshots also constitute an important part of online gaming, given its transient nature. Pearce and Artemesia (2009) studied the community of an online game named Myst: The Gathering of Uru which was shutdown following a poor critical reception, low sales and a plethora of technical problems. The remaining fans rebuilt parts of the game in other online worlds, such as Second Life and There.com. This was possible because players had taken screenshots of the previous game to document it, especially towards the end of its life. My research project was centred on Final Fantasy XIV, an online game that also received very bad press to the point where the company who created it, Square Enix, decided to rebuild. Consequently, changes to the game became very regular and only amplified the recording habits of its players. Screenshots became an important part of remembering different parts of the game, its history and events that the player and their group of friends took part in.

This included one of the most enthusiastic players I interviewed, Barrel,[1] who had started playing the game during its early testing phase. When a game is in development players are invited to test its capabilities in order to provide feedback to developers on how the game runs on different computers and their experiences of the game's content. Being involved with such testing holds prestige for gamers as participation is often via invitation only, and Barret was quick to send me pictures of his involvement. He also sent other screenshots tracking his subsequent experiences in the game. In some ways, he used the screenshots to establish his credibility with me as a knowledgeable, skilful gamer. Moreover, this authority was important for establishing his place within the wider community and his group of friends. Final Fantasy XIV contains informal player groups called Linkshells, where like-minded players socialize and play the game together. In other MMORPGs, these are also known as guilds. Barret's Linkshell consisted of other advanced, knowledgeable players who similarly enjoyed challenging themselves (e.g. by traversing the toughest terrain, or fighting the hardest enemies). His screenshots would have formed an important part of proving and maintaining his credibility with the Linkshell. Such players often kept a collection of screenshots, much like a photo album, that formed evidence of their acts in the game. Taylor (2006) noted a similar trend with forum signatures which are pictures of the avatar situated at the bottom of every message written by the player. These pictures often contain information about the avatar's achievements in the game for other players to see. Barret's screenshots performed a similar role in his interactions with other players and such image sharing further illustrated the potential for photo elicitation. The section below will discuss how to conduct photo elicitation interviews online.

The process of email interviewing

Interviewing online takes two forms: asynchronously, which is predominantly conducted via email and the interviewer and interviewee offer their replies at different times, or synchronously via chat taking place in real-time. Asynchronous email interviews have gained popularity due to their technical ease, and their potential to generate reflexive discussions (James and Busher, 2006). Respondents are given plenty of time to consider their responses, though it can encourage respondents to linger on a reply, in contrast to quick-fire answers in synchronous interviews (James and Busher, 2006). Part of the attraction of email interviewing remains its accessibility. Unlike other means of researching online, very little specialist knowledge is required, especially given the widespread nature of email use. Consequently, email interviewing can seem like a relatively easy option, in comparison to the bigger budget and deeper expertise required for other forms of online research. The following examines the process of conducting online photo elicitation interviews in more depth drawing on my experiences with this method.

Having identified two fan forums for the game, I contacted the forum administrators regarding the possibility of conducting interviews with some of their users. The message included details of my research aims, and information about myself such as my status as a gamer and researcher, as well as a link to my e-portfolio on the department website for more information. The first to consent to my request was a forum for a fan-run wiki site whose members were devoted to finding and displaying information about the game. This has since been taken over by the company gamerescape.com. Many forums for video games are part of larger companies which run multiple websites for gaming. This included the second to agree, namely the Final Fantasy XIV forum in the ZAM network, which is one of the biggest websites for online gaming, including all of the biggest online games in North America and Europe.

Prior to starting the interviews I underestimated the number of respondents that would be interested in participating. Other online researchers suggest that a form of incentive is required to encourage potential respondents for online interviews (Sanders, 2005). However, I could not offer anything to encourage participants, and thus anticipated few respondents. In the first group of interviews conducted in January 2011, 12 players participated. Forum moderators assisted in placing the thread requesting volunteers, as well as posting a message in the thread to confirm that I had sought their permission. The opening message of the thread was in a similar vein to the original request sent to the moderators, offering a brief description about me and the aims of the research. Some of the volunteers came forward in this thread, whereas others contacted me through private messaging on the forum or emails. The next group of interviews was conducted in the first two weeks of February 2011 with 23 respondents. The ZAM forum moderators were also helpful in identifying the best section for my thread, and again posted in the thread confirming that I had negotiated access with them. One further interview was elicited in late February from a friend of one of the respondents who contacted me separately. In total, 36 interviews were conducted in this phase of the research.

I asked respondents about their preferred mode of contact, suggesting MSN messenger, Skype, email or private messaging. Most opted for email or forum messaging and implied that such modes of communication were more private, and easier to fit in around their other commitments compared to Skype, as well as the time difference since most of the respondents were from North America. For example, one respondent replied during his lunch hour at work, and another would wait until her young daughter was in bed. Using email interviewing also enabled me to quickly copy the interview into Word, then import into NVivo for coding. Further to the above discussion of online communication being taken on its own merits, it was also important to take the respondents' wishes into account when considering communication with them as part of the interview process.

Two issues associated with asynchronous methods are worth examining: the level of directness permitted by the exchange and the time taken to complete the interview process. While respondents may benefit from time to reflect on the answers they give (James and Busher, 2006), some researchers have noted that such interview can be time-consuming (Kivits, 2004; Orgad, 2005; James and Busher, 2006). The onus remains on the researcher to reply quickly, otherwise the respondent may interpret a slow response as disinterest and decide to drop out (Orgad, 2005). An offline interview may take a few hours, followed by many more in transcription, but an asynchronous interview may take months (Kivits, 2004; Orgad, 2005; James and Busher, 2006). My experience was more fortunate in that my respondents replied much more regularly to my questions, which may be in part due to their very regular online social interaction. Furthermore I had allowed the respondents to select their preferred mode of contact, which may have resulted in a more positive interview experience for them.

Nevertheless, online interviewing can permit a greater level of directness as a result of the medium itself. O'Connor et al. (2008) highlight the ease with which one can as for age, sex and location (abbreviated to 'asl') online. Asynchronous interviews can encourage greater levels of disclosure due to the lack of facial cues and the perception of anonymity (Suler, 2004; Joinson, 2005). Nevertheless, the lack of face-to-face interaction has been cited as a cause for concern when building rapport with respondents (Bryman, 2008). Orgad (2009) forcibly argues that such concerns about computer-mediated communication stem from fears around disembodiment. Computer-mediated communication is still posited as 'a constrained version of face-to-face embodied interaction' (Orgad, 2009, p.48). Ultimately, online social research is mediated by the same technological constraints that accompany online social interaction, such as the lack of face-to-face interaction in certain situations. Moreover, this project involved a consideration of the avatar in the research encounter via photo elicitation. The avatar is considered to be much the same as the corporeal body by the players themselves, and points towards the potential for visual methods involving the avatar to encourage respondents to reflect on online embodiment and identity. Nevertheless, the decision to conduct interviews in this manner and the lack of face-to-face contact also had ethical implications that need to be examined.

The ethics of online interviews

The first ethical issue concerns how a respondent feels about an online interview. It can be harder to tell if the respondent is upset by a line of questioning in the absence of visual and aural cues (James and Busher, 2006). Having said that, my list of questions did not contain anything sensitive that would obviously cause offence; most questions concerned the respondent's avatar and its role in the game, as well as their online friends and interactions. By allowing respondents time in which to consider their replies, they can decide what they should include. Unlike face-to-face interviews, it is easier for the respondent to withdraw from the interview altogether by simply ceasing to reply. Moreover, the lack of face-to-face interaction can mean that the interview is less affected by power relations between researcher and respondent. The ability to easily withdraw from the interview/research potentially offers the respondent a more equal position. Nevertheless, in the present study I was still situated as a white woman of a similar age to many of the respondents, and affiliated with a university in the UK, who ultimately benefited from the research encounter. Yet, the relationship was not just one-way as suggested by my respondent Laguna, when he signed off a message with the following[2]:

> Anyway, Emma, thank you for taking the time to read my response. Feel free to ask any more questions as long as the length of the response isn't an issue!

Laguna wrote lengthy replies and kept asking if I minded reading his 'soapbox' musings, which he claimed filled his normally empty lunch hour. The implication here is that I still have a degree of power, as he wishes to make sure that his responses are what I want to hear, and that it does not cause me undue effort to read his answers. While this partly affects the validity of the interview data where the respondent wants to produce 'pleasing' material, the lack of visual cues can equally leave the respondent unsure of the researcher's reaction. At the same time, the interview helped him to pass the time at work, so he benefited from the exchanges too.

Another ethical issue concerns whether the researcher should keep attempting to contact a respondent who has ceased replying. In some instances, it is hard to know whether the respondent has merely forgotten to reply due to pressing concerns elsewhere in their lives, or whether they wish to withdraw from the study completely (James and Busher, 2006). Orgad (2005) suggests emailing participants to remind them about the interview, however I felt quite awkward about that. A handful simply stopped replying, but I was wary of appearing to be 'spam' in their inboxes, that is, continuing to contact them in a disrespectful or annoying manner. I opted not to send reminder emails, which may have meant that a few interviews were not wrapped up properly. The majority did reach a natural end, and I sent a message thanking them for their participation. The remainder of the chapter concerns the potential for photo elicitation online in the study of online embodiment and identity.

Avatars and identity in online photo elicitation interviews

As discussed above, photo elicitation interviews work well if the respondent has a personal connection to the image in question (Harper, 2002). For a number of respondents, the personal connection to the avatar was as much corporeal as mental. Players have a significant emotional and psychic investment in their avatars (Taylor, 2006; Boellstorff, 2008; Pearce and Artemesia, 2009), however my research also revealed a powerful embodied aspect to the relationship. This investment in personal avatars confirmed that photo elicitation using screenshots could be a fruitful direction for the research. Some of the interviewed players always constructed an avatar that bore a resemblance to their facial features, while others needed an avatar that was similar in physical size otherwise they could not 'think through' how their avatar would behave in particular situations. I asked interviewees if they could send a picture of their avatar at the start of the interview. Most sent at least one screenshot, often with the avatar facing forwards, like a typical self-portrait or 'selfie'. A handful also sent further screenshots to illustrate their points throughout the interview. I similarly shared some of my own screenshots to illustrate certain points, such as when I wanted to talk about avatar appearance. This approach prompted discussions with respondents, and in some instances helped to clarify my points, as well as theirs. Using screenshots also tapped into the visual culture of these players who routinely shared screenshots as part of their regular interaction with others. The portrait style screenshots initially sent by respondents at the start of the interviews were often accompanied by an explanation of how the avatar resembled them. Selphie explained how she designed her avatar's face as follows:

> As far as her facial features were concerned, I kinda wanted her to look like me. I have a round face, which she has, and a similar nose.

> She's kinda a mix of me and then this fantastical part of me that
> I could never be.

Selphie emphasized her points by sending two images – one of herself
and one of her avatar. Both were portrait style pictures, and she was
facing forward in both of them.

For some respondents, only a particular physical characteristic needed
to be replicated online. Barret emphasized that he needed to have an
avatar embodiment that matched his own larger size, even if the avatar
did not need to necessarily have a facial resemblance.

> When character creation is an option i spend a bit of time creating
> something that i think looks good. when there are various races to
> choose from i normaly pick the big brutish type. going back to my
> lite rp [lite roleplay] i am a big guy in real life. Its easier for me to
> think through a big guys decisions.

What was most interesting about Barret's account concerned his body
type and that of the avatar. To illustrate the relationship, he sent
a picture of himself to compare with the avatar and emphasize his
larger size. In this way, he tied the appearance of the avatar to his
own embodiment, using the photo to reinforce the continuity between
his offline and online self. In the photo elicitation interview, photos
and screenshots form proof of the player's 'true' identity and further
illustrate the points being made by the player in question.

Other respondents also spoke of approaching their avatar in a similar manner. Montblanc stated in an interview that he preferred shorter
avatars otherwise the avatar would not 'feel' right to him.

> I cannot and do not see myself as particularly strong so a bulky char-
> acter isn't right. Nor do I see myself as very cartoony or serious. I see
> myself as an inbetween. The hair has to be just right (to actually
> match my own hair to an extent). I'm also not very tall, so a tall
> character would not do.

The avatar's embodiment can affect how the player behaves in online
games. It could be argued that these players seek to make their physical
bodies visible online, which complicates the popular notion of disembodied online communication, especially with regard to predominantly
text-based email.

Another respondent, Laguna, went one step further by creating an avatar that looked as much like himself as possible.

Creating a character that shares my likeness keeps me grounded in reality and allows me to make an honest representation of myself, i.e. 'What you see is what you get'. I developed this outlook back when I was playing FFXI [Final Fantasy XI] years ago. My character was an Elvaan Paladin [an Elven Warrior avatar and the tallest race in the game], I was the owner of a large linkshell at the time, and people looked up to me for guidance and leadership. I also made efforts to become an expert in the game and received a great deal of respect; something I never really had in life being a man of smaller stature at 5'5'. I took it all in, chalking it up to the fact that I was a reliable, adept player. Later on, I met with a few linkshell members at a get-together with my friends, and I got remarks along the lines of 'wow, I really expected you to be taller' or 'who is this little guy, and where is the badass?' I treated it as friendly taunts, but as time passed, they would ignore me more often than not while we played and began to look down on me. It was a wake-up call to realize appearance was a major factor in getting all that respect I thought I had earned. Since then, Ive always felt the need to show myself accurately and receive approval despite my shortcomings much as I do in life.

Laguna now creates avatars that resemble him much more closely following this experience in the previous Final Fantasy online game. His account also further emphasizes the relationship between the player and avatar and how it can be viewed in the eyes of other players.

Additionally, photo elicitation interviews pose a challenge to the notion of the digital lacking a face-to-face component where the researcher and respondent actually have a form of visual interaction. Most interviewees assumed that other players would have a physical resemblance to their avatar, even if they were aware of cases where this was not true. Boellstorff et al. (2012) suggest that researchers undertaking avatar-based research must be mindful of how their avatar will be construed by other players, such as its race and gender. This precaution also applies to the embodied characteristics of the researcher's avatar in the game itself, but also in a photo elicitation interview involving images of the researcher and the researched avatars. The majority of players felt the need to have some form of resemblance to their avatar, and would have assumed I would too. This points to the potential for considering online images as part of an individual's identity that are not necessarily images of the user, but can still be used in photo elicitation interviews online. Using screenshots also invokes the visual culture that exists in gaming where images form a regular feature of interaction, as well as tapping into the relationship between avatar and player to open up the discussion around identity and embodiment.

Conclusion

Online social research methods must not be divorced from the existing social research methods canon which has much to offer those conducting research on online communities. Rather than continuously seeking the novel or innovative, this chapter reflects upon the value of revisiting existing social research methods, namely visual methods that remain relatively under-developed with regard to online research, as well as a reconsideration of online interviewing. One of the main issues associated with Internet research remains the problem of comparison with offline social research. The criticism of online research focuses on the lack of face-to-face interaction and the accompanying visual or aural cues that are normally present in offline research encounters such as interviews or participant observation. In conducting research online, the process is always mediated through the same technological constraints that shape online identity and communication, but which also make such research so interesting. This point is often missed in the critique of online research that compares such methods to offline methods and finds them unfairly wanting. Here, my core argument has been that we ought to seek ways to research online communities on their own terms, while drawing on existing research methods, refashioned to reflect online modes of communication and its affordances. Online social interaction retains a strong visual aspect even away from video-based communication, as can be seen in the example of the gamers above. In online gaming, the avatar is assumed to resemble the player to some extent, and for many players, it is important to project their offline identities and embodiment into online spaces in this way. The avatar provides a fascinating link between the player and the game itself that can also be used to explore the relationship between online and offline life. Moreover, the screenshots of the avatar are as meaningful to the players as pictures of themselves and are easy to incorporate into a photo elicitation interview. Visual sociology has much to offer online research methods to better examine the different layers of communication between members of an online community.

Notes

1. Respondent names or usernames are substituted with names from the Final Fantasy series.
2. Quotations from respondents are reproduced verbatim from email interviews.

References

Banks, M. (2001) *Visual Methods in Social Research*. London: Sage.

Baym, N. (2009) 'A call for grounding in the face of blurred boundaries', *Journal of Computer-Mediated Communication*, 14(3), 720–3.

Boellstorff, T. (2008) *Coming of Age in Second Life*. Oxford: Princeton University Press.

Boellstorff, T., Nardi, B.A., Pearce, V. and Taylor, T.L. (2012) *Ethnography and Virtual Worlds: A Handbook of Method*. Princeton: Princeton University Press.

Bryman, A. (2008) *Social Research Methods* (3rd edition). Oxford: Oxford University Press.

Bushman, B.J. and Anderson, C.A. (2009) 'Comfortably numb: Desensitising effects of violent media on helping others', *Psychological Science*, 20(3), 273–7.

Erkenbrack, E. (2012) 'Discursive engagements in world of warcraft: A semiotic analysis of player relationships', in D.G. Embrick, J.T. Wright and A. Lukacs (eds.) *Social Exclusion, Power and Video Game Play: New Research in Digital Media and Technology*. Lanham, MD: Lexington Books, pp.23–40.

Garcia, A.C., Standlee, A., Bechkoff, J. and Cui, Y. (2009) 'Ethnographic approaches to the Internet and computer-mediated communication', *Journal of Contemporary Ethnography*, 38(1), 52–84.

Giddings, S. (2007) ' "I'm the one who makes the Lego Racers go": Studying virtual and actual play', in S. Weber and S. Dixon (eds.) *Growing Up Online: Young People and Digital Technologies*. Basingstoke: Palgrave Macmillan, pp.37–50.

Harper, D. (2002) 'Talking about pictures: A case for photo elicitation', *Visual Studies*, 17(1), 13–26.

Hirsch, M. (1999) 'Introduction: Familial looking', in M. Hirsch (ed.) *The Familial Gaze*. London: University Press of New England, pp.xi–xxv.

Hum, N.J., Chamberlin, P.E., Hambright, B.L., Portwood, A.C., Schat, A.C. and Bevan, J.L. (2011) 'A picture is worth a thousand words: A content analysis of Facebook profile photographs', *Computers in Human Behavior*, 27(5), 1828–33.

James, N. and Busher, H. (2006) 'Credibility, authenticity and voice: Dilemmas in online interviewing', *Qualitative Research*, 6(3), 403–20.

Joinson, A. (2005) 'Internet behaviour and the design of virtual methods', in C. Hine (ed.) *Virtual Methods: Issues in Social Research on the Internet*. Oxford: Berg, pp.21–34.

Kivits, J. (2004) 'Researching the informed patient', *Information, Communication and Society*, 7(4), 510–30.

O'Connor, H., Madge, C., Shaw, R. and Wellens, J. (2008) 'Internet-based interviewing', in N. Fielding, R.M. Lee and G. Blank (eds.) *The Sage Handbook of Online Research Methods*. London: Sage, pp.271–89.

Orgad, S. (2005) 'From online to offline and back: Moving from online to offline relationships with research informants', in C. Hine (ed.) *Virtual Methods: Issues in Social Research on the Internet*. Oxford: Berg, pp.51–65.

Orgad, S. (2009) 'Question two: How can researchers make sense of the issues involved in collecting and interpreting online and offline data?', in A. Markham and N. Baym (eds.) *Internet Inquiry: Conversations about Method*. London: Sage, pp.33–53.

Pearce, C. and Artemesia (2009) *Communities of Play: Emergent Cultures in Multiplayer Games and Virtual Worlds*. London: MIT Press.

Pink, S. (2007). *Doing Visual Ethnography: Images, Media and Representation in Research* (2nd edition). London: Sage.

Pink, S. (2012) 'Visual ethnography and the Internet: Visuality, virtuality and the spatial turn', in S. Pink (ed.) *Advances in Visual Methodology*. London: Sage, pp.113–30.

Rose, G. (2013) 'On the relation between ' "visual research methods" and contemporary visual culture', *The Sociological Review*, 62(1), 24–46.

Sanders, T. (2005) 'Researching the online sex work community', in C. Hine (ed.) *Virtual Methods: Issues in Social Research on the Internet*. Oxford: Berg, pp.67–79.

Shontell, A. and Yarow, J. (2014) *Mary Meeker's Stunning 2014 Presentation on the State of the Web*, http://www.businessinsider.com/mary-meekers-2014-internet-presentation-2014-5?IR=T, date accessed 22 November 2014.

Suler, J. (2004) 'The online disinhibition effect', *CyberPsychology and Behavior*, 7(3), 321–6.

Taylor, T.L. (2003) 'Intentional bodies: Virtual environments and the designers who shape them', *International Journal of Engineering Education*, 19(1), 25–34.

Taylor, T.L. (2006) *Play Between Worlds: Exploring Online Game Culture*. London: MIT Press.

10
Digital Stories and Handmade Skills: Explorations in How Digital Methods Can Be Used to Study Transmissions of Skill

Victoria Tedder

Introduction

While the chapters in this book consider a multitude of ways that digital landscapes are used to connect and create, it remains important that the material relationship of digital contexts/the digital landscape is not lost. Socio-materiality is considered by others within this text, with Knox exploring the impact of massive online open courses (MOOCs) upon educational research. However, this chapter faces the challenge of conceptualizing ways in which skills and ways of engaging with materiality can be taught and expanded upon within the digital landscape. With qualitative research taken from my PhD, this chapter will focus on skill as an area of study lacking a thorough engagement with new technologies. In a discussion of methods for understanding the transmission and development of skills, an argument is made that the materiality of learning digitally has been largely overlooked. Case studies of different crafters and home growers will be used because of their large online presence and the interrelationship between crafting and growing. This chapter therefore provides an opportunity for incorporating the digital landscape in research on skill, thus prompting discussion about potential sources of data, about relationships between the digital and the material, and also raise discussion regarding ideas of digital co-presence. The skills and activities considered within this chapter broaden our understanding of how embodied actions are learnt through digital skill transference and in doing so enables further consideration of both embodiment and materiality within digital spaces.

Literature review of skill

The acquisition of a skill is based on an individual's active engagement with their surroundings. This includes working *with* objects, materials and tools – as opposed to simply using them for a task (Ingold, 2000, 2001). As such, skill acquisition is part of a larger engagement with different skills and actions. Here it is particularly important to acknowledge that an ecological approach towards skill acquisition is needed (Ingold, 2007) so that we can fully comprehend the different ways in which skill is enacted; or the ways in which the acquisition of skill is shaped by other kinds of material, physical and biological agency. This is particularly the case when considering gardens whereby the relationships between plants and humans cannot be viewed as unidirectional. Skilled relationships with tools also need consideration as they are relationships which require constant adjustment and sensory correction.

The clear prerequisite of a skill is that the actions need to be known to such an extent that they become familiar to the actor, and are thus more than a mechanical coupling of action and material. Skills are based on a familiarity with an action to the point that individual movements become natural. This can be interpreted as part of the reason why individuals find it difficult to explain the component actions of their skills. Essentially, in order to achieve a lightness of hand they have moved beyond the point of conscious action.

Ingold (2000) claims that skill acquisition is not problem solving. Taking the example of the bag-making Telefol people of New Guinea, Ingold (2000) claims that the 'problem' has already been solved. The skill is the enactment of this solution. This enactment of the design solution will involve more problem-solving when difficulties arise and in order for this to be a skill rather than a mechanical undertaking of the task, ways of improving and dealing with mistakes must be learnt. Sennett (2009) claims that skills need to be considered within a body of other skills rather than one task. For Sennett (2009) the idea of problem solving is important, but instead he regards it as an on-going process of developing skills. For example,

> the open relation between problem solving and problem finding...builds and expands skills, but this can't be a one-off event. Skill opens up in this way only because the rhythm of solving and opening up occurs again and again.
>
> (Sennett, 2009, p.38)

However, this kind of problem solving may be impacted by the way in which machines are used and the methods which are utilized to learn skills in formal settings, thus creating a different set of skills such as how to respond to a particular tool to gain a certain desired effect. Individual skills therefore need to be understood within the context of other skills. However, this may be difficult in application to digital learning.

Ingold (2001) states that teachers and students need to be co-present for to be taught. He argues that this includes being taught how to hold your body in order for the skills to be learnt:

> the novice's observation of accomplished practitioners is not detached from, but grounded in, his own, active, perceptual engagement with his surroundings. And the key to imitation lies in the intimate coordination of the movement of the novice's attention to others with his own bodily movement in the world.
>
> (Ingold, 2001, p.21)

In addition to the importance of the body's role, the sensory nature of the activities being considered should also be a focus. This is particularly key to this chapter due to the sensory nature of the activities described, the impact of muscle memory on skills, and also the feel of wool and thread (as well as the occasional pin prick) along with the experience of dirt under fingernails and aching backs. Therefore, as argued by Sennett (2009) and Ingold (2000, 2007), sensory memory and the way in which learning occurs through experience, is extremely important. Haptic knowledge (the process of learning through touch), and our struggles to understand and articulate the skills stemming from this knowledge, is a significant aspect of understanding how bodily experiences can be used within research. Similarly, Grasseni (2004a, 2004b, 2005) and Ingold (2000, 2007) claim that work is learnt through the movements we carry out when attempting to achieve an end product. However, Ingold (2001) argues that the context of movements is important, as the movements are being consciously imitated by the actor in order to become known; this mimesis creates a lightness of hand allowing for greater expression. This is problematic when contemplating whether direct movements are being actively learnt or are simply the results of habitus. For example, the act of knitting a stitch requires the individual who is attempting to teach the action to pinpoint certain markers which need to be achieved for the stitch to work. However, the actions which the body is carrying out to create these end results, movement by movement, are harder to transmit in the way which was exemplified by Ingold (2007) who used the example of learning knots. Instead, Bourdieu argues that movements are transmitted and *are* a form of embodied knowledge and thus points to how the cultural can also be interpreted individually (see Sweetman 2009). Following this discussion of the different ways in which skills are embodied, it is therefore possible to integrate the cultural and biological, thereby recognizing skill as a form of embodied knowledge and physicality leading to forms of knowledge (Downey, 2011).

The body is often absent from our visions of skill. Leder (1990) described how the body can go in and out of awareness when learning a skill, which is in keep with Ingold's (2007) reference to a 'lightness of hand' and his claim that it is this loss of awareness of bodily movements which leads to the mastery of a skill. This linking of the loss of bodily awareness with proficiency in a skill is certainly commonplace. Leder (1990) has argued that this 'dys-appearance' of the body lead to it becoming only acknowledged through pain. Yet the embodiment of learning actions lays at the centre of our understanding to how actions are passed from one to another.

The absence of the body from academic and other understandings of how skills are acquired can partly be explained by a lack of language for describing the technical actions involved in the bodily enactment of skills. This is improving as seen from the work of Wolkowitz (2006) and McDowell (2009) who have explored the importance of the body in work. In addition, the importance of materiality has been observed by Pettinger (2006) in relation to retail. Here materiality is seen alongside other processes of creating meaning within the retail setting, in response to Sayer and Walker's (1992) exploration of the circulation of goods. As demonstrated above, it has tended to be anthropologists who have taken this area seriously, including the likes of Downey (2011), Ingold (2000, 2001, 2007) and Grasseni (2004a, 2004b, 2005). This research needs to be taken on board by sociologists of work. In particular by those who want there to be a greater focus on the body, including the ways in which we can understand actions which are difficult to articulate without resorting to mere representation.

The power associated with our conceptions of skill needs consideration. There are two issues of concern; first if we are to give power to the idea that there has been a separation of head and hand we must consider the consequences of this, as this may lead to a further emphasis on such a division, and create this reality. In essence, we need to be careful that we do not consider skill simply as an actor whom imposes their will on both tools and materials. Particularly for work concerning cultivation, we need to view these actions as working along *with* such materials. The ways which we can see skills as being learnt and practised created these discussions around the codification (and I would also often claim commodification) of skilled practices, as changing their value but also their skilled value, which thus creates a greater understanding of how people are able to use hobby crafts, ranging from the tensions within this to the skills that they gain. As such, the issues that surround skill raise more questions regarding our assumptions of what is skilled work and what is not, and how our economic concerns and gendered notions affect this. Of particular concern is the relationship between hobbies and skilled work as these hobbies reside within a place where work can certainly become skilled yet, are often seen as not possessing the respect that craftsmanship and skill are given.

Within my conceptions of craft, I will define it as the on-going development of a skill. This follows the idea that to be a craftsman (or woman) there must be a sense of exclusivity about the task, that is you devote yourself to learning this skill. This is particularly the case when considering the levels at which actions are learnt whereby some participants are highly skilled to the point of being instructors in their craft. These limits can be seen as being indicative of something other than craftsmanship or a very certain form of craftsmanship such as that expected within an apprenticeship. The classifications of skill and craftsmanship within leisure are then ambiguous within current conceptions.

The way in which leisure activities are here being discounted from skilled status acts as a reinforcement of the discounting of crafts associated with femininity (Parker, [1987] 2010). Actions such as embroidery, knitting and other domestic crafts are often simply written off as unskilled work in part due to the lack of debates where they are classified as skilled (Parker, [1987] 2010).

Although actors should not automatically be considered as craftsman, being discounted due to definitions which are based on employment is prejudiced. Within the craft groups interviewed there was an acknowledgement of this power balance and a history of overlooking skills. This was noted also as part of an effort to change the perception of these actions. Others noted that men involved in traditionally female work, such as embroidery, have received increasing attention.

New challenges

Within my PhD research I set myself the task of researching communities of crafters and growers, and their current popularity. I conducted a traditional ethnography and oral history interviews (collecting over 45 hours' worth of interviews) with 30 individuals from three different groupings to consider their formation, these included: craft activists, community gardens and those who crafted and/or grew at home. Here the space in which communities are digitally created soon became clear. This was a way of connecting, creating events at which to meet in person, but also a place to share ideas, skills and create. Such a position was initially chosen due to pragmatism rather than a methodological standpoint because of the nature of the activity carried out concerning growing and crafting tasks online. The research took the form of an online ethnography; spending time in online social spaces such as forums, Facebook and Twitter to see the forms of interaction taking place as well as seeing presentations which were made on blogs while keeping a field diary. Both the craft activists and those who make and grow at home had strong online presences which enabled me to make contact and gain information before a face-to-face interview and also to continue data collection and correspondence with participants once the interview was completed. This helped me to understand new developments within participant's lives and helped the sample stay dynamic, and can be seen as a continuation of ethnography within a virtual environment (Kendall, 1999; Hine, 2000). Of course such a process was not simply one way. Due to the nature of social networking, participants also got to know my life which lead to greater levels of trust for some participants during the interview stage and greater engagement with the project afterwards. Throughout the research I carried out growing and crafting activities and learnt new skills from those I was working with while conducting the research. However, by inviting participants into part of my life as well as experiencing some of theirs I felt the need to take care in re-evaluating the relationships and attempted to establish some distance for analysis.

While ethnographic practice is the most practical way of gaining an understanding it also has ethical problems within the digital world where informed consent is problematic. The use of digital methods has brought increased awareness of ethical issues, whereby care has been taken to use sources which are well acknowledged as being public spaces, for example the use of blogs (Hewson et al., 2003) or information which participants allow me access to. Online presence has also caused difficulties in regard to anonymity of participants who use micro-blogging sites such as Twitter, social networking sites such as Facebook, as well as blogs to discuss being part of the research with the awareness that those small communities of others involved may read the project, this has also been noted by DeLorme, Sinkhan and French (2001) arguing that use of digital methods makes identifying participants easier. Within this field, this is overcome by only quoting those who have also been interviewed and given permission for their digital output to be considered alongside these interviews and face-to-face ethnographic work. Due to the large variety of different sources of data, this has happened in several ways using computer-aided analysis and paper-based sources.

For the computer-aided analysis I used NVivo, commercially available software which aids qualitative analysis. This has been beneficial due to the large amount of data generated and the different types of data that research comprises of. NVivo accepted all of my data forms and so allowed connections to be recorded in a simple way between them all. This tool was used for making these links clear and easily searchable. Coding in this sense has allowed themes to emerge rather than demonstrating the number of times a certain phrase or response happened, which would be impractical and erroneous within qualitative work.

Throughout my research I have kept fieldwork diaries. During certain times, the diaries have been carried out directly using NVivo, allowing me to link images and parts of interviews. In this way direct links were able to be made as research was on going. Additionally, at other times, fieldwork notes were also produced on paper, this was particularly the case when it was vital to write down first impressions. The tactile nature of needing to write, draw and make demonstrations on paper as part of the process of analysis should also not be understated. This is a vital part of gaining an understanding before such ideas can be fully put into words and something that has been particularly useful. The crucial notion has been not to be constrained by either but be able to use both as needed. This multi-usage has also been significant for getting to know the data.

While there were several platforms used by the sample and each allowed for a different form of interaction, the sharing and development of skills within this area proves problematic given the research set out in the literature review. This is problematic not simply due to a current gap whereby digitally based skills can be rethought of in an altered fashion. Rather there is an exclusion from the definition of skilled work within these activities due to their communities not having the same sense of co-presence, dealing with the same materials or following the same cultural patterns in their craft production.

As such, I am arguing we need to rethink the way in which skill is conceptualized but beyond that and more applicably for digital methods, I am making the case that digital exploration can allow us to consider actions and skilled tasks with greater precision and depth which would have previously taken many months. This is partly due to technological advances which the researcher but also to technology altering the ways in which participants present and discuss their work, gaining an increased level of awareness of action and reflexivity of influences.

Methodological opportunities

YouTube

An interesting method of passing on knowledge has been through the use of video sharing websites. While YouTube and Vimeo are popular there has also been an additional creation of sites which contain videos on a particular craft, such as Ravellery which focuses on knitting, and other sites which consider paper crafts and stitching. This use of video is an innovation based on a number of technical advances from the recent ubiquity of hardware to video record from webcams on laptops to mobile phones. This is coupled with an increased high speed broadband that allows both the fast uploading and downloading of video-recorded material. These developments have allowed the amateur to play with such resources in a similar way that crafters are often playing with a variety of techniques and materials. However, their innovation is more important from our consideration of skill both in the individual development of knowledge and in the formations of communities based around such techniques. In the growth of individual knowledge, the use of video technology has allowed crafters to gain a new perspective on their practice. Being able to record actions gives the opportunity to view activity again, yet this time without the burden of carrying it out allowing for an increased awareness of the outsider but in a manner which can be repeated, slowed down and sped up or recorded again from different angles. This outsider view allows the crafter greater understanding of themselves in order to improve but also to gain greater understanding to enable the passing on of knowledge. This is a reflexive process through which creators need to consider their own actions in minute detail in order to have the understanding to pass on to others. One crafter I interviewed explored her own use of video to discover how she was causing pain to her fingers during a particular stitch. This mediated approach allowed the slowing down of a movement and watching at a different angle she was able to observe and alter her stitching.

Forums

Another space where digital innovation has impacted skill transfer has been within forum spaces. While the written sharing of skills is certainly nothing new the immediate interaction and quick building of a community is of interest. We can again see spaces which have developed for specific crafts alongside those which are more general with boards focusing on specialist embroidery techniques alongside those considering all Christmas crafts. Here techniques are explored but often from a problem solving or information gathering perspective. Working to use the collective knowledge of members in order to improve one's own understanding is a common feature of communities of skill, yet this digital setting to makes use of other Internet-based advice such as websites or videos along with personal written or visual understanding. In addition to asking for advice we can also see that forums are used to explore the potentials of a medium, they are then places where innovations and new projects can be shown for feedback and praise. This is using the visual elements of the forums to great effect but also only allows for the poster to pick and choose how these images are created and uploaded. For instance, areas where a skill may not have been fully mastered may be hidden or highlighted depending on how the poster is trying to position themselves within that community of skill. We can then see that while there is an opportunity for a direct response from other skilled persons this may not be fully accurate in relation to the whole of an object in comparison to being co-present with that item.

Blogs and micro-blogging

Another very different depiction of skill and the materiality surrounding it is present within blogging and micro-blogging. While blogging allows creators greater space to explore their stories and the items they have made it does not allow for the same level of feedback we may see on forums, or videos, or even micro-blogging. This level of interaction can even be turned on or off in the form of comments under posts. As such, we can begin to question if blogs on skill face the same problems as books on their topic, whereby they create a two-dimensional image of material activities which are then hard to learn from or interpret into day-to-day experience. Despite this blogging can be argued to have a great approachability, whereby readers are able to interact with and ask questions of the writer when problems arise. However, while blogging participants discussed a love of this interaction with readers there was the acknowledgement that this was impossible as the site grew and it became impossible to reply to all emails. Blogs can be seen as allowing for a greater reflexivity of action, showing the development of skills over time as the creator gains further understanding and experience. While blogging allows for a mediated understanding of activities there is greater room for exploration of mistakes and problems than we can see in print media as well as exploring the way in which these are learnt from. Micro-blogging (e.g. Twitter) on the other hand allows for an immediate and community building form of communication which is totally unsuitable for spreading skills using these alone. However, it is important to acknowledge that these methods of social media interaction are not used alone but rather in conjunction with other blogs or websites, individuals' blogs or micro-blog videos alongside written pieces.

Case study: Bringing historical skills alive

A shared history is a way of creating communities of skill particularly when viewing groups coming together such as crafters on forums and specific websites such as Ravelry, Etsy and Craftster. Each of these popular websites has sections for historical crafting. One case I will focus on is the re-creation through a knitting forum of a piece of knitting named 'The Queen Susan Shawl'.

While exploring the digital archives of the Shetland museum in 2009 a member of a forum came across a beautiful shawl which was duly posted to the forum to see if other members knew more about the pattern or how to make it. Although the pattern was not recognized, the attractiveness was and so the group joined together to work out a pattern for the shawl. Artistic and practical decisions were made throughout the process leading to the pattern not being an exact replica but instead a 'respectful' reproduction. Little was known about the makers of the shawl when work first began; the Shetland museum was contacted for more information leading to speculative histories of those who designed and created the piece, apart from the photographer and his family history of knitting and lace work little was known for certain. It seems that could not keep the group from bringing the pattern back into something material, one of the key instigators described the process of creating the pattern as taking ten weeks from start to finish with three levels of participation: a core group of experienced knitters, a secondary group who made test swatches to explore if their stitches created a similar effect, and then a third group who helped to make decisions and cheerlead the process along. Once the process was finished one contributor commented:

> I'm feeling a little weepy here. Think of it- a piece knitted before the turn of the last century, designed by a close group of family/friends living in an isolated area, preserved in a photograph, being recreated

by a far-flung band brought together by technology and a love of this craft.

(Comment posted on a knitting forum)

This expresses the emotional connection between an imagined past and the present, but also the processes which this digital connection to the skills involved had allowed. Thus these groups were able to share their different knowledge of knitting, wool and history to create anew an item they had only seen in images.

Through the use of all of the mediums described above this disparate group has been able to design and adjust patterns from site, using a multitude of previous knowledge and access to different resources. They have then been able to exchange and develop upon each other's skill base to learn the techniques needed for creating such work. In this sense we can see that communities of practice where skills are formed as a web of knowledge are possible within this online space.

Discussion

The case study previously discussed suggests that there are a number of ways in which a digital methodology can improve our understanding of a skill. Yet it remains important to recognize that this is not simply an optional area to consider but a place where skills are developed and transferred, and are of great importance to any whom are considering these tasks. While stressing the importance of digital consideration of skill, this section will explore some of the current gaps within our methodology and hope to explore some of the possible advances in our knowledge. There is currently a lack of understanding of how skills continue to be used after they have been learnt. While this chapter opens with a discussion of skill that involves the in-depth knowledge of the area, it is understood that a great many people will begin the journey to become skilled in actions without ever become masters. It is currently unknown what relationship that digital learning of actions will have with the number of people who are never able to fully develop their knowledge of task, whether by choice or due to the methods of learning available to them. This would be important to consider as it would help us understand in further depth the relationship that digital learning of action could end up having with different areas of this process.

Second, current research has been unable to explore the relationship between skills and their development when participants are only exposed to digital sources of learning. Instead current work has only considered relationships which have utilized digital sources alongside other more traditional methods, such as being taught the basics by family and friends or gaining an understanding in formal education. It is then impossible to accurately tell what influence digital learning on its own has on the development of skill.

Finally, there has been a slow uptake in exploring the effects that digital learning has on action. While domestic crafts have been spoken about here we can see that the resources explored above have been used for task such as cooking, sports techniques, learning to play instruments and even meditation. These tasks all adapt to the mediums in different ways yet the digital methods for learning techniques and gaining feedback on these need to be explored in greater depth to both gain further understanding of skill mediated by computers and also of the skill itself.

This use of digital methods has also generated feedback into a continuation of methodological advances. This can be explored in two main ways; first through understanding of the importance of tactility and the role this can take within digital exploration and second within the use of technology for reflection of action.

While often not fully recognized, our digital explorations are based in materiality. Whether this be through the use of fingers typing on a keyboard or the experience of the location in which the interaction is taking place. This understanding becomes increased when skills are considered which involve interaction with materials. The relationship between wool, needle hand and eye becomes further complicated when cameras and screens are added into the mix. This relationship can then alter the ways in which we consider these methods and the need to explore them in relation to material relationships. Video, still image, and the written word has given makers the opportunity to consider both the motivations and linkages where their work connects them to others and ideas before, but also acts as a way of exploring the skills and methods involved. This then becomes a reflective process whereby skills are altered and acted upon both from this exploration of the maker's own experience but also from the feedback of others.

Conclusion

This chapter has set out to explore the contribution that digital methods can make to the exploration of skill and ways of engaging with materiality, and how skill can be taught and expanded upon within this digital landscape. It has shown that while makers and practitioners have used the digital sphere to explore, learn and share skills alongside developing a self-examination of their work, this has not prompted empirical research which is focused on skill using digital understanding of material work. Through the use of case studies of different crafters and home growers the argument has been built that the understanding of this area is rich, but that it is currently coming out of work by practitioners and so sorely lacks sociological rigour. There is however much needed discussion about potential sources of data that can be used in this area as well as discussions regarding the relationship between the digital and material, and ideas of digital co-presence. While this chapter has outlined some of the methods which are currently being used, the need for further research has been argued throughout. There is also an ardent acknowledgement that this is an ever-evolving field conscious effort is needed to keep expanding and developing upon methodology, and thus make the best use of the ways in which the topics being studied are also altering through the use of these activities. Through the use of further digital ethnography greater understanding can be established on both how the transfer of skills has changed when occurring digitally and also the impact that communities of skill have upon the digital realm.

References

DeLorme, D., Sinkhan, G., and French, W. (2001) 'Ethics and the Internet issues associated with qualitative research', *Journal of Business Ethics*, 33(4), 271–86.

Downey, G. (2011) ' "Practice without theory": A neuroanthropological perspective on embodied learning', *Journal of the Royal Anthropological Institute*, 16(1), 22–40.

Grasseni, C. (2004a) 'Skilled landscapes: Mapping practices of locality', *Environment and Planning*, 22(5), 699–718.

Grasseni, C. (2004b) 'Skilled vision: An apprenticeship in breeding aesthetics', *Social Anthropology*, 12(1), 41–55.

Grasseni, C. (2005) 'Designer cows: The practice of cattle breeding between skill and standardization', *Society and Animals*, 13(1), 33–50.

Hewson, C., Yule, P., Laurent, D. and Vogel, C. (2003) *Internet Research Methods: A Practical Guide for the Social and Behavioural Sciences*. London: Sage.

Hine, C. (2000) *Virtual Ethnography*. London: Sage.

Ingold, T. (2000) *The Perception of the Environment: Essays on Livelihood, Dwelling and Skil*. London and New York: Routledge.

Ingold, T. (2001) 'Beyond art and technology: The anthropology of skill', in M.B. Schiffer (ed.) *Anthropological Perspectives on Technology*. Albuquerque: University of New Mexico Press, pp. 17–31.

Ingold, T. (2007) 'Materials against materiality', *Archaeological Dialogues*, 14(1), 1–16.

Kendall, L. (1999) 'Recontextualizing "Cyberspace": Methodological considerations for on-line research', in S. Jones (ed.) *Doing Internet Research: Critical Issues and Methods for Examining the Net*. London: Sage.

Leder, D. (1990) *The Absent Body*. Chicago: University of Chicago Press.

Parker, R. ([1987] 2010) *The Subversive Stitch: Embroidery and the Making of the Feminine*. London: I.B. Tauris and Co Ltd.

Pettinger, L. (2006) 'On the materiality of service work', *Sociological Review*, 54(1), 48–65.

Sayer, A. and Walker, R. (1992) *The New Social Economy: Reworking the Division of Labour*. Oxford: Blackwell.

Sennett, R. (2009) *The Craftsman*. London: Penguin.

Sweetman, P. (2009) 'Revealing habitus, illuminating practice: Bourdieu, photography and visual methods', *The Sociological Review*, 57(3), 491–511.

Wolkowitz, C. (2006) *Bodies at Work*. London: Sage.

Part IV
Digital Research: Challenges and Contentions

Introduction to Part IV

The problem: What are the implications of bringing digital methods into the mainstream?

So far, the chapters in this collection have explored the potential of digital methods for expanding and enhancing the possibilities for social science to engage with contemporary social life. They have also critically reflected upon the adoption of digital technologies, as methodological innovations bring new challenges along with opportunities. It is tempting to be 'carried away' with the exciting possibilities of digital data without considering epistemological implications and ethical consequences. As digital methods move into the mainstream, how do we ensure that our research is theoretically informed, methodologically rigorous and ethically responsible? A critical social science approach is needed to engage with these matters so that research is not conducted for its own sake but responsibly adopted.

As discussed in the opening chapter, there are some clear practical challenges in adopting digital methods, such as a constantly changing online environment with the on-going emergence of new data and new tools. There are also some fundamental methodological questions. One issue of concern is treating digital tools as 'black boxes' without critical interrogation of the sort of knowledge that is being produced, and who might benefit from this. There are important political and ethical questions over how methods are taken up. This section presents three chapters with different foci and approaches but with common goals in considering the implications of mainstreaming digital social research. The chapters outline contentious issues of power, ethics, working with vulnerable groups, privacy and inequalities in adopting digital methods. The challenges discussed range from the repercussions of conceptualizing the 'impact' of technology and data-driven approaches; balancing the potential of digital methods to give young people a voice with ensuring they do not come to any harm; and the key ethical concerns associated with Internet-mediated research.

Case studies: Contentions in digital social science

The widespread availability of digital data and ease of access to digital tools means that both obtrusive and unobtrusive research can engage with a range of populations, both global and local. Yet there are numerous points of caution to note. For instance, it is crucial to interrogate the provenance of data in unobtrusive research. Obtrusive methods need to carefully consider the relationships with participants. Both kinds of research have a duty of care to do no harm. The chapters in this section detail the challenges *of* digital methods, but also offer challenges *to* social scientists in thinking about how these methods are adopted.

Jeremy Knox's paper highlights the importance of critical reflection on how digital methods are taken up and theoretically engages with the relationship between technology and society. In a review of trends in educational research into massive open online courses (MOOCs), Knox raises wider concerns regarding data being taken at face value. Thanks to the rise in the adoption of MOOCs, research into these forms of learning is moving into the mainstream of educational studies, but Knox suggests problems with its view of technology as passive and inert that has 'impacts' on society, as well as with a data-driven approach. To illustrate these points, and to put forward an alternative socio-material approach, Knox explores two problematic elements of current research into MOOCs. First, he draws attention to the issues of power and representation in the world map visualizations of MOOC adoption that, without critically exploring the data that are used to generate these maps, can mask ongoing inequalities and the 'data-colonialism' of acquiring student data. Second, Knox suggests that attempts to capture and classify student participant in MOOCs simultaneously focus on the students (rather than the technology) but also allow the technological issues to drive this classification. Consequently, Knox argues for interrogation of code, algorithms and software in MOOC research that recognizes the technological process that generate data (see also Brooker et al., this volume). In keeping with the overall theme of this book, Knox stresses the value of seeing the social as already digital, rather than viewing online research as a distinct subfield, and suggests a more theoretically driven approach to understanding the relationship between humans and technology.

The way that technology is embedded in everyday life has particular resonance for children and young people who, as Emma Bond and Stuart Agnew note in their chapter, lead increasingly mediated lives. The authors address the mainstreaming of two issues – a child-centred approach to research and digital methods – and focus on how the latter can facilitate the former. In a project to explore young people's experiences of education, Bond and Agnew demonstrate a range of ways that social media can be used in research with children and young people, including fostering participation and providing creative tools for data collection. Their multi-modal approach shows the potential of digital methods for providing spaces for children's voices to be heard and seen as active participants in the research process on one hand; and the practical issues associated with trying to achieve this while protecting children from potential risks. One of the ways that young people could express themselves was using a 'virtual scrapbook' on Pinterest, which presented some potential problems with ensuring confidentiality and anonymity of the young participants, and also preventing cyberbullying and inappropriate content. Their technical problem-solving demonstrates how such issues can be overcome with ethical safeguards while retaining a focus on collaboration and acknowledging young people's agency.

Claire Hewson's chapter addresses these and other ethical challenges that need to be considered when using online digital methods. Her paper traces the emergence of a consensus surrounding the need for specific ethical guidelines for Internet-mediated research that recognize the enhanced risks. While these are guided by the basic principles of social science research, the innovations afforded by digital research mean that researchers are not as familiar with the particular issues that may arise and have fewer precedents to draw upon. Hewson advocates a contextual approach rather than strict rules in Internet ethics and offers a valuable account of best practice in outlining the debates and controversies in both obtrusive and unobtrusive methods, addressing issues of privacy and confidentiality, illustrated with reference to case studies. The impact of the recent Facebook 'emotional contagion' study that generated public anxiety and outrage over perceived intrusion is used by Hewson to highlight the challenges of dealing with ethical issues in institutionalized mainstream ethical safeguarding processes such as research ethics committees. Looking to practical guidance informed by existing research such as that offered by Hewson is crucial in order to develop a recognition of the importance of key ethical principles in digital methods.

The challenges of methodological innovation

Common to all three chapters is an engagement with methodological innovation and critical interrogations of digital data and tools. For researchers with an interest in taking up these challenges, the authors offer the following points to assist with negotiating this terrain:

- Bringing digital research into the mainstream offers new opportunities but also novel challenges. The chapters in this section suggest how to respond to such concerns through technical innovations to solve ethical problems, ensuring we pursue critical perspectives on technology informed by theory, and developing best practice in resolving ethical dilemmas.
- It is vitally important to engage with critical social science perspectives on the politics and power of methodologies, for example when dealing with research relationships with children and young people or considering how global inequalities may be reproduced. Digital data are not politically neutral, and we need to consider what data is produced, when, by whom and for what purpose.

11
What's the *Matter* with MOOCs? Socio-material Methodologies for Educational Research

Jeremy Knox

Introduction

Massive open online courses (MOOCs) are fully online programmes of study, usually offering free participation, and often attracting enrolments in the tens or hundreds of thousands. Following partnerships between the prominent MOOC platforms and a number of elite universities, MOOCs have attracted unprecedented media attention and played an unparalleled role in surfacing issues of online education into the 'mainstream'. In the words of Pappano's often-cited *New York Times* article, 2012 was for education 'the year of the MOOC' (2012). The dramatic rise in attention was perhaps encapsulated by the UK universities minister David Willets publicizing his support for MOOC partnerships (Coughlan, 2013), and Daphne Koller, head of the US-based MOOC organization Coursera appearing at the G8 Global Innovation Conference (UKTI, 2013). No more simply a trend within the narrow field of educational technology, the MOOC seemed to have become international news. Thus, while critical responses to the MOOC have highlighted the long histories of technological innovation (Logue, 2012), and indeed 'open' education (Peter and Deimann, 2013) overlooked in the hyperbole, these high-profile courses have done much to place the 'online' at the centre of educational concerns. As the recent report from Universities UK asks, is the MOOC 'Higher Education's digital moment?' (Universities UK, 2013).

However, for all the talk of disruption and revolution, the emerging research of MOOCs has largely conformed to orthodox educational approaches, and the technology itself remains significantly under-theorized. The next section will suggest that MOOC research is limited by the tendency to render technology passive and inert; not only in the MOOCs undergoing examination, but also in the research process itself. Such deterministic inclinations (Kanuka, 2008) fail to engage with the complex and nuanced ways in which human beings and technologies shape and influence each other, and result in an over-emphasis on social factors, human intention and agency, ultimately producing an impoverished understanding of the complex contingencies involved in MOOCs. Subsequently, I propose socio-material theory as a more coherent approach to the analysis of relationships between humans and technology prevalent in MOOCs. Two prominent trends in MOOC research will be discussed: world map visualizations and the analysis of 'active' and 'passive' student behaviour. These examples will illustrate two dominant assumptions that are occupying the 'mainstream' of MOOC research: a tendency to focus exclusively on students, either through the measurement of behaviour or through the study of experience, and a reassertion of data-driven methods commensurate with post-positivism and behaviourism. As such, a socio-material analysis will offer alternative methodological perspectives that might transform the research of MOOCs, and of digital methods more generally.

MOOC research

To date, MOOC research has largely conformed to an orthodox *anthropocentrism* and a problematic *representationalism*. The first is an inclination to focus exclusively on human beings as the site and measure of educational concerns. Thus, a number of large-scale quantitative analyses of student behaviour (Breslow et al., 2013; Perna et al., 2013; Ho et al., 2014) have been countered by more qualitative methods, concerned with ethnographic studies of student networking (Saadatmand and Kumpulainen, 2014), or phenomenological accounts of participation (Adams et al., 2014). Yet what of 'the digital' in this supposed moment of the MOOC? If this is indeed the time when educational technology hits the mainstream, how is the role of technology being understood? Drawing on the work of Hamilton and Friesen (2013), elsewhere I have argued that open education projects such as the MOOC tend to instrumentalize technology, positioning it as a transparent means to access educational content or forming social networks (Knox 2013, 2014). As such, the technology is subordinated to, and measured against, the educational aims of its human users. This underlying orientation establishes a fundamental separation between the social and the technological, and importantly, builds-in a constraint for educational enquiry that is limited to examining whether a particular technology has improved education or not (Hamilton and Friesen, 2013). In precisely this way, educational research preoccupies itself with considering the 'effects' and 'impacts' of technology (Selwyn, 2011), rather than developing a clear position on the technology itself. Research of the MOOC appears to have followed this trend, and for all the talk of 'digital moments', as we shall see, a rather conservative focus on retention rates, achievements and modes of participation has come to the fore.

Embroiled in the MOOC phenomenon is also the emergence of a data-driven approach that appears to reassert a problematic *representationalism* in educational research. I use this term here to refer to the idea that data are assumed to straightforwardly (re)present an external reality; that points of measurement can be easily extracted from a given situation, with no loss of fidelity, and can continue to portray that reality in an extracted form. MOOCs have been associated with 'big data' from their earliest incarnations (Fournier et al., 2011), and the subsequent scale of participation in the more high-profile offerings has motivated further media enthusiasm for the disruptive potential of computational methods in education (Guthrie, 2013). While a culture of Silicon Valley 'solutionism' (Morozov, 2013) is enfolded in the project of the MOOC itself, that is, seeking to resolve long-standing social dilemmas through technological fixes, I suggest that a belief in the emancipatory power of data may also be solidifying as a powerful 'common sense' which influences how digital methods in education can be understood. Following Anderson's well-known contention that '[w]ith enough data, the numbers speak for themselves' (2008, n.p.), a critical response to big data has been gaining increasing traction in the social sciences, and notably within Internet Studies (see boyd and Crawford, 2012). Critical responses in education are needed, where the analysis of big data are often formulated as 'Learning Analytics', and suggested to be 'essential for penetrating the fog that has settled over much of higher education' (Long and Siemens, 2011, p.40). However, as Williamson contends, '[s]tatistics, collected and analysed in databases, provide a new kind of powerful knowledge, one that is seemingly rigorous, reliable and objective, that can be used to count and control education' (Williamson, 2014b, n.p.). What is important here is the assumed incontrovertibility of data, such that the processes which produce it are often not questioned. Once again, technology (this time as the tool of research) in this moment of the MOOC runs the risk of being instrumentalized, where algorithms are positioned as the transparent means to revolutionizing educational insights.

In the next section I suggest that perspectives from socio-material theory (Fenwick et al., 2011) provide a basis from which to critically examine anthropocentrism and representationalism in digital education research. Such theorization offers productive ways of approaching methods that can not only begin to recognize the influence and agency of technology in the domains under study, but can also recognize the same complex relations in the instruments of research.

A socio-material method

Socio-material theory is beneficial for digital methods in two important ways. First, it provides a theoretical basis from which to account for broad human and non-human factors, rather than a narrow focus on the social, or the individual learner. In other words, the material world is given as much consideration as the social world, hence 'socio-material'. For the purposes of this chapter, I consider technology to involve aspects of the material, or non-human. Second, agency is positioned as something distributed among the relations between humans and non-humans, rather than located exclusively in the former. This means that technology can be considered to act in ways not reducible to the intention of human users or designers.

A socio-material position can be understood as deriving from a post-foundational philosophy that not only decentres the human subject, but also counters the notion of essential characteristics. These two inter-related aspects are crucial here, providing the theoretical capacity to tackle the issues of anthropocentrism and representationalism identified previously. First, the socio-material is concerned with shifting an engrained focus on the 'social' to one which views the human and non-human as equivalent; as similarly in need of examination and analysis. Quite simply, this means that to consider something as socio-material, one does not necessarily begin with examining the human beings involved, or indeed assume that coming to understand the social will be equivalent to understanding the situation. Second, and relatedly, this decentring of the subject is premised on a relational ontology, which views such things as human beings, objects, properties and boundaries to be *produced* through relational assemblages, rather than having intrinsic properties. As Fenwick et al. suggest, such things of the world emerge 'simultaneously in webs of interconnections, among heterogeneous entities: human and non-human, social discourses, activities and meanings, as well as material forces, assemblages and transformations' (Fenwick et al., 2011, p.2). In other words, all things are considered the effects of relational co-constitution, rather than possessing essential characteristics.

From such a perspective, the representational inclinations of research are challenged. From a socio-material perspective, there is no genuine essence of an event to be *re*-presented through method, only a continual practice so far (Fenwick et al., 2011), of which research is a contingent part. Thus, instead of a representational logic to research in which 'the world is brought into being by humans who go about knowing and naming observation-independent objects with attributes' (Scott and Orlikowski, 2013, p.78), we might say that a socio-material approach is more concerned with *how* the subject-researcher and the research object have been produced as such. As Barad has suggested, representationalism 'marks a failure to take account of the practices through which representations are produced' (2007, p.53).

Significantly, this socio-material perspective provides a useful counter to instrumentalism, destabilizing 'the widespread account of technology as stable singular tools separate from and under the control of human beings' (Sørensen, 2009, p.32). Following Scott and Orlikowski, code itself can be considered active in shaping online space (2013). This is a perspective established in 'software studies' (see Dodge et al., 2009), and requiring theoretical engagement in education.

While the decentring of the human subject involves a significant challenge to orthodox education (Fenwick et al., 2011), and the questioning of representationalism may dispute the deep-rooted convictions of researchers in many disciplines, I suggest that such exploration offers new and rich insights for those concerned with 'digital methods'. The following examples are intended to problematize the assumed simplicity and transparency of data analysis and expose the technology that is often rendered invisible in such processes; what we might then term the 'materialist dynamics of oppression, exclusion, transgression and agonism that are at play but often overlooked in educational processes' (Fenwick and Edwards, 2013, p.60).

MOOC maps

A significant trend in MOOC research has been the attempt to identify the location of participants. Multi-coloured visualizations of world maps generated from enrolment statistics (or 'heat maps') seem to be *de rigueur* in research associated with the major MOOC platforms (see Breslow et al., 2013; MOOCs@Edinburgh Group, 2013; Perna et al., 2013). These visualizations appear to direct our attention towards the extent of international interest in MOOCs, and ostensibly depict the geographical whereabouts of enrollees. This is particularly apparent in the visualization produced by Breslow et al., which, rather than uniformly coloured nation states and their boundaries, displays nodes supposedly representing individual student locations (2013, p.18). What these visualizations seem to show us is a world-wide, universal interest in MOOCs, despite the noticeable absences from the African continent. However, to simply understand such images as straightforwardly representing human involvement in MOOCs is to divert attention away from crucial questions about the involvement of technology: both of inequitable global infrastructure and of the processes that drive such data analysis itself. The MOOC maps of the world are an example of the increasing ways in which 'data has been mediated into a variety of visualizations, diagrams, charts, tables, infographics and other forms of representation that make education intelligible to a wide variety of audiences' (Williamson, 2014b, n.p.). The trend of visualization is one premised on the idea that the image conveys meaning more directly; that the truth of data is better seen than read. As Williamson suggests, '[t]he capacity to mobilize data graphically as visualizations and representations, or "database aesthetics", amplifies the rhetorical, argumentative and persuasive function of data' (2014a, n.p.). However, when the data collection method behind such visualizations is examined, a much more complex landscape of the MOOC is revealed.

One significant factor is the use of IP address data as the primary means of analysing participant location in MOOC research (Kizilcec et al., 2013; Perna et al. 2013; Ho et al., 2014). Kizilcec et al. (2013) acknowledge the use of a third party database service, 'GeoLite', to match the IP address data with specific geographical locations. This indicates a multi-layered process, involving a range of distributed data capture and analysis procedures. Not only are the specific locations of individuals generalized into the predefined regions defined by the database, such as cities, but the accuracy in identifying those particular areas can vary according to the local Internet infrastructure. A quick scan of the GeoLite accuracy data reveals significant inconsistencies between countries (MaxMind, 2014), indicating the problems with assuming that IP address location is a standard and uniform process. For example, Venezuela's accuracy score of 31 per cent appears considerably lower than the 84 per cent of the United States (MaxMind, 2014). What appears to be exposed here is not a world of universal access, but a world of complex inconsistencies. Ho et al. offer some more insight into the complications of this process: 'The country was located by IP address or, if the IP address is missing, the country was located by the parsed mailing address submitted at initial edX registration, if possible' (2014, p.25). Perna et al. include a disclaimer in their research that states: 'Only registrants with valid IP addresses were included in the analysis' (2013, p.30). Consequently, the accuracy of these visualizations are called into question, along with the processes of authentication that decide who is represented and who is not.

The identification of location might be better understood as the result of contingent relationships between the particular location an individual might be in at the point of enrolment (or indeed the point of measurement), the arrangement and quality of the local Internet infrastructure, and the numerous data capture processes that populate the databases that supposedly identify the IP address position. The actual whereabouts of the MOOC participants appears to be only one small factor in this complex entanglement of national, political and technological relations, yet it is undoubtedly the location of human beings that we are meant to infer from the visualizations of MOOC enrolments. Taken at surface value, the maps appear to suggest a pan-human bond around educational participation, while the world is offered as the passive backdrop to MOOC expansion. However, if the MOOC is indeed a project concerned with emancipation through education, with breaking down barriers to access, the methods employed to produce the world maps act to mask the material infrastructures that are involved in producing regional inequalities, and that often act to restrict access. This is the matter embroiled in the visualization of MOOC participation, and it *matters*. The method of identifying location is not a neutral instrument which makes the world of the MOOC increasingly transparent. It is a procedure which produces a particular and narrow fabrication of the world; one which conceals vast inconsistencies in education with a colourful veneer of universalism.

So, do these MOOC data 'speak for themselves', or does they speak for an agenda of corporate promotion and a vested interest in global expansion? An algorithmic form of power (Williamson, 2014a), I suggest, must be recognized in such visualizations. They produce a spatial representation of the MOOC that appears more concerned with portraying the global reach of MOOC participation than the complexities and inequalities of access. Moreover, what is also made starkly visible in this world of the MOOC are those territories *not* currently participating. The grey or hollow landmasses portrayed by Perna et al. (2013) and Breslow et al. (2013) appear thus as zones ripe for colonization by the MOOC brand. As Williamson contends, 'powerful visualizations are now being deployed to envision and diagrammatize the educational land-scape "out there", and to make it amenable to having things done to it' (2014b, n.p.).

Critical responses to big data and the MOOC are emerging. Watters has questioned the motives of MOOC expansionism on the grounds of profiteering from the personal data of students. In doing so, she challenges the connotations of the term data 'mining' and asks: 'how do we make sure that education technology isn't poised simply to extract value from students?' (Watters, 2013, n.p.). This 'colonialist ori-entation' of the MOOC project suggests an alternative reading of the world visualizations. Rather than the acquisition of geographical ter-ritory, MOOCs appear to be involved in a 'data-colonialism' through the systematic capture of participation statistics, from which income can ultimately be generated. In other words, rather than coloniz-ing remote nation states, we might understand the MOOC platform organizations as concerned much more with acquiring the personal data of distant populations. Such data include when and where an individual might have accessed specific content, how long particu-lar resources were viewed, or how successful a student has been; data collection that avoids the restrictions imposed on formal education (Watters, 2013). As such, the MOOC maps can be understood as dia-grams of the data collection strategy itself, marking the extent of the colonialist reach and the range of potential value extraction. This interpretation is not meant to be totalizing, and nor is it a call to cease the creation of visualizations. Rather, it is an appeal to delve beneath the surface of data, to take visualization seriously, and to ques-tion and interrogate the software functions, code and algorithms that produce them.

Quantifying 'active' participation

Perhaps the most prominent theme in discussions of the MOOC is the reports of dramatically low retention rates (Parr, 2013). Research has sug-gested that less than 10 per cent of those who enrol on MOOCs go on to complete the course (Jordan, 2014), statistics which have moti-vated large-scale examinations of the activities of MOOC participants. With such a large majority seeming to 'fail' in MOOCs, there has been a palpable rush to categorize student groups and quantify participant behaviours, frequently drawing on the large datasets generated by the platform software.

In reporting on the University of Pennsylvania's MOOCs offered through the Coursera platform, Christensen et al. suggest: 'there are no robust, published data that describe who is taking these courses and why they are doing so. As such, we do not yet know how transformative the MOOC phenomenon can or will be' (2013, p.1). This central concern for profiling MOOC participants is mirrored in the University of Edinburgh's report on its Coursera offerings (MOOCs@Edinburgh Group, 2013), as well as research emerging from the edX platform (Breslow et al., 2013; Ho et al., 2014), which have reported characteristics such as the age, gender, and educational background of MOOC enrolees. The way to understand MOOCs appears to be through examining the human beings that undertake them. Premised on the idea that open access education attracts students with differing motivations, further studies of student activity within these courses have suggested different categorizations of MOOC participation. Waite et al. (2013) propose relationships between experienced and novice participants, while Ho et al. suggest four categories of 'certified', 'only explored', 'only viewed' and 'only registered' (2014). In a study of one particular MOOC, Milligan et al. (2013) identified a similar 'active participation', 'passive participation', and 'lurking'.

Such a focus on 'active' and 'passive' forms of behaviour situates these studies within theories of learning that are grounded in psychologism and behaviourism, and which retain the human being as the exclusive focus of research. However, while such an approach attempts to establish a narrow definition of what might be 'active' in the MOOC, it can also be understood to contradict its own anthropocentrism by basing such measures on specific aspects of the platform software. For example, Ho et al. are unambiguous about this, stating: 'To become a "viewer," a registrant must merely "click" on the courseware. To become an "explorer," the viewer must click on content within half or more of the chapters' (2014, p.12). In other words, 'viewing' and 'exploring' are not behaviours that are distinct from, or exist independently to, the features of the MOOC platform. Rather they are produced as the result of specific interactions with the software. The question then is whether we can consider such 'active' participation as an intrinsic characteristic of the individual MOOC student, or as a quality derived from a combination of human activity, platform design, and data-capture strategy. From this latter perspective, 'viewing' and 'exploring' are already socio-material entanglements. I therefore suggest that research methods need to acknowledge the distributed meshwork of software designers, platform code, MOOC students, and data collection algorithms involved in this kind of study. Rather than 'discovering' particular human behaviours, methods might work towards understanding how the 'active' learning subject of the MOOC is *produced*.

Our understanding of the 'MOOC learner' is being shaped by assumptions already encoded in the platform software, which, despite a range of offerings from different organizations, tend to structure divisions between content (largely in the form of video lectures), formal assessment, and discussion fora (Rodriguez, 2013). Thus, the design of the platform itself conditions a 'normal' mode of participation, based on persistent activity and course completion, while other ways of engaging in MOOCs are marginalized. Ho et al.'s designations are exemplary here, applying 'only' to all but the 'certified' category (2014), ranking participation according to diminishing resemblance to the norm. Participation is quite clearly ordered by an intensity of engagement with the platform software, from a normal 'active' to an abnormal and peripheral loitering.

However, far from actually embracing different educational motives, this categorization of MOOC participation tends to preserve a core and authentic mode of conduct, and casts all others as lesser variants, or even deviant behaviours, as in the lowest class of 'lurkers'. The problem here lies precisely in the assumption that such methods are exclusively identifying human behaviour. When we analyse how these categories are produced, we see that it is primarily the data that determines the outcome, not anything that the human participant might actually have been doing at the time. For example, the categories of 'lurking', 'only registered' or 'passive' are produced only as a *lack* of the presence of data indicating 'active' participation. For example, when one watches a video, answers a multiple choice question, or simply clicks a link within the MOOC platform, or any of the other predetermined measures of participation, one is actively producing data that can be labelled as 'active'. But the other categories of participation do not come about through the production of alternative data. Rather they are inferred by the *absence* of the very same indicators. One is produced as a 'lurker' precisely by *not* behaving in the ways predetermined as 'normal learning'. Such 'passivity' cannot therefore be understood very accurately as simply the conduct of MOOC students. It is better recognized as a complex process of classification resulting from multiple contingencies, including human activity, but also requiring specific elements of the platform software and particular data analysis procedures. 'Lurking' is not simply 'human', it is a socio-material enactment produced from algorithmic processes that are entangled with educational ideas about what it is to be 'active' in online study. Methodological approaches might look to engage with precisely the kind of analysis outlined here; one that works to expose and acknowledge the active and constitutive role of technology, both in the domains being researched, as well as in the methods themselves.

Implications for research

While it seems unlikely that MOOCs themselves will have the disruptive effects on educational provision often promised in their promotion, the data-driven methods of research described here have the potential for more profound consequences. As educational institutions seek to broaden their online and distance learning provision, as well as increase the online systems used for teaching on campus, the profusion of student data may provoke the intensification of computational analysis in education. Where these digital methods populate the 'mainstream' of educational research, and gain traction though the promise of efficiency-savings and greater accuracy, critical voices are required.

The enfolding of ever more digital data in our understanding of education necessitates a clearer understanding of the processes through which it is produced, but also how it acts to constitute the practices of teaching and experiences of learning. As the examples in this chapter have highlighted, data can be used in powerful ways to surveil, categorize and 'speak for' students, for the purposes of acute educational intervention. The socio-material critique I have demonstrated here is one way of working to expose the practices of data production, such that any educational decision to intervene might be based on more than simply the data representation. In just such a way, 'mainstream' educational research needs to develop a critical awareness around the growing ubiquity of digital data: not to assume its 'face value', but to acknowledge the contexts and contingencies of its production.

The two examples in this chapter also suggest productive methodological explorations with relevance beyond educational research. First, a socio-material approach involves looking beyond the human being as the sole focus of data collection and analysis. Moving away from entrenched commitments to the idea that it is exclusively human beings that constitute the measure and limit of research may expose the significant non-human forces and influences that shape our work. The socio-material encourages a perspective which views the social and technological to be always and already implicated in one another, rather than separate entities that 'interact'. Digital technologies are a recent and potent example of this relationship: algorithms and databases increasingly pervade and organize social life, at a much more fundamental level than simply the act of 'using' technology. In other words,

I suggest that it is becoming increasing difficult to study 'social life' that is *not* acted upon by algorithms, such as those that govern financial transactions, influence state policies, or help to design cities. From such a perspective, there is a need for 'mainstream' research in the social sciences to acknowledge the *social as already digital*, rather than assuming the 'Internet' or the 'web' to be a distinct sub-domain of study.

Second, the value of a socio-material approach is in the focus on *how* things are produced, and this encourages a critical emphasis on the processes that construct research data, rather that the things they are assumed to represent. The prevalence of the digital is not just in that which we study, as suggested above, it is also increasingly in the methods we use to undertake research. Where social life is increasingly 'online', 'mainstream' methods must engage more with the capture, analysis and presentation of digital data. However, to assume that powerful data mining and analysis methods are simply transparent instruments of research maintains a problematic user determinism, in which the agency of the technology is excluded. The importance of a socio-material approach is precisely in in exposing the gap between the research object and its representation, by tracing the ways that data are produced and accounting for the non-human agencies involved. Therefore, shifting 'from questions of correspondence between descriptions and reality (for example, do they mirror nature or culture?) to matters of practices, doings, and actions' (Scott and Orlikowski, 2013, p.78), may expose the situated and conditional factors involved in data computation methods. For example, important work is to be done in tracing the assumptions already built-in to data-driven analysis. As in the examples in this chapter, that may involve uncovering manifestations of power rather than assuming the inherent transparency of computation.

Conclusions

It is perhaps easy to see how these initial forays into the big data domains of the MOOC might translate into more established methodological regimes of Learning Analytics: the capture, analysis and presentation of large datasets representing student behaviour. Long and Siemens warn of 'gaping holes of delayed action and opportunities for intervention' (2011, p.32), and the promise of increasing efficiencies wrought through computational analysis may motivate a hurried response. Nevertheless, questions remain about how such a 'mainstream' method of digital education research might be occupied and what kind of disciplinary practices will become established within it.

Instead of social scientists, the new social experts of the social media environment are the 'algorithmists' and big data analysts of Google, Facebook and Amazon, and of new kinds of data analysis start-ups, intermediaries and 'policy labs' that work across the technology, social scientific and policy fields.

(Williamson, 2014a, n.p.)

While one conclusion might be that education is too important to be left to the 'algorithmists', I am not sure that the future of educational research would be as exciting without them. I have offered a critique of data-driven methods in this chapter, but the intention is certainly not to suggest the dismissal of such approaches or their practitioners, and a retreat to established small-scale enquiries. What may be genuinely new about global and 'massive' educational endeavours such as the MOOC is precisely that which occurs outside and in-between human experience (Knox, 2014). These are activities which might only be revealed through large-scale data analysis techniques. The way forward for digital methods in education is not to reassert a rift between qualitative and quantitative methods, but to seek their commensurability. This means not positioning ethnography 'as the Other to big data' (Boellstorff, 2013, n.p.), but rather as a vital opportunity to push digital methodology in new interdisciplinary directions. Acknowledging that data *produces* educational realities should open possibilities for working *productively* and critically, with data, not against it.

References

Adams, C., Yin, Y., Madriz, L.F.V. and Mullen, C.S. (2014) 'A phenomenology of learning large: The tutorial sphere of xMOOC video lectures', *Distance Education*, 35(2), 202–16.

Anderson C. (2008) 'The end of theory: The data deluge makes the scientific method obsolete', *Wired Magazine*, http://archive.wired.com/science/discoveries/magazine/16-07/pb_theory, date accessed 1 February 2011.

Barad, K. (2007) *Meeting the Universe Halfway: Quantum Physics and the Entanglement of Matter and Meaning*. London: Duke University Press.

Boellstorff, T. (2013) 'Making big data, in theory', *First Monday*, 18(10), http://firstmonday.org/ojs/index.php/fm/article/view/4869/3750.

boyd, d. and Crawford, K. (2012) 'Critical questions for big data', *Information, Communication & Society*, 15(5), 662–79.

Breslow, L., Pritchard, D.E., DeBoer, J., Stump, G.S., Ho, A.D. and Seaton, D.T. (2013) 'Tudying learning in the worldwide classroom: Research into edX's first MOOC', *Research and Practice in Assessment*, 8(2), 13–25.

Coughlan, S. (2013) 'UK enters global online university race', *BBC News Business*, http://www.bbc.co.uk/news/business-24109190, date accessed 9 December 2013.

Dodge, M., Kitchin, R. and Zook, M. (2009) 'How does software make space? Exploring some geographical dimensions of pervasive computing and software studies', *Environment and Planning A*, 41, 1283–93.

Fenwick, T., Edwards, R. and Sawchuk, P. (2011) *Emerging Approaches to Educational Research: Tracing the Sociomaterial*. Abingdon: Routledge.

Fenwick, T. and Edwards, R. (2013) 'Performative ontologies: Sociomaterial approaches to researching adult education and lifelong learning', *European Journal for Research on the Education and Learning of Adults*, 4(1), 49–63.

Fournier, H., Kop, R. and Wiley, D. (2011) 'The value of learning analytics to networked learning on a personal learning environment', *In First International Conference on Learning Analytics and Knowledge*. Banff, Alberta, Canada, http://dl.acm.org/citation.cfm?id=2090131, date accessed 3 August 2013.

Guthrie, D. (2013) 'The coming big data education revolution', *US News*, http://www.usnews.com/opinion/articles/2013/08/15/why-big-data-not-moocs-will-revolutionize-education, date accessed 23 August 2014.

Hamilton, E.C. and Friesen, N. (2013) 'Online education: A science and technology studies perspective', *Canadian Journal of Learning and Technology*, 39(2), http://cjlt.csj.ualberta.ca/index.php/cjlt/article/view/689/363.

Ho, A.D., Reich, J., Nesterko, S., Seaton, D.T, Mullaney, T., Waldo, J. and Chuang, I. (2014) 'HarvardX and MITx: The first year of open online courses', in HarvardX and MITx Working Paper No. 1, http://harvardx.harvard.edu/multiplecourse-report.

Jordan, K. (2014) 'Initial trends in enrolment and completion of massive open online courses', *International Review of Research in Open and Distance Learning*, 15(1), 133–60.

Kanuka, H. (2008), 'Understanding e-learning technologies in practice through philosophies in practice', in T. Anderson (ed.) *The Theory and Practice of Online Learning*. Edmonton: AU Press, pp.91–118.

Kizilcec, R. F., Piech, C., and Schneider, E. (2013). 'Deconstructing disengagement: analyzing learner subpopulations in massive open online courses', in *Proceedings of the Third International Conference on Learning Analytics and Knowledge*, New York, NY, USA: ACM, pp. 170–179.

Knox, J. (2013) 'The limitations of access alone: Moving towards open processes in education technology', *Open Praxis*, 5(1), 21–9.

Knox, J. (2014) 'Digital culture clash: "Massive" education in the E-learning and Digital Cultures MOOC', *Distance Education*, 35(2), 164–77.

Logue, A. (2012) 'Higher Ed disruption: Not so new', *Inside Higher Ed*. https://www.insidehighered.com/views/2012/10/08/essay-evolving-ideas-about-technology-and-education.

Long, P. and Siemens, G. (2011) 'Penetrating the fog: Analytics in learning and education', *EDUCAUSE Review*, 46(5), 31–40.

MaxMind (2014). *GeoIP2 City Accuracy*. https://www.maxmind.com/en/geoip2-city-accuracy, date accessed 10 September 2014.

Milligan, C., Littlejohn, A. and Margaryan, A. (2013) 'Patterns of engagement in connectivist MOOCs', *Journal of Online Learning and Teaching*, 9(2), 149–59.

MOOCs@Edinburgh Group (2013) *MOOCs@Edinburgh 2013 – Report #1*, https://www.era.lib.ed.ac.uk/bitstream/1842/6683/1/Edinburgh_MOOCs_Report2013_no1.pdf, date accessed 21 May 2014.

Morozov, E. (2013) *To Save Everything, Click Here: Technology, Solutionism, and the Urge to Fix Problems that Don't Exist*. London: Allen Lane.

Pappano, L. (2012) 'The year of the MOOC', *The New York Times*, http://www
.nytimes.com/2012/11/04/education/edlife/massive-open-online-courses-are
-multiplying-at-a-rapid-pace.html, date accessed 11 October 2013.

Parr, C. (2013) 'Mooc completion rates "below 7%"', *Times Higher Education*,
9 May 2013. http://www.timeshighereducation.co.uk/news/mooccompletion
-rates-below-7/2003710.article, date accessed 11 May 2013.

Perna, L., Ruby, A., Boruch, R., Wang, N., Scull, J., Evans, C. and Ahmad
S. (2013) 'The life cycle of a million MOOC users', *MOOC Research Initiative
Conference*, http://www.gse.upenn.edu/pdf/ahead/perna_ruby_boruch_moocs
_dec2013.pdf, date accessed 17 February 2014.

Peter, S. and Deimann, M. (2013) 'On the role of openness in education:
A historical reconstruction', *Open Praxis*, 5(1), 7–14.

Rodriguez, O. (2013) 'The concept of openness behind c and x-MOOCs (Massive
Open Online Courses)', *Open Praxis*, 5(1), 67–73.

Saadatmand M. and Kumpulainen, K. (2014) 'Participants' perceptions of learning and networking in connectivist MOOCs', *Journal of Online Learning and
Teaching*, 10(1), 16–30.

Scott, S. V. and Orlikowski, W.J. (2013) 'Sociomateriality – Taking the wrong
turning? A response to mutch', *Information and Organization*, 23(2), 77–80.

Selwyn, N. (2011) *Education and Technology: Key Issues and Debates*. London:
Continuum International Publishing Group.

Sørensen.E. (2009) *The Materiality of Learning: Technology and Knowledge in Educational Practice. Series: Learning in Doing: Social, Cognitive and Computational
Perspectives*, New York: Cambridge University Press.

UKTI (2013) 'Daphne Koller, Stanford University at Global innovations conference, June 14 2013', *UK Trade and Investment*, http://youtu.be/_jPHGwFCrvs,
date accessed 1 October 2014.

Universities UK (2013) 'Massive open online courses: Higher education's digital moment?', https://www.gov.uk/government/uploads/system/uploads
/attachment_data/file/240193/13-1173-maturing-of-the-mooc.pdf,   date
accessed 11 October 2013.

Waite, M., Mackness, J., Roberts, G. and Lovegrove, E. (2013) 'Liminal participants and skilled orienteers: Learner participation in a MOOC for new
lecturers', *Journal of Online Learning and Teaching*, 9(2), http://jolt.merlot.org
/vol9no2/waite_0613.htm.

Watters, A. (2013) 'Student data is the new oil: MOOCs, metaphor, and
money', *Hack Education*, http://hackeducation.com/2013/10/17/student-data
-is-the-new-oil/.

Williamson, B. (2014a) 'The end of theory in digital social research?',
DML Central, http://dmlcentral.net/blog/ben-williamson/end-theory-digital
-social-research, date accessed 10 May 2014.

Williamson, B. (2014b) 'New centers of data visualization in education', *DML Central*, http://dmlcentral.net/blog/ben-williamson/new-centers
-data-visualization-education, date accessed 21 July 2014.

12
Towards an Innovative Inclusion: Using Digital Methods with Young People

Emma Bond and Stuart Agnew

Introduction

This chapter outlines an innovative research project undertaken in 2013, which employed digital methods in order to enable children and young people to contribute to a countywide enquiry into educational attainment and provide them the opportunity to express their views on their educational experiences. Until relatively recently, childhood was neglected by mainstream social research and, while societal attitudes have moved away from the fifteenth-century proverb that 'children should be seen and not heard', young people's views are still largely ignored in educational reform. Recent developments in children's rights to participation have, however, provided a catalyst for developing enhanced child-centred and, arguably, more creative research methods. These have begun to supersede previous research approaches which accorded criticism for conceptualizing children as incompetent, unreliable and incomplete, as mere objects to be studied (Hill et al., 1996).

The study incorporated a multi-modal methodological approach which drew on creative methodologies (see e.g. Barker and Weller, 2003) and exploited the opportunities afforded by digital methodologies, virtual environments and social media to not only encourage young people's participation in the research but also, importantly, provide an online space to publish their contributions and their views. However, this participatory methodological approach was far from straightforward in practice. This chapter considers the ideology of researching childhood and children's everyday experiences, as informed by the social studies of childhood and the increasing influence of Article 12 of the United Nations Convention of the Rights of the Child (UNCRC) and the actual reality of undertaking a multi-modal study which included using digital methods.

Kellett et al. (2004, p.330) suggest that 'from a rights-based agenda, the perspective of children as social actors places them as a socially excluded, minority group struggling to find a voice'. Kellett et al.'s (2004) argument reflects very neatly the starting point for the study discussed here which, following a rights-based approach and viewing children as active social agents, set out to give voice to children and young people in Suffolk as part of a countywide enquiry into educational attainment. Specifically, this study aimed to recognize children whose 'social roles, relationships and interactions are generated in the dynamism of people engaging with one another' in addition to adults (Mavers, 2011, p.3). As such, their understanding and perspectives should provide valuable insights into any proposed educational reform agenda in the county. The use of social media and digital methods facilitates children's agency in an environment that is familiar to their everyday practices. We do not argue in this chapter that the use of digital methods should supersede more traditional approaches but that they offer new opportunities to enable children's voices to be heard.

Background to the study

Educational attainment remains at the forefront of both political debate and public discourse, and the media has provided a platform for the competitive climate that currently dominates the educational arena in the United Kingdom (BBC, 2012). Statistical data in published league tables and key performance indicators rank counties comparatively with each other nationally and schools locally. Local authorities are increasingly challenged with the task of continually seeking to maintain educational outcomes at a time when they have diminished control over schools following academization[1] and in progressing educational standards at a time when schools are facing a harsh economic environment and increasing financial cutbacks.

In Suffolk, a county of average size and population, the major concern at the time was not one of a decline in educational attainment, but one of a decline in relative educational attainment in the county due to a slower increase in attainment than the rest of England. This situation was partly due to the substantial increases in attainment being made in London and by some urban local authorities at both KS2 and GCSE levels. A countywide independent enquiry commissioned by Suffolk County Council and led by The Royal Society for the encouragement of Arts, Manufactures and Commerce (RSA) was launched in 2012 that aimed to make recommendations in order 'to achieve a significant and sustained improvement in pupil attainment and young people's employability' (see Suffolk County Council, online). In late modern society, the restructuring of education to create a highly skilled and knowledgeable workforce has been at the centre of educational reform (France, 2007). However, the *child* in these debates and much political and indeed, public discourse on educational attainment is positioned as the *becoming child* (see James et al., 2010) – the child as the future citizen.

While the enquiry involved a multitude of different stakeholder groups across the county and developed solution groups including councillors, head teachers, school governors and local employers, it failed to successfully engage young people in the initiative in spite of the requirements of the UNCRC (Article 12) and Children Act (1989, 2004) that highlight that children have the right to be consulted in matters affecting their lives. This is a fundamental issue not only due to the legal obligations placed upon the County Council but also as a result of the 'unique body of knowledge [children have] about their lives, needs and concerns, together with ideas and views which derive from their direct experience' (Lansdown, 2011, p.5). Thus, while education is often commonly conceptualized as something that is done *to the child*, and *the child* remains positioned from this perspective as a passive recipient, we set out to undertake this study from a rights-based perspective (in line with the social studies of childhood), positioning the child as an active, social *being* as opposed to *becoming* (see James et al., 2010 for further discussion); and the use of more innovative methodologies offer the opportunity to adopt this perspective in a way that mainstream methods may not.

Our approach

della Porta and Keating (2008) suggest that the term 'approaches' is helpful in designing a methodological perspective and when considering which research methods to use rather than a particular single method, and, as such, we adopted this view accordingly. Our approach was participatory. Working in partnership with RSA fellows in Suffolk, the study adopted a collaborative, community/organization-based philosophy throughout the project, which was underpinned by a robust framework designed and developed in consultation with young people themselves. This highlighted a preference for a multi-method approach using both traditional creative data collection strategies and virtual networks (developed through a range of online and social media platforms). Once launched, the study successfully engaged 568 young people in the project over a six-week period. The limited timeframe available to collect data for the study provided us with a considerable challenge; however, we believe that we were able to access a much larger participant sample than traditional means alone by actively engaging young people and raising the profile of the study via social media networks. This provided young people with the opportunity to produce contributions that appealed to them, in a format that they believed best suited the message that they wanted to get across. The multi-modal (see Kress, 2010; Archer and Newfield, 2014) contributions included writing, poetry, art and film and an open access 'virtual online scrapbook' was set up to provide an arena for their voices to be heard. Scrapbooks have been very successfully used in researching media with children and young people (Bragg and Buckingham, 2008), and we used a 'virtual online scrapbook' which had a number of benefits and added considerable value to the study and the methodological approach adopted. By presenting young people's contributions on the open access platform 'Pinterest', young people could view the responses received, confirming to contributors that their voice was being exhibited to decision makers and potentially inspire others to engage with the study.

Academic discourses on digital environments, new media technologies and virtual spaces have flourished in recent years and the Internet and social media have emerged not only as new topics of research but also as research methods. The advantages of adopting a multi-method or mixed methods approach to social research is well established (see Plano Clark and Cresswell, 2008), and more recently using social media and online platforms has further shifted the menu of research strategies towards a potentially rich eclectic mix of both traditional and non-traditional offline and online methods (see Hewson et al., 2003; Johns et al., 2004; Fielding et al., 2008; Bryman, 2012; Hine, 2013). Furthermore, such multi-method approaches and the adoption of such methodologies that draw on young people's strengths, rather than focusing on what they are unable to do, allow issues of power and social exclusion to be addressed. There is a wealth of evidence that young people are progressively more active with online environments (Livingstone et al., 2011), and the increasing use of Internet-enabled mobile devices (Bond, 2014) suggests that using social media and online platforms to successfully engage with young people in addition to traditional approaches would be effective and potentially empowering.

However, in considering innovation in qualitative research, it is fundamentally important to reflect on what we, as researchers, actually aim to achieve and to consider whether or not our methodological approach is appropriate for our aims. Recent theoretical developments in understanding childhood which position the child/young person as an active, competent and knowledgeable expert have led to methodological developments in childhood research which draw on these characteristics and celebrate children's unique viewpoints (see James et al., 2010) and, as such, our methodological approach suited the aims of the study.

Study aims and research design

This study, funded by the RSA and Suffolk County Council, explored children's subjective experience of education within Suffolk. It investigated this aspect of their social world within the framework of qualitative research (see Atkinson, 1993), which places an emphasis on meanings and stresses the socially constructed nature of reality (Denzin and Lincoln, 2011). The methods used by qualitative researchers exemplify a common belief that they can provide a deeper understanding of the social phenomena than would be obtained from purely quantitative data (Silverman, 2012) and the rich detail they provide assumes an interpretivistic approach (May, 2011).

The study aimed

- to give voice to Suffolk's young people so that they can influence the policy and strategy that will impact on their ability to achieve the future they want;
- to use our influence to ensure that young people's voices are heard and thereby enable them to realize their own power; and
- to create, identify and respond to opportunities to support young people in achieving what they hope for.

In order to achieve the aims outlined above, the study adopted a three-tier networked approach which drew on

1. existing professional networks (the RSA Fellowship, University Campus Suffolk (UCS), Suffolk County Council and Children's groups and organizations in the county);
2. social networks (asking those involved in the project to share the information with their friends and acquaintances); and

3. virtual networks and digital platforms (developed through a range of online and social media platforms).

This networked approach intended to ensure that information about the project reached as many young people in the county as possible in a very short timeframe and that the data were generated through creative activity-based focus groups and through social media platforms to encourage young people's individual contributions online. A dedicated website was created to provide a central point of reference and incorporated large and clear links to our other, more interactive, online content. The website was deliberately simple and was (during the consultation phase) largely a project information platform for young people. Activity on the website produced 2,124 visits during February and March 2013.

At the time of the study, Facebook reported approximately 40,000 users younger than 20 years in Suffolk, 80 per cent of which access Facebook via mobile devices. As such we undertook a Facebook advertising campaign targeting Suffolk Facebook users within this age range. An outcome of the campaign was over 26,000 young people viewing the project's Facebook Page and over 200 young people accessing the website by clicking on the Facebook advertisements in six weeks. Twitter was also used as a means of posting quick updates and links to relevant content elsewhere online in order to help generate a little buzz.

To create an online presence via a virtual scrapbook, the project design team identified the specific requirements in order to comply with the project governance, safeguarding and ethical practice, with special emphasis placed upon email submissions, content and contributor handling and integration to other platforms (especially social media). The project needed to be easily accessible, able to be used by a diverse range of people and be useable on both computer and mobile devices. It was essential that it encouraged multi-modal content presentation yet simultaneously would permit the aggregation of yet unknown artefact types and would support an ability to combine free accounts, if needed, to host content or direct links (pins) from the scrapbook to the original content.

The use of recognizable and mature platforms enabled a stable network presence, existing security models, features and techniques implicit with the platforms. In addition, a dedicated domain name was obtained for the central web pages to meet validity and credibility needs of the project. Detailed information about the research, the people involved and contact details were given on the site to give the project a clear online identity and a digital presence. This ensured search engine and user experience consistency by using the same term throughout. Andrejevic suggests that 'if art is a creative, expressive way of organising information of all kinds, from works and images to body movements, the Internet provides artists with a vast new pallet of possibilities' (2000, p.127). The range of social media and digital methods adopted in the study can be viewed as component parts of this 'new pallet'.

Children, technology and social research

We used a multi-modal approach (see Kress, 2010), and while the adoption of creative child-centred methods is widely accepted in the field of childhood and youth studies, using online and digital methods to research children's everyday experiences remains less well established. Online methods are, however, increasingly used in social science research as Kozinets (2010) in his account of *Netnography* (online ethnography) highlights:

> Our social worlds are going digital. As a consequence, social scientists around the world are finding that to understand society they must follow people's social activities and encounters onto the internet and through other technologically-mediated communications.
>
> (Kozinets, 2010, p.1)

The social embeddedness of technology is discussed at length by Warschauer (2004) and is now increasingly embedded in social research as Gaiser and Schreiner argue: 'when we think of research we typically think of researcher and participant. The Internet, however, appears to be transforming the role of researcher and those being researched' (2009, p.159).

Furthermore, children and young people themselves are increasingly living what Livingstone (2002) suggests are media-saturated lives and are spending more and more time online (Ofcom, 2012). Livingstone et al.'s (2011, p.2) extensive research across more than 25,000 European children and their parents found that 'internet use is increasingly individualized, privatised and mobile'. In the United Kingdom, Ofcom (2012) found that since 2011 smartphone ownership had increased among all children aged 5–15 and that from the age of 12 onwards smartphone ownership outstrips ownership of other mobile phones (Ofcom, 2012). Therefore, as patterns of communication and interaction change and virtual spaces become more and more embedded in children's everyday lives, we are also beginning to see similarly shifting patterns of interaction in researching children's everyday experiences.

Crowe (2012), for example, examines how young people interact with technologically created environments and argues that in research terms online spaces share many of the characteristics of material space. These technologically created research environments have opened up a wealth of new research possibilities and expanded the possibilities for young people to engage with research. For example, Weller (2012) demonstrates the role of online and digital spaces in facilitating qualitative longitudinal research with teenagers, and Carrington (2008) used blogs in a study of childhood, text and new technologies. She argues for a view of 'text as 'active' rather than as an artefact and an acceptance that children's lives are lived across multiple sites that require sophisticated blending and use a variety of literate practices' (Carrington, 2008, p.151). boyd (2006) highlights the role of the blog as a space for research opportunities and for performing an identity, and Snee (2012) uses blog analysis very effectively as a way of accessing very rich, in-depth naturally occurring data on young people's construction of identity through their gap year experiences. Online gaming offers another example of a research method that is gaining much interest in the social science community. Facer et al. (2004) investigated experiential learning through mobile gaming with children. More recently, Ringrose et al. (2012) used Facebook to explore young people's experiences of sexting. These examples are far from an exhaustive list but highlight the growing use of digital methods in childhood research across a wide range of topic areas and with an increasing age span with diverse groups. While we did not set out to replicate these techniques in our study, these changing research approaches reflect young people's use of online space in their everyday lives generally and influenced the design of this study in that they provided robust examples of how different digital methods have been successfully used in research with young people.

Evaluating the use of digital methods in children's research

While many children and young people have access to digital technologies (see Ofcom, 2012), others do not and digital divides remain. Therefore, in considering the use of digital methods in researching children's lives and experiences it is important to remember that although recent technologies, especially mobile Internet technologies, have transformed children's access to virtual environments and digital convergence has made it far easier to produce and share content online, not all children have the same opportunities or even motivations to engage with digital environments equally (Bond, 2014).

Furthermore, in the shift towards using online/digital methods in research, the relationship with other research approaches should not be forgotten. Hine (2013) also emphasizes that the relationship between virtual research methods and more conventional research approaches should not be ignored, and in order to be as inclusive as possible, our project combined both creative and digital methods. By drawing on established elements of ethnography and visual methods widely used in research with young people (see Allan, 2012), we encouraged contributions from young people in whatever form they felt happy to express themselves in, and these included film, photographs, drawing, rap, poetry among others. We also used a variety of social media to advertise the project and collect contributions including Facebook and Twitter, a dedicated website, email, text and YouTube.

The activity-based focus groups used child-centred techniques that were based on examples of methods favoured by children themselves (see Barker and Weller, 2003; Wyness, 2012), as they tend to be based on non-traditional approaches to research (Corsaro, 2011). Mavers (2011, p.5) highlights that children when 'given the space to explore and experiment, we see inventiveness, originality, and ingenuity of their drawing and writing'. This was a key aspect of the data collection method employed by the study as we believed that providing a creative environment, children and young people would explore and express their experiences of education in Suffolk.

These methods have been successfully employed by a growing number of social science researchers in a variety of contexts (see e.g. Barker and Weller, 2003; Barker and Smith, 2012; Coombs, 2014). Such creative child-centred research methods reflect the educational philosophy of Reggio Emilia and 'the hundred languages of children', in that children have many different ways of expressing themselves and it is we, as adults, who are limited and arguably less competent in how we express ourselves (North American Reggio Emilia Alliance online). They also draw on skills associated with the concept of *divergent thinking* as argued in Robinson's (2010) *Changing Educational Paradigms* lecture.

However, while using this combination of methods was successful in fostering participation, we had a number of practical and ethical issues that needed careful consideration and during the study. Initially we had to resolve the practical implications of the research, setting up the digital tools and designing a research framework for data collection and storage. The relationship between maximizing potential participation in research while ensuring protection of those participating is an uneasy one in research practice and can be ethically problematic in a project of this nature.

Practical and ethical issues in maximizing participation

Ethical approval for the research was gained from the Research Ethics Committee of UCS, and careful management of the study ensured that participants were protected throughout the project. Only two specified academic researchers had access to the children's submissions and analysed the raw data. Undertaking research with children and young people may give rise to potential ethical issues (see Kimmel, 1998; Wyness, 2012). Aspects of child protection, the role of the researcher and questions of responsibility, confidentiality and how to deal with the potential disclosure of information, the possibility of abuse by a researcher or possible exploitation through the research process require special consideration (Thomas and O'Kane, 1998). The challenge of maximizing participation using digital methods while ensuring protection, including anonymity and confidentiality, required careful deliberation both in the research design and throughout the study. Concerns over the potential for cyberbullying of both children and teachers and the possibility of uploading inappropriate content meant that the online environments we used for the study had to be carefully moderated and checked for the disclosure of personal information, safeguarding issues (e.g. being bullied) or any inappropriate or offensive content. Thus, mindful of data protection and ethical considerations, all contributions were submitted centrally via a specifically designed technical pathway developed by RSA fellow Kevin Mitchell and could only be accessed and seen by the research team at UCS, who then coded the contributions and moderated them for any inappropriate content before the contributions were published online at 'Pinterest' (see Bond and Agnew, 2013 for details).

This study respected the competence of young people in a number of ways: we worked collaboratively with young people at the design stage, thus maximizing the likelihood that those that participate will be fully informed so that they are able to make an active and informed decision to participate. The language used to describe the study and the data collection tool was kept deliberately focused, and the three main research questions were, 'What is learning like in Suffolk? What do you hope for in your life? What would help you make that happen?' Where contributions were provided in more creative traditional forums, we engaged young people in practical methods such as drawing, exhibitions and poetry. This approach is recognized by Alderson (2014) as a way of valuing the contributions that children and young people can provide, and the use of an online space – a 'digital scrapbook' – ensured that their viewpoints were valued, displayed and seen directly by policy makers and a wider public audience.

Using digital methods added an additional aspect to developing our ethical framework, and the relationship between childhood, risk and digital spaces has been the focus of much recent research, public discourse and political debate (Livingstone et al., 2011; Bond, 2014). Gillies and Robinson's (2013) research highlights how fostering participation and developing 'child-centred' approaches can be problematic when displaying or publishing art work, poems and opinions. Mand (2012) also suggests that art-based methods seek to include children's voices, but that in representing and giving space to children's voices some 'voices' are muted or lost due to spatial restrictions and adults' agendas. These studies usefully highlight that while the development of child-centred/non-traditionalist approaches is seen as ethical and inclusive from a theoretical perspective, they can be less than straightforward in practice. The concerns highlighted by Gillies and Robinson (2013) and Mand (2012) were also pertinent to our study, and the use of Pinterest enables us to overcome these problems. Čopič (2008, p.114) suggests that 'ICT can contribute to the democratization of culture, making better access to the means for cultural production and dissemination'. The use of 'Pinterest' to publish the young people's contributions arose in reality from an ethical dilemma – how to ensure that the multi-modal and very varied and different contributions in a multitude of formats could be acknowledged, valued and displayed and allow the young people's voices to be heard. All too often, when using mainstream methods, their voices are lost, ignored or buried in a research report or academic journal hardly accessible for public viewing.

Concluding thoughts

Children's lives and the contemporary cultures of childhood are indeed attracting both academic research and political debate, and there is an increasing awareness of the importance of fostering children's meaningful participation in both arenas of action (Hutchby and Moran-Ellis, 1998). Meaningful dialogue is essential to participation, and 'innovations in technology are, once again, shaping how adults and youth interact with each other in school, at home, and at large' (Goldman et al., 2008, p.185). Pimlott-Wilson (2012) also points out:

> The importance of dialogue cannot be lost even with the adoption of visual and activity-based methods. Creative methods generate

knowledge and about participants' lives and social experiences, and thus their creations cannot be understood in isolation. In order for visual representations to express the meaning of their author, a level of dialogue is needed rather than researchers attaching their own interpretations to the productions made by participants. Together the combination of visual methods with narration can offer deeper insights than either one can provide alone.

(Pimlott-Wilson, 2012, p.146)

The use of creative art-based digital and material methods, with traditional verbatim data from focus groups, and text-based written contributions combined to form a detailed, rich and comprehensive insight into the children's views and experiences. We received 568 contributions from children and young people across Suffolk over a six-week period, and analysis of the multi-modal data revealed three main themes around their educational experiences, cultural capital and their future aspirations.

The research study presented in this chapter was, on reflection, effective not only in enabling children's views to be heard but also in highlighting to local councillors and policy makers the importance of listening to children. Mulgan (2012, p.35) defines social innovation as 'new ideas (products, services and models) that simultaneously meet socially recognized social needs (more effectively than alternatives) and create new social relationships or collaborations, that are good for society and enhance society's capacity to act'. Our study offers an example of a new social relationship and collaboration in that the use of digital methods allowed the voices of young people to be directly heard by policy makers, educators and the local education authority.

It is still too early to speculate whether or not our study will ultimately contribute to innovation in transforming education in Suffolk, but while using digital methods is a relatively new component in the shifting paradigm of social research, especially in relation to children and young people, they can offer more choice of methodological approaches and greater accessibility to both social researcher and participants. Our study and discussion presented in this chapter provides an example of how, in using multiple and varied technologies including digital and social media technologies, the views and experiences of a relatively large group and previously ignored stakeholders – in our case children and young people – could be successfully sought and, most importantly, heard. Our argument is not that digital methods should be seen as superior or more effective than traditional creative method with children but rather as a part of the research method toolbox. A more recent section of the toolkit, perhaps, but an increasingly important one and one in which many children themselves feel familiar with and are skilled in using. As Goldman et al. (2008) observe:

> the mix of social, cultural, and digital technologies brought youth to new levels of participation – levels that surprise, inspire, and even threaten the adults who support their demographic engagement. Technologies, as communication vehicles, serve as platforms for dialogue, discourse, and connection. By using a mix of technologies educationally, youth learn to represent themselves without being confined to the structures that keep them out of the public debate, or tokenising their 'voices' as pure, and therefore either true or naïve.
>
> (Goldman et al., 2008, p.203)

Our study was certainly not without its limitations, but we hope it did achieve what it set out to accomplish and ameliorate the dearth of children's voices in considering the rich landscape of educational experiences in Suffolk. We hope that our discussion in this chapter will provide other researchers or educators with some ideas of what can be done and what some of the potential challenges may be. It offers an insight into the reality of undertaking research of using digital methods with children and young people within the wider context of the more major developments in using creative and child-centred methods in studying children's experiences in their everyday lives.

Note

1. Academy schools are state-funded schools in England, which are directly funded by central government (specifically, the Department for Education) and independent of direct control by the local authority.

References

Alderson, P. (2014) 'Ethics', in A. Clark, R. Flewitt, M. Hammersley and M. Robb (eds.) *Understanding Research with Children and Young People*. London: Sage, pp.85–102 .

Allan, A. (2012) 'Doing ethnography and using visual methods', in S. Bradford and F. Cullen (eds.) *Research and Research Methods for Youth Practitioners*. London: Routledge, pp.66–89.

Andrejevic, M. (2000) 'Art in cyberspace: The digital aesthetic', in D. Gauntlett and R. Horsely (eds.) *Web.Studies* (2nd edition). London: Arnold, pp.127–36.

Archer, A. and Newfield, D. (eds.) (2014) *Multi-Modal Approaches to Research and Pedagogy Recognition, Resources and Access*. New York: Routledge.

Atkinson, D. (1993) 'Relating', in P. Shakespeare, D. Atkinson and S. French (eds.) *Reflecting on Research Practice*. Buckingham: Open University Press, pp.58–69.

Barker, J. and Smith, F. (2012) 'What's in focus? A critical discussion of photography, children and young people', *International Journal of Social Research Methodology*, 15(2), 9–103.

Barker, J. and Weller, S. (2003) ' "Is it fun?" Developing children centred research methods', *International Journal of Sociology and Social Policy*, 23(1–2), 33–58.

BBC (2012) *Q and A: School League Tables*, http://www.bbc.co.uk/news/education -15282371.

Bond, E. (2014) *Childhood, Mobile Technologies and Everyday Experiences Changing Technologies = Changing Childhoods*. Basingstoke: Palgrave Macmillan.

Bond, E. and Agnew, S. (2013) *My Education: The Good the Bad and the Ugly. A Report on the Findings from Shout Out Suffolk!* www.ucs.ac.uk/shoutoutsuffolk.

boyd, d. (2006) 'A Blogger's Blog: Exploring the definition of a medium', *Reconstruction: Studies in Contemporary Culture*, 6(4), http://reconstruction.eserver.org /064/boyd.shtml.

Bragg, S. and Buckingham, D. (2008) 'Scrapbooks' as a resource in media research with young people', in P. Thomson (ed.) *Doing Visual Research with Children and Young People*. London: Routledge, pp.114–31.

Bryman, A. (2012) *Social Research Methods*. Oxford: Oxford University Press.

Carrington, V. (2008) ' "I'm Dylan and I'm not going to say my last name": Some thoughts on childhood, text and new technologies', *British Educational Research Journal*, 34(2), 151–66.

Coombs, S. (2014) 'Death wears a T-Shirt – Listening to young people talk about death', *Mortality: Promoting the Interdisciplinary Study of Death and Dying*, 19(3), 284–302.

Čopič, V. (2008) 'Digital culture in policy documents: The national(istic) perception of cultural diversity – The case of Slovenia', in A. Uzelac and B. Cvjetičanin (eds.) *Digital Culture: The Changing Dynamics*. Zagreb: Institute for International Relations, pp.113–26.

Corsaro, W. (2011) *The Sociology of Childhood* (3rd edition). California: Pine Forge Press.

Crowe, N. (2012) 'Virtual and online research with young people', in S. Bradford and F. Cullen (eds.) *Research and Research Methods for Youth Practitioners*. London: Routledge, pp.162–81.

della Porta, D. and Keating, M. (2008) 'Comparing approaches, methodologies and methods. Some concluding remarks', in D. della Porta and M. Keating (eds.) *Approaches and Methodologies in the Social Sciences A Pluralist Perspective*. Cambridge: Cambridge University Press, pp.316–22.

Denzin, N.K. and Lincoln, Y.S. (eds.) (2011) *The Sage Handbook of Qualitative Research* (4th edition). London: Sage.

Facer, K., Joiner, R., Stanton, D., Reidz, J., Hullz, R., and Kirk, D. (2004) 'Savannah: mobile gaming and learning?', *Journal of Computer Assisted Learning*, 20, 399–409.

Fielding, N.G., Lee, R.M. and Blank G. (eds.) (2008) *The Sage Book of Online Research Methods*, London: Sage.

France, A. (2007) *Understanding Youth in Late Modernity*. Maidenhead: McGraw-Hill.

Gaiser, T.J. and Schreiner, A.E. (2009) *A Guide to Conducting Online Research*. London: Sage.

Gillies, V. and Robinson, Y. (2013) 'Developing creative research methods with challenging pupils', *International Journal of Social Research Methodology*, 15(2), 161–73.

Goldman, S., Booker, A. and McDermott, M. (2008) 'Mixing the digital, social and cultural: Learning, identity, and agency in youth participation', in D. Buckingham (ed.) *Youth, Identity and Digital Media*. Cambridge, MA: MIT, pp.185–206.

Hewson, C., Yule, D., Laurent, D. and Vogel, C. (2003) *Internet Research Methods: A Practical Guide for the Social and Behavioural Sciences*. London: Sage.

Hill M., Laybourn, A. and Borland, M. (1996) 'Engaging with primary-aged children and their emotions and well-being: Methodological considerations', *Children and Society*, 10, 129–44.

Hine, C. (2013) *The Internet*. Oxford: Oxford University Press.

Hutchby, I. and Moran-Ellis, J. (1998) *Children and Social Competence Arenas of Action*. London: Routledge.

James, A., Jenks, C. and Prout, A. (2010) *Theorizing Childhood*. Cambridge: Polity.

Johns, M.D., Chen, S.L.S. and Hall, G.J. (eds.) (2004) *Online Social Research: Methods, Issues and Ethics*. Oxford: Peter Lang.

Kellett, M., Forrest, R., Dent, N. and Ward, S. (2004) 'Just teach us the skills please, we'll do the rest: Empowering ten-year-olds as active researchers', *Children and Society*, 18, 329–43.

Kimmel, A.J. (1988) *Ethics and Values in Applied Social Research*. London: Sage.

Kozinets, R.V. (2010) *Netnography Doing Ethnographic Research Online*. London: Sage.

Kress, G. (2010) *Multi-Modality: A Social Semiotic Approach to Contemporary Communication*. London: Routledge.

Lansdown, G. (2011) *Every Child's Right to Be Heard*. London: UNICEF and Save the Children.

Livingstone, S. (2002) *Young People and New Media*. London: Sage.

Livingstone, S., Haddon, L. Görzig, A. and Ólafsson K. (2011) *Risks and Safety on the Internet: The Perspective of European Children Full findings and Policy Implications from the EU Kids Online Survey of 9–16 year olds and Their Parents in 25 Countries*. LSE, London: EU Kids online.

Mand, K. (2012) 'Giving children a "voice": Arts-based participatory research activities and representation', *International Journal of Social Research Methodology*, 15(2), 149–60.

Mavers, D. (2011) *Children's Drawing and Writing: The Remarkable in the Unremarkable*. London: Routledge.

May, T. (2011) *Social Research Issues, Methods and Research* (4th edition). Buckingham: Open University Press.

Mulgan, G. (2012) 'The theoretical foundations of social innovation', in A. Nicholls and A. Murdock (eds.) *Social Innovation: Blurring Boundaries to Reconfigure Markets*. Basingstoke: Palgrave Macmillan, pp.33–64.

North American Reggio Emilia Alliance (n.d.) http://reggioalliance.org/.

Ofcom (2012) *Communications Market Report*, http://stakeholders.ofcom.org.uk/binaries/research/cmr/cmr12/CMR_UK_2012.pdf.

Pimlott-Wilson, H. (2012) 'Visualising children's participation in research: Lego Duplo, rainbows and clouds and moodboards', *International Journal of Social Research Methodology*, 15(2), 135–48.

Plano Clark, V.L. and Creswell, J.W. (2008) *The Mixed Methods Reader*. London: Sage.

Ringrose, J., Gill, R., Livingstone, S. and Harvey, L. (2012) *A Qualitative Study of Children, Young people and 'Sexting' A Report for the NSPCC.* http://www.nspcc .org.uk/Inform/resourcesforprofessionals/sexualabuse/sexting-research-report _wdf89269.pdf.

Robinson, K. (2010) *Changing Educational Paradigms.* http://www.thersa .org/events/rsaanimate/animate/rsa-animate-changing-paradigms?gclid= CIGLzaqewsACFRHLtAodUl0AeA.

Silverman, D. (2012) 'Research and theory', in C. Scale (ed.) *Researching Society and Culture.* London: Sage, pp.29–44.

Snee, H. (2012) 'Youth research in Web 2.0: A case study in Blog analysis', in S. Heath and C. Walker (eds.) *Innovations in Youth Research.* Basingstoke: Palgrave Macmillan, pp.178–94.

Suffolk County Council (online) *Raising the Bar.* http://www.suffolk.gov.uk/your -council/plans-and-policies/raising-the-bar-briefing/about-raising-the-bar/.

Thomas, N. and O'Kane, C. (1998) 'The ethics of participatory research with children', *Children and Society*, 12, 336–48.

Warschauer, M. (2004) *Technology and Social Inclusion Rethinking the Digital Divide.* London: MIT Press.

Weller, S. (2012) 'Evolving creativity in qualitative longitudinal research with children and teenagers', *International Journal of Social Research Methodology*, 15(2), 119–33.

Wyness, M. (2012) *Childhood and Society* (2nd edition). Basingstoke: Palgrave Macmillan.

13
Ethics Issues in Digital Methods Research

Claire Hewson

Introduction

This chapter addresses issues of ethical research practice in the context of the recently emerging range of methods which use the Internet to support the creation of primary research data – variously referred to as online methods, digital methods and *Internet-mediated research* (IMR) (here, the latter term will be used). Social and behavioural researchers started devising and piloting IMR methods from around the mid-1990s, with surveys, experiments, interviews and observational studies all being represented in early pioneering attempts (e.g. Hewson, 1994; Bordia, 1996). Since then, IMR methods have flourished, expanding in volume, interdisciplinary reach and range of methodological approaches (as discussed in the introduction to this book). In particular, the emergence of 'Web 2.0', as discussed in Chapter 1, has facilitated the recent expansion of unobtrusive methods, including those involving data 'mining' or 'harvesting' (often requiring the use of complex computer algorithms), which can lead to what have become known as 'big data' sets (see Part I, this book). Such unobtrusive approaches, which make use of the digital traces of peoples' online behaviours (typically, without obtaining consent), have led to debates regarding what is appropriate ethical practice in an IMR context; in particular, a salient issue has been the distinction between what should be considered 'private' and 'in the public domain' in an online context.

Obtrusive research methods in IMR (where informed consent *is* obtained) have also created new challenges and debates regarding what is ethical practice (as discussed further below). Some of the difficulties which can arise may not be immediately obvious to researchers accustomed to gathering data using traditional offline methods, creating the need for IMR-specific guidelines which highlight issues and caveats. The ethical issues which emerge in an IMR context may also potentially lead to new ways of thinking about ethics in traditional (offline) research contexts, for example by highlighting ambiguities in what constitutes 'public' and 'private' spaces, or questioning the distinction between 'real' and 'pseudonymous' identities. The impact of such debates in transforming traditional conceptions of ethical research practice remains largely to be seen. A key tenet of the present chapter is that striving to specify a predefined set of 'online research ethics rules' is not very useful. Rather, researchers need to carefully assess a number of key considerations, and make decisions, within the context of any particular research project. The present discussion is intended to be of use to IMR researchers, students and Research Ethics Committees (RECs) when planning, designing and assessing an IMR research study. To this end, some practical guidance on best practice procedures across a range of methodological approaches is offered throughout.

Ethics issues in Internet-mediated research

Existing IMR ethics guidelines

Early pioneers using IMR methods often focused primarily on methodological issues, rather than ethical considerations (Peden and Flashinski, 2004). However, it soon became apparent that a number of pressing issues, both in applying existing ethical standards and in resolving novel issues that emerge in an IMR context, required attention. In 1999, the report of a workshop convened by the American Association for the Advancement of Science (AAAS) was published (Frankel and Siang, 1999), which highlighted the following key issues in online research ethics: complexities in gaining informed consent; the use of 'anonymous', or pseudonymous, identities; exaggerated expectations of privacy; the blurred public–private domain distinction. The report also questioned the applicability and interpretation of existing 'human subjects' research guidelines in an IMR context. Taking *autonomy, beneficence* (maximizing benefits, minimizing harm) and *justice* as basic ethical principles for directing research with human participants, the AAAS document identifies several enhanced risks in IMR: dubious reliability and validity of data; greater scope for leakage of research participants' personally identifiable data; difficulty in implementing robust informed consent and debrief procedures; ambiguities over what is 'in the public domain' online.

Since this early discussion paper, several professional bodies have published ethics guidelines for IMR, including the Association of Internet Researchers (AoIR, formed in 1998) (Markham and Buchanan, 2012 [*version 2*]); the American Psychological Association (APA) (Kraut et al., 2004); the British Psychological Society (BPS, 2013 [*version 2*]). Similar to the AAAS document, the BPS (2013) guidelines identify some basic ethics principles for research with human participants – *respect for the autonomy and dignity of persons; scientific value; social responsibility; maximizing benefits and minimizing harm* – and discuss particular issues which can arise in adhering to these principles in an IMR context. Discussions of ethics in IMR can also be found in journal papers (e.g. Rodham and Gavin, 2006), book chapters (e.g. Ess, 2007) and online resources and guidelines (e.g. see the information available at *Exploring Online Research Methods* (NCRM, n.d.); also the IMR-specific guidelines of various university ethics committees, locatable by searching online). Also noteworthy is the cross-disciplinary journal dedicated to the topic, *International Journal of Internet Research Ethics* (IJIRE, n.d.). The next section now discusses the main IMR ethical issues requiring consideration, as identified in the existing literature.

Obtrusive IMR methods

Gaining informed consent

In situations where participants are actively recruited to knowingly take part in a research study, informed consent is required, and participants must be given the right to withdraw their consent, during or after participation (within a reasonable timescale), and must be suitably debriefed once participation is complete. In IMR, ensuring these procedures are implemented effectively can be problematic for a number of reasons. Most fundamentally, reduced levels of researcher control compared with many offline contexts, due to the non-proximal nature of the interaction, can raise various issues. While non-proximal methods are also commonly used in some types of offline research, such as postal surveys, a unique feature of IMR is that it allows far greater levels of interactivity while maintaining high levels of anonymity and reduced identifiability and traceability of participants. Thus, an online experiment could potentially take place in a rich, interactive 3D environment, without the researcher knowing the (offline) identities of participants, or having any means of tracing them after completion of the study – or, perhaps most significantly, if they withdraw and choose to exit part way through. Likewise, online surveys can be (and often are) placed in publically accessible locations for participants to discover and complete while remaining totally anonymous (apart from perhaps the logging on an IP address) and untraceable. IMR interview and focus groups involve participants being remotely present, rather than actually present with the researcher as in offline face-to-face contexts, often interacting only via typed text, using asynchronous or synchronous discussion/chat software. Obtrusive observational studies, such as ethnographic research within a discussion forum or online virtual world, allows participants to remain relatively anonymous, compared with offline face-to-face approaches.

This distinct feature of IMR can lead to the following problems in devising effective informed consent procedures: ensuring, verifying and documenting that participants have actually read and understood consent information; ensuring and verifying that participants are eligible to give consent, for example they are not underage, or are unable to give consent for some other reason. Various solutions and good practice suggestions have been offered to address these difficulties. Presenting consent information in a way that is accessible (clear and easy to read), informative, but not over-lengthy, should help encourage engagement from participants. In the case of web-based surveys and experiments, providing an initial page with this information – which should be informative but succinct – is effective. To check for understanding, including a bulleted list of statements to endorse (e.g. using check boxes) is a useful strategy (BPS, 2013). To avoid participants simply going through and ticking 'yes' to all statements, varying the appropriate response (e.g. 'yes', or 'no') can be effective. A final check box indicating explicit consent to take part in the study is a good way of keeping a record that consent has been formally obtained (it can be useful to include this again at the end of a survey or experiment, to double check).

For other obtrusive methods, such as disclosed ethnographic observation within an existing discussion forum, reliably contacting *all* participants to gain consent can be problematic. Different strategies are possible, including sending an email to all listed members of a discussion forum, or posting an 'opt-in' or 'opt-out' message to the group (it is generally good practice, and netiquette, to go through group moderators before taking any of these actions). If discussion group *archives* are being used, the email method may be best able to catch members who have been inactive for some time, or since left the group (though dormant email accounts, and transmission errors, mean this approach is not foolproof). Where discussion groups are larger, reliably contacting all contributors becomes increasingly difficult (leading some researchers to argue that undisclosed approaches which waive informed consent are justified: see further discussion below). Creating a dedicated research study site to which potential participants are invited, for example, by posting adverts to an existing group, can be an option if the research study design permits (obtaining consent on entry to the site, for example). This approach also allows greater researcher control over the security and confidentiality of research data gathered (discussed further below). However, it might not always be appropriate, for example where more 'naturalistic' settings are desired.

Ensuring that consent gained from participants is actually 'valid' raises particular difficulties in IMR, due to the diminished verifiability of participant characteristics. Using sampling methods that are less likely to reach and attract certain groups, such as those under the required consent age, can be useful. A careful risk assessment of the possible harm that may result from access by participants ineligible to give consent should also be carried out. For example, research which is particularly sensitive, or involves adult themes, should be considered higher risk. The BPS (2013) guidelines outline some specific good practice strategies, including asking for age information prior to presenting study materials, so participants who do not meet the minimum age requirements can be redirected and blocked from re-entering the study (e.g. this can be achieved using cookies). In high-risk situations, additional safeguard measures can be used, such as verifying participant characteristics (and perhaps also recording consent) offline (BPS, 2013), or using methods which maximize levels of identifiability, such as Skype interviews. However, in some cases it may be decided that the risks are too high to allow the study to be conducted online. Research which involves obtaining parent/guardian consent should not to be ruled out in IMR; instead, it requires especially careful (see Hessler et al., 2003 for an example).

Withdrawal and debrief

Implementing effective withdrawal and debrief procedures can be problematic in IMR. In web-based surveys and experiments, a participant (typically) interacts remotely with an automated program (or HTML form), without any researcher presence, and often anonymously with no subsequent way of being traced or contacted (this is the case, at least, with many of the publically available web surveys readily accessible at sites such as Online Psychology Research UK (OPR UK, n.d.)). In such situations, there is no way for the researcher to know whether the participant has engaged with the debrief information presented (usually placed on the final page of the survey/experiment, and offering researcher contact information). In cases where a participant withdraws early, ensuring debrief can become even more problematic since exiting by closing a browser precludes the debrief page being presented at all. Providing a clearly visible 'withdraw' button on each page of a survey (or experiment) and urging participants to use this if they wish to exit early can help, and allows redirection to a debrief page (at least this is an option in many of the most popular current online survey software packages). Adding a question asking participants if they are happy for any partial submitted data to be used is also useful, since using these data could violate withdrawal rights if participants do not want their partial responses to be used; on the other hand, not using partial responses may violate respect for the autonomy of individuals, and the time they have given the study, if they did wish their (incomplete) answers to be used. In IMR, it is often harder (than in many offline contexts) for a researcher to ascertain whether participants may have left a study in a state of distress, or discomfort, so paying particular attention to developing robust, reliable withdrawal and debrief procedures is important. Trade-offs can emerge, for example allowing post-study withdrawal requires being able to identify an individual's set of responses, but such traceability can conflict with anonymity requirements. Existing guidelines (e.g. BPS, 2013) offer some advice on the methods available (e.g. using an email address, or password, for identification purposes) and when they might be useful. Different approaches will suit different contexts; for example, if deception is involved, then ensuring debrief becomes more urgent, so maximizing traceability at the expense of anonymity might be appropriate.

Even in contexts involving greater levels of researcher involvement, such as online interviews, focus groups, participant observations, and so on, similar withdrawal and debrief issues can arise, since participants can leave mid-study without any explanation. However, in these contexts a researcher is more likely to notice withdrawal when it occurs and detect any adverse reactions from participants during the study. Ensuring a means of contacting any participants who might disappear in this way is advisable, so that debrief information can be sent, and follow-up questions and checks offered (e.g. regarding a participant's well-being). Knowing whether participants are happy for their existing contribution to be used as research data is also important, especially in contexts where removing the contribution of one person (e.g. from a discussion group) can be challenging, and perhaps detrimental to the quality of the data gathered. Contacting participants in these situations may not always be straightforward, even in cases where an email address has been obtained (see above for barriers to the use of email to contact participants). Membership of existing online groups and virtual spaces is fluid and ever-changing. An avatar in SecondLife might be there one day, and gone the next, similar to a participant in a discussion forum or mailing list group. The safest strategy is for researchers to use procedures which maximize the identifiability and traceability of research participants; this is especially important for very sensitive research where risk of harm to participants is greater. Setting up a dedicated research site which participants access with a username/password, linked with a valid email address, can be an effective strategy (a temporary email address could be provided, which can be set forward to a more permanent account, if greater anonymity is desired).

Ensuring confidentiality

In both obtrusive and unobtrusive (see below) IMR methods, a number of threats to the confidentiality of participants' data go beyond what is normally present in offline research (Reips and Buffardi, 2012). Risks include hacker access, transmission errors (e.g. if using email) and third-party control (e.g. if using server-hosted online study software solutions). Traditional offline approaches which store data on local media storage devices, or in hardcopy form (e.g. pen and paper questionnaires), are not subject to these risks. Most crucially, in IMR, careful measures are needed to minimize the risk of participants' *personally identifiable* data being accessed by an unauthorized third party. One established way of maintaining confidentiality is to make sure all individual responses collected are anonymous, so that even if the data are accessed (e.g. by third-party providers, or hackers), responses cannot be traced back to the individuals who produced them. However, in IMR, potentially identifying information is more likely to be automatically recorded as part of the data collection process; for example, online survey software often stores information about IP addresses alongside responses (though in some packages, such as SurveyMonkey, this feature can be turned off), and posts to online discussion groups typically are accompanied by a username associated with an email address. Compare this with a laboratory-based experiment, where participants take part on a local computer provided by the researcher and are assigned a 'code name/number' which is only linked with their responses by a separate coding sheet, used only by the researcher. The IMR researcher thus needs to carefully consider additional risks, solutions and precautionary measures, following the guidance available in existing texts (e.g. Hewson et al., 2003).

Stripping away any potential personally identifying information from datasets at greater risk of third-party access is one important safety measure and can work well when the datasets, and any original source material from which they were drawn (e.g. a dedicated, private discussion forum), are fully under the control of the researcher. In cases where data are sourced from or stored using third-party services, such as hosted survey or experiment software, or public online discussion forums, additional complications emerge. Here, the researcher is unable to access and remove personally identifying information from the original data sources, so particularly careful consideration must be given to dissemination practices, due to the durability, traceability and searchability of these original sources. For example, publishing verbatim quotes from a public online discussion forum could lead to them being traced back to source, viewed in context, and individual authors being identified, posing a serious potential threat to participant confidentiality. The problem is further compounded if the researcher publishes the name of the original source (e.g. website address or social network site [SNS] name) alongside the reported research findings. For this reason, it has been suggested that source material information should not be given, and that quotes should not be used, or at least should be carefully paraphrased (BPS, 2013). Objections to these recommendations refer to such constraints sometimes being detrimental to research goals. On balance, risks associated with traceability and identifiability of participants must be weighed against the research benefits of disclosure during dissemination.

The traceability of individual's data should also be considered in terms of the local equipment individuals use to participate in a study, since computers store traces of the activity that occurs on them. Interacting with a web browser can leave traces, including the text responses given to survey questions, on the local computer which was used; this means other users of the same computer equipment may be able to retrieve and view these responses. Researchers should assess the extent to which it is their duty to inform participants (e.g. in the debrief, or consent, information) that this is the case, and offer advice and guidance on how to remove such traces, where this is possible. Finally, the leakage of researcher interpretations of participants' responses is another consideration to be taken into account – given the enhanced accessibility of published research reports online these days, there is greater risk that a research participant, or someone who knows them, might locate such interpretations. This means that extra care might be needed to protect the personal identities of research participants in published reports of findings (and this applies equally to offline studies whose findings are disseminated in ways that make them more publically accessible).

Unobtrusive IMR methods

The public–private domain distinction online

The issue of when the traces of online activity left behind by individuals should reasonably be considered 'in the public domain', and thus arguably available for use as research data without gaining informed consent, has been and remains deeply controversial (e.g. see Brownlow and Dell, 2002). A number of factors and considerations come into play in attempting to answer this question, and as always, decisions must be guided by the particular research study context. As with obtrusive methods, key factors to consider in unobtrusive IMR are risks of harm to participants caused by the research, for example through making personally identifiable information (particularly where this is sensitive, such as illegal activities) more likely to be discovered and disseminated, and likely benefits of the research. A key consideration, which relates to the principle of *autonomy*, is ascertaining users' own *perceptions* and *expectations about* what is public and private online (Markham and Buchanan, 2012; BPS, 2013). However, user perceptions still remain largely unknown. A study which set out to investigate privacy perceptions, using an experimental paradigm, is reported by Hudson and Bruckman (2004). They entered chat rooms and either posted a message alerting participants that they wished to log their discussions (with opt-in or opt-out conditions) or simply lurked (remained present not posting anything). They received hostile responses in both cases, but were kicked out *less often* when they simply entered and lurked, leading them to argue that non-disclosure is justified in order to be able to carry out valuable research. However, other researchers have reported different, more positive, outcomes when entering chat rooms to observe discussions and gather research data, both in 'lurking' contexts (e.g. Rodino, 1997) and where permission was requested (e.g. Madge and O'Connor, 2002). Further research is clearly needed on this topic, since knowing what the privacy expectations of users of online interactive spaces are (which likely vary individually and culturally) is fundamental to reaching conclusions on the public–private distinction debate (Ferri, 2000). It is worth noting that, strictly speaking, anything covered by copyright law is *not* in the public domain (BPS, 2013), which would render readily 'accessible' content such as Facebook posts, Tweets and various other social media sources, not 'publically available' for use as research data. In terms of ethical research practice, a more common conception is that anything which is accessible to anyone, without the need for explicit permission, is 'in the public domain'. Legalities such as copyright and data protection laws are important to keep in mind, but may not necessarily dictate what constitutes good ethical research practice (see later example below).

People's awareness of the extent to which their online activities are logged and made available for third-party access needs consideration. If individuals are unaware that their contributions (e.g. to a discussion group), or activity traces, can be accessed and viewed, they may engage in disclosures and/or behaviours that they otherwise would not submit. Furthermore, traces that were once private can later become public (BPS, 2013), without a person's knowledge or permission. Another important point is that given the nature of online communications, and the settings in which they take place – for example, simultaneously in a private space such as a bedroom and in a public online discussion forum – they may be perceived as both 'private' and 'public' at the same time. This might lead to greater candour and disclosures than individuals might engage in if in an offline fully public setting. All the aforementioned considerations complicate the issue of when it is acceptable, ethically, to use online information that is readily available. In particular, with all the 'unknowns' about user perceptions, knowledge, expectations, and so on, assessing likely *levels of harm* in doing so can be difficult. Fundamentally, deciding what is 'in the public domain' is complex and contextual, and in ambiguous cases researchers must exercise their judgement to assess a range of factors (as mentioned above, for example, sensitivity of the data) to make appropriate decisions which serve to minimize risks and maximize benefits. As noted in both the BPS (2013) and Markham and Buchanan (2012) guidelines, a context-dependent, bottom-up, flexible approach is appropriate when dealing with ethics decisions in IMR, in general, and this is the approach advocated here.

Practical considerations are also important – for example, it may often not be practical (or indeed possible) to reliably contact all individuals who have contributed information to a potential data source (e.g. as in an archived discussion forum), due to the fluid nature of individuals' presence in online spaces (as well as dormant emails addresses, transmission errors, etc.). The *scientific value* of a piece of research may also be compromised by disclosure, due to interfering with the authenticity of participants' behaviours, and thus reducing ecological validity (as reported by Reid, 1996, in an observational study in an MUD (Multi-User Dungeon) environment). Finally, the principle of *social responsibility*, particularly avoiding disrupting existing social structures, becomes relevant here – one argument against disclosure in observational research online being that it may harm group members by fostering suspicion and mistrust.

The above discussion has indicated the complexity of making decisions about when it is ethically appropriate to gather data unobtrusively, without disclosure, from online sources. An illustration of the contrasting approaches that have been taken can be found in comparing two very similar ethnographic studies of pro-anorexia support groups. Fox, Ward and O'Rourke (2005) contacted moderators and group members of a pro-anorexia website to fully disclose their intentions to follow discussions, using participant observation methods, and use these as research data. Permission was granted, and they report gathering valuable data using this approach. Brotsky and Giles (2007), on the other hand, argue that disclosing their intentions as researchers in a similar study (also following discussions on a pro-anorexia website) would have compromised the integrity of the research. Hence, they went undercover, one researcher posing as a plausible persona within the group for some time before going on to gather data from members' posts which were then used as research data (and published, including using quotes from group discussions). The latter approach is highly controversial (indeed, the author has encountered reactions of outrage when reporting on this study in seminar sessions). Nevertheless, the authors present clear arguments for adopting this stance and acquired REC approval for the study. Interestingly, moderators may even sometimes block attempts to disclose research intentions to discussion group members, as reported by Tackett-Gibson (2008), who intended full disclosure (to observe online communities engaged in exchanging drug-use information), but was given permission by group moderators only to lurk and carry out observations unobtrusively, and access stored discussion archives. This relates back to the principle of social responsibility and avoiding disrupting existing social groups. As noted earlier, it is good practice to contact moderators before proceeding with an observation study of an online group, and they may well have particular insights into whether disclosure is likely to disrupt, damage or benefit a particular group.

Ensuring confidentiality

The topic of confidentiality in IMR was discussed above in relation to obtrusive methods. As noted, the particular issues with Internet data collection, in comparison with many offline methods, relate to storing data securely, maintaining participant anonymity (so individual responses are not personally identifiable) and using dissemination procedures that do not entail a high risk of allowing data to be traced back to source (such as an active online discussion forum used as a site for ethnographic research). In unobtrusive methods, where informed consent is typically not obtained (as discussed above), ensuring data confidentiality arguably becomes most crucial. Thus, when informed consent is gained, participants can be warned of any risks and may be willing, for example, to agree to anonymized quotes being disseminated, or in some cases to waive anonymity (e.g. some activist or marginalized groups are keen for their voice to be heard). However, when traces are 'harvested' as data without an individual's consent, making sure that these data cannot be linked back to an identifiable person becomes especially crucial (e.g. BPS, 2013). In cases where large, quantified, aggregate datasets are gathered, such as from Google searches, web page browsing activity, shares on Twitter, SNS links, and so on, risks of data becoming personally identifiable are typically at their lowest. As long as the researcher takes steps to strip away any potentially identifying information (such as IP addresses, email addresses, usernames, etc.), then storing and disseminating such large datasets poses minimal risks to the individuals who provided the data.

Risks will often be higher in qualitative research studies, however, particularly those which source linguistic data from online discussion forums, and in these cases the aforementioned considerations (such as whether to reveal names and locations of sources or use verbatim quotes) require careful attention. Again, a range of contextual factors will come into play in assessing risks and making appropriate, ethically sound decisions; these include the sensitivity of the research topic, and data, how vulnerable the individuals involved are, how beneficial the research is, and so on. The core principle repeated in the BPS (2013) guidelines is pertinent here, which is that a researcher should assess all key relevant factors and 'ensure that ethics procedures and safeguards are implemented so as to be proportional to the level of risk and potential harm to participants' (BPS, 2013, p.8). As mentioned earlier, sometimes legal requirements and good ethical practice may seem to be in conflict; for example, copyright legislation may dictate attributing authorship for any online documents sourced (e.g. personal blogs and homepages), which might be in conflict with requirements to maintain anonymity and confidentiality to protect individuals. Some further discussion of legal issues in IMR can be found in BPS (2013) and Markham and Buchanan (2012).

Case study: Manipulating Facebook users' moods

In a recent study on 'emotional contagion', Kramer, Guillory and Hancock (2014) examined the effects on individual Facebook users' moods of manipulating the 'emotional valence' of content on their News Feeds. The published findings from this research led to controversy over the ethical soundness of the methods employed, and a good deal of media attention and public comment (generally highly critical). For example, *The Guardian* reports: 'Lawyers, internet activists and politicians said this weekend that the mass experiment in emotional manipulation was "scandalous", "spooky" and "disturbing"' (*The Guardian*, 2014). What the researchers did was to take advantage of the way in which users' Facebook News Feeds are filtered, using a ranking algorithm, to select and present a subset of all the possible News Feed posts available (which Facebook uses to try to show users the content they will find most relevant and engaging). In an experimental manipulation, a random selection of users' (close to 700,000) News Feeds were adjusted to reduce the amount of emotional content presented; the study reports finding that reducing positive emotional expressions led people to produce fewer positive and more negative posts, and reducing negative expressions led to the opposite effect. In an editorial response published by the journal soon after the study appeared in print, it was recognized that the study had raised questions about the principles of 'informed consent', 'opportunity to opt out' and personal privacy. Legally, the use of Facebook users' personal data is sanctioned by the Data Use Policy, which they agree to upon signing up. However, as noted earlier, adherence to legal requirements does not necessarily translate into ethical research practice.

A number of key points about the study are worth highlighting: Facebook News Feeds are routinely manipulated, so the present intervention was an extension of this practice; the effect sizes were extremely small (but nevertheless statistically significant due to the sheer sample size); the published findings used aggregate, fully anonymized data. These features could be used to justify the study as very low risk, in terms of potential harm to participants, and it is unlikely that any of the randomly selected Facebook users suffered any significant disruption or harm as a result of the study intervention. However, the publication and dissemination of the findings (including the media hype regarding the implications) led to a good deal of public anxiety and outrage at the findings and their implications. Interestingly, while REC (typically known in the United States as *Institutional Review Board*) approval for the study was sought, it was exempted from the review process, since it used archival data collected by Facebook for internal purposes (it is not clear to what extent the research team had input into this process, however). This IRB decision could be challenged, depending on the details of the research design process, and the nature of the collaboration between

Facebook and the research team. Such relatively novel digital methods research contexts remain a challenge for IRBs, in the absence of a set of established ethics guidelines. Clearly, there are presently ambiguities regarding how to deal with the research use of data collected online by private entities such as Facebook.[1]

Conclusions

This chapter has highlighted and discussed a number of key ethical issues identified as requiring extra care and attention in digital methods research, some of which may not be immediately obvious to the researcher accustomed to conducting research in offline contexts. Issues can emerge in properly applying existing ethical guidelines in IMR, to ensure robust and rigorous procedures to enable adherence to established ethics principles, as well as in tackling new challenges that emerge within an online context. Key issues include deciding what is public and private online; devising robust informed consent, withdrawal and debrief procedures; and protecting participant confidentiality. As researchers continue to explore, pilot and debate IMR procedures and their ethical implications, principles and guidelines will evolve, and new procedures and ways of thinking about ethics will emerge, potentially impacting upon the way researchers think about research ethics in offline contexts.

Digital methods are still in their relative infancy, and so are the ethical guidelines that have been developed to date. As highlighted by the 'emotional contagion' Facebook study, the issues can be varied and complex. What is institutionally sanctioned may still be seen as ethically problematic. Furthermore, researchers may disagree on key points, such as whether publically accessible traces of online behaviour can be considered available for use as research data without gaining consent from those who produced them. What does seem apparent is that no set of 'online ethics rules' for IMR is likely to be forthcoming; rather, flexibility in applying some broader key principles within the context of particular research study designs is required. Changing online landscapes, practices, new research data and researcher experiences will continue to shape the evolution, revision and refinement of ethical principles and guidelines for digital methods research.

Note

1. Interested readers should be able to find further discussions by conducting an appropriate Google search; the first author of the paper, Adam Kramer, has also posted a personal response on his own Facebook Page (accessible at

the following link, at the time of writing: https://www.facebook.com/akramer /posts/10152987150867796).

References

Bordia, P. (1996) 'Studying verbal interaction on the Internet', *Behaviour Research Methods, Instruments and Computers*, 28(2): 149–151.

BPS (2013) *Report of the Working Party on Conducting Research on the Internet: Ethics Guidelines for Internet-Mediated Research*. British Psychological Society, INF206/1.2013, http://www.bps.org.uk/system/files/Public%20files /inf206-guidelines-for-internet-mediated-research.pdf.

Brotsky, S.R. and Giles, D. (2007) 'Inside the "Pro-ana" community: A covert online participant observation', *Eating Disorders: The Journal of Treatment and Prevention* 15(2), 93–109.

Brownlow, C. and O'Dell, L. (2002) 'Ethical issues for qualitative research in on-line communities', *Disability and Society*, 17(6), 685–94.

Ess, C. (2007) 'Internet research ethics', in A. Joinson, K. McKenna, U. Reips and T. Postmes (eds.) *Oxford Handbook of Internet Psychology*. Oxford: Oxford University Press, pp.487–502.

Ferri, B. (2000) 'The hidden cost of difference: Women with learning disabilities', *Learning Disabilities: A Multidisciplinary Journal*, 10(3), 129–38.

Fox, N., Ward, K. and O'Rourke, A. (2005) 'Pro-anorexia, weight-loss drugs and the Internet: an "anti recovery" explanatory model of anorexia', *Sociology of Health and Illness*, 27(7), 944–71.

Frankel, M. and Siang, S. (1999) *Ethical and Legal Issues of Human Subjects Research on the Internet – Report of a Workshop*. Washington, DC: American Association for the Advancement of Science, http://www.aaas.org/spp/sfrl/projects/intres /report.pdf date accessed January 2013.

The Guardian (2014) 'Facebook reveals news feed experiment to control emotions', *The Guardian*, 30 June 2014, http://www.theguardian.com/technology /2014/jun/29/facebook-users-emotions-news-feeds.

Hessler, R. M., Downing, J., Beltz, C., Pelliccio, A., Powell, M., and Vale, W. (2003) 'Qualitative research on adolescent risk using email: A methodological assessment', *Qualitative Sociology*, 26(1), 111–24.

Hewson, C.M. (1994) 'Empirical evidence regarding the folk psychological concept of belief', in *Proceedings of the Sixteenth Annual Conference of the Cognitive Science Society*. Atlanta, Georgia, pp.403–408.

Hewson, C.M., Yule, P., Laurent, D. and Vogel, C.M. (2003) *Internet Research Methods: A Practical Guide for the Social and Behavioural Sciences*. London: Sage.

Hudson, J. and Bruckman, A. (2004) ' "Go Away": Participant objections to being studied and the ethics of chatroom research', *The Information Society*, 20(2), 127–39.

International Journal of Internet Research Ethics (IJIRE) (n.d.) http://ijire.net/.

Kraut, R., Olson, J., Banaji, M., Bruckman, A., Cohen, J. and Cooper, M. (2004) 'Psychological research online: Report of board of scientific affairs' advisory group on the conduct of research on the Internet', *American Psychologist*, 59(4), 1–13.

Madge, C. and O'Connor, H. (2002) 'On-line with e-mums: Exploring the Internet as a medium for research', *Area*, 34(1), 92–102.

Markham, A. and Buchanan, E. (2012) *Ethical Decision-Making and Internet Research. Recommendations from the AoIR Ethics Working Committee (version 2)*, http://www.aoir.org/reports/ethics2.pdf.

National Centre for Research Methods (NCRM) (n.d.) 'Online Research Ethics', *Exploring Online Research Methods* http://www.restore.ac.uk/orm/ethics /ethcontents.htm.

Online Psychology Research UK (OPR UK) (n.d.) http://www.online psychresearch.co.uk.

Peden, B.F. and Flashinski, D.P. (2004) 'Virtual research ethics: A content analysis of surveys and experiments online', in E. Buchanan (ed.) *Readings in Virtual Research Ethics: Issues and Controversies*. Hershey, PA: Information Science Pub, pp.1–26.

Reid, E. (1996) 'Informed consent in the study of online communities: A reflection on the effect of computer-mediated social research', *Information Society*, 12, 169–74.

Reips, U.-D. and Buffardi, L. E. (2012) 'Studying migrants with the help of the Internet: Methods from psychology', *Journal of Ethnic and Migration Studies*, 38(9): 1405–24.

Rodham, K. and Gavin, J. (2006) 'The ethics of using the Internet to collect qualitative research data', *Research Ethics Review*, 2(3), 92–7.

Rodino, M. (1997) 'Breaking out of binaries: Reconceptualizing gender and its relationship to language', *Journal of Computer-Mediated Communication*, 3(3), http://jcmc.indiana.edu/vol3/issue3/rodino.html, date accessed January 2013.

Tackett-Gibson, M. (2008) 'Constructions of risk and harm in online discussions of ketamine use', *Addiction Research and Theory*, 16(3), 245–57.

14
Digital Methods as Mainstream Methodology: Conclusions

Helene Snee, Christine Hine, Yvette Morey, Steven Roberts and Hayley Watson

One of the dangers of writing about innovative digital research is that, by definition, the field is subject to ongoing transformations. The pace of technological change is such that both digital social life and digital tools will have developed since the research reported in this collection was conducted. As noted in the introduction to Part III, this is further complicated when we consider some of the debates concerning exactly what is meant by 'methodological innovation'. Wiles et al. (2013, p.19) note that while some authors reserve the term for new methodologies, others such as Taylor and Coffey (2008) also consider extensions to existing methods as innovative. Moreover, questions arise as to whether these developments are innovative if they remain on the margins, or whether this occurs only when they have been more widely adopted (Wiles et al., 2013, p.19). We have taken a broad approach to innovation by considering how the 'mainstream' – by which we mean established social science research – is being supplemented and extended by digital methods. As such, this collection has focused on two core points of innovation: the existing social science *methodological repertoire* and the *conceptual* mainstream or established social science *issues and concerns*.

This chapter critically explores the notion of the relationship between innovative and mainstream research, before considering the contributions made in this collection to five key questions: Who has access to digital data? What is the role of disciplinary boundaries in relation to innovative research? Why is it important to understand the origin of digital data and digital tools? What do digital methods and digital tools have to offer in comparison with 'mainstream' research? What are the ethical challenges associated with digital methodological innovation?

In order for digital methods to become a part of mainstream methodology, it is necessary for social scientists to acknowledge the barriers as well as the drivers that help to prohibit and facilitate such innovative measures in social science research. As part of this discussion, we draw on the outputs from the seminar series 'Digital Methods as Mainstream Methodology', the catalyst for this edited collection (Roberts et al., 2013). We conclude by reflecting upon the status of 'the digital' in contemporary social science research. As we considered in the introductory chapter (Chapter 1), and as highlighted in many of the contributions to this volume, we cannot look at methodological innovation in isolation but need to understand these processes in their social, cultural and political context (Wiles et al., 2013).

Reflections on innovations in digital methods

It is clear that there exists a plethora of ways in which digital methods are instrumental in methodological innovation as well as conceptual development. However, what is just as apparent is that there is no easy disentangling of the methodological and the conceptual/theoretical and that digital methods blur a number of distinctions/binaries: online and offline, traditional and new, quantitative and qualitative, data collection field and method and so on.

Following from the above, many of the chapters in the collection problematized the notions of innovation and the mainstream. A further complicating factor is that the platforms, tools, devices and social practices we associate with the digital, and digital methods, have undergone (and are undergoing) different periods of mainstreaming for publics, the scientific community and commercial organizations. The Internet became a mainstream phenomenon with the advent of accessible web browsers from 1993 onwards (Naughton, 2000). In 2003, social networking sites went mainstream as Shirky (in boyd and Ellison, 2007, p.216) bemoaned the emergence of 'yet another social networking service'; while the uptake of iOS and Android-enabled smartphones and other digital devices has been unprecedented from 2010 onwards.

The pace of change in digital environments and technologies has, in turn, impacted upon elements of social interaction and modes of sociality. In Chapter 1, we referenced van Dijck's (2013) notion of 'platformed sociality' to characterize the ways in which social networking sites offer means for users to connect with one another and leave persistent traces of their activities. It is tempting to consider whether the uptake of smart devices, which allow users to access social networks virtually anywhere and at any time across a range of devices, might consequently be characterized as a 'multi-platformed sociality'. New platforms and increased possibilities for connectivity may retain older elements of sociality (a user profile based on demographics, interactions with acquaintances and known others, conventions of offline social interaction observed – e.g. Facebook). They also give rise to newer forms of social interaction (user profile based on post-demographics or demographics of taste, interactions with unknown others or communities of interest, interaction based on rapid generation and exchange of pertinent information and content – for example, Twitter).

To bring all of the above together – rather than trying to discuss methodological innovation separately from mainstreaming and modes of sociality – it is possible to identify five interrelated areas where these issues coalesce in the chapters. These may be broadly conceptualized as issues related to access and gatekeeping; disciplinary boundaries and internal constraints; analytics and tools; methods and concepts; and ethics.

Access and gatekeeping

Digital research is not restricted to being an exercise solely conducted by those within academia. We are seeing increasingly innovative approaches to digital research beyond the academic realm and such activities might present challenges to professional practice. Many of the most dramatic innovations in digital methods particularly using 'big data' are happening within commercial organizations and are not necessarily shared with academic researchers (Savage and Burrows, 2007).

The chapters by Bruns and Burgess (Chapter 2) and by Knox (Chapter 11) were both concerned with the question of who has access to big data sets and the implications of this access for the kinds of research questions that are asked and the methods of analysis that are undertaken. Bruns and Burgess discussed the ways in which Twitter has been widely adopted as a tool for public communication and debate and the significant opportunities it offers for research (e.g. crisis communication and the relaying of information in emergency situations). They then highlighted the difficulties that scientific communities face in trying to access data on Twitter due to considerable access fees and limitations placed upon the functionality of the public Application Programing Interface (API) by the platform. The divide between private market research organizations (who can afford commercial access fees) and the scientific community (who have to make do with the public Twitter

API) has resulted in a condition of precarity for Twitter research. Limited access to Twitter data both constrains the development of research areas in the social sciences and shapes the broader research agenda as commercial parties are more likely to invest in research that offers a clear return on investment. Similarly Knox was concerned with the big data sets generated by massive open online courses (MOOCs). While these have the potential to feed into learning analytics and digital education research, Knox argued that is presently unclear who will conduct this research in the future – if this role is solely occupied by algorithmists and big data analysts how will this shape the digital education research agenda? In both instances, innovation in digital technologies and the mainstream uptake of these technologies and platforms also present barriers to social science research.

Disciplinary boundaries and internal constraints

One way forward could be building partnerships between academia and industry, thereby serving to complement one another in their pursuit for innovations in digital research (Roberts et al., 2013). However, social scientists may (quite rightly) be cautious of collaborations with organizations that are market-driven and potentially contribute to the marginalization of discipline areas as methodological specialists (Savage and Burrows, 2007). This raises questions about the role of disciplinary boundaries in facilitating or constraining methodological innovation. In his discussion of the practice of prototyping, Estalella (Chapter 8) highlighted the way in which innovation often occurs outside of the disciplinary boundaries of the social sciences. Drawing on Marres's (2012) argument about a redistribution of social science methods, Estalella argued that social science researchers must recognize and be open to non-conventional forms of expertise (such as those held by amateurs, hackers and non-scholars). Furthermore, Estalella identified an ethos of hospitality and openness underlying the practice of prototyping and innovation more broadly. A willingness to experiment, the embracing of uncertainty and failure, and perhaps above all, the sharing of knowledge and practice, are not characteristics traditionally associated with social science methods that have become part of the canon.

To explore the potential of digital methods, it seems that interdisciplinary work will become increasingly important. One point for consideration is whether potential collaborations may result in larger research teams in the social sciences along the natural science model (Roberts et al., 2013). This may offer opportunities for early career researchers, but may also have implications for career progression since recognition for shared publications and interdisciplinary outputs is not yet well developed in mainstream social science (the UK Research Excellence Framework submissions would be a case in point). Thus a key practical consideration is how to embrace collaboration while maintaining the security of the progress of the researcher within his/her career.

Moreover, the relevance of digital research can be compromised by extended publication timescales. New formats of dissemination, the increased uptake of open access publishing options and the increasing availability of raw open data may however, help to drive change. Crucially, it can be productive to bring together digital and traditional 'offline' methods in a central space, such as through conferences and journals (rather than isolated conferences and journals celebrating the digital) to help provide greater visibility and attention to the benefits and challenges associated with digital research (Roberts et al., 2013).

Analytics and tools

Related to a shift in attitude and practices surrounding disciplinary boundaries is an accompanying shift in perceiving and working with the analytics and tools that generate digital methods data and findings. Training research students at both undergraduate and postgraduate level in interdisciplinary work and advances in digital research methods will be increasingly important. Moreover, a challenge for the digital methods community is to identify the skills required to engage with technology, and there is a need for training and guidance in how to take this forward. In Roberts et al. (2013), we suggested that in order to foster good practices and encourage further innovation within digital research methods, there is a need for further engagement with research students as well as the sharing of good practices in training approaches across the academic sector. However, we would also point to the need to consider the 'Social Life of Methods' (Savage, 2013). Such work highlights the need for critical engagement; of not viewing digital tools as 'black boxes', but to consider 'the affordances and capacities which are mobilized in and through methods themselves... methods become both the object of social scientific interest as well as the inevitable vehicles for social scientists of different hues to practise their trade' (Savage, 2013, p.5).

In this vein, Brooker, Barnett, Cribbin and Sharma (Chapter 3) argued that researchers engaged in data collection and visualization using social media analytics are reliant on computational and technical processes and that researchers do not necessarily understand or explicitly engage with the ways in which these processes inform their findings. They argued that as researchers we need to start thinking about data as not just data but as an *assemblage* of technical and social processes, which have interacted to produce datasets. The authors advocated thinking of data in terms of assemblages and processes that are, furthermore, always unfolding. Similarly, Estalella (Chapter 8) invoked the notions of socio-material or socio-technical assemblages to refer to the social, material and technological processes involved in digital methods and the generation and analysis of digital data.

Methods and concepts

Aside from a few notes of reservation about limitations associated with the use of certain digital methods, many of the contributors explored the ways in which digital methods extend, supplement or enhance existing methods and concepts in innovative ways. For example, the contributions included reflections on the collapsing of the sites and tools for data collection and the widening of participation as a result of different modes of recruitment and data collection. Additionally, two chapters reflected on the ways in which existing social science theories, concepts and methods can be extended and repurposed through their deployment in digital terrains.

Stirling (Chapter 4) considered the way in which her use of Facebook for conducting an ethnography of Higher Education students in the UK collapsed traditional ethnographic divisions between field site and data collection tool. Drawing on Hine's (2007) notion of connective ethnography, Stirling argued that the digital field site of Facebook constituted an extension of the traditional field site and should therefore be conceived as supplementing or enhancing a mainstream method. Hope (Chapter 5) discussed the way that mixed mode (both online and offline) recruitment and data collection ensured the participation of a much wider range of parents than would have been the case otherwise (e.g. full-time workers, the geographically distant, male participants). She found that it was possible to establish rapport across all interview modes (telephone, face-to-face, Voice over Internet Protocol (VoIP) and email) but that certain methods and platforms (e.g. VoIP) were more suited to participants with greater digital know-how and confidence. Similarly, Bond and Agnew (Chapter 12) found that the use of creative art-based digital and material methods combined with the use of traditional verbatim data from focus groups and written contributions allowed them to capture the views of children and young people – a demographic whose voices often remain unheard. A few notes of caution were sounded by de Roock, Bhatt and Adams

(Chapter 7) who argued that researchers need to be proficient in the use of different digital research tools for data collection, management and analysis, but that the interpretation of data findings still relied heavily on human input. This was echoed by Sajuria and Fábrega (Chapter 6) who explored whether the analysis of public opinion on Twitter could be used to complement traditional opinion polls and found that sentiment analysis tools are incapable of detecting sarcasm and irony.

From a slightly different perspective, the chapters by Hutchinson (Chapter 9) and Tedder (Chapter 10) extolled the value of revisiting and repurposing existing social science methods and theories which have much to offer researchers using digital methods. Hutchinson argued that visual theory and sociology had much to offer research on the links between gaming avatars and identity in photo elicitation interviews conducted asynchronously via email. Tedder focused on the ways in which sociological understandings of skill development and transmission were extended by considering how material and physical processes involved in skilled activity are learned in digital environments. Alongside the task of exploring the implications of online phenomena for theories of the self, society, identity and culture, it is therefore beneficial for different methods to interconnect and inform each other, including those of the 'mainstream' (Roberts et al., 2013).

Ethics

As noted by Nind et al. (2012), there are often tensions between methodological innovation and research ethics. Consequently, all of the above arguments about the innovation and mainstreaming of digital research methods cut across the issue of ethics. Much debate already exists concerning ethical practice in the digital realm, particularly in what is considered to be private versus what is public. Increasingly, the argument that 'it's in the public domain' for use of online data without informed consent is not seen as an acceptable, universal rationale, as evident in the processual approach to decision-making advocated by the Association of Internet Researchers (Markham and Buchanan, 2012). Although ethical questions are context-dependent, an overarching awareness of online ethics is clearly an important issue for the social science community (Roberts et al., 2013). Hence, Hewson argued in Chapter 13 that the ongoing changes in online environments, platforms, applications, tools and devices, publics, modes of data and analysis, and research topics necessitate an evolving set of guidelines and principles for digital research ethics.

Conclusion

Based on the contributions to this collection, innovation in digital methods involves more than simply the discovery of the 'new' and more properly follows a recursive trajectory in which methods are repurposed, revisioned and revisited. The mainstreaming of methods, platforms and environments occurs at different points for different stakeholders. This produces a layered, multi-platformed, complex setting for social science researchers in which decisions about whether to use offline or online methods have been replaced by a much larger number of decisions and possibilities. As time progresses, there is a need to raise awareness of the value of digital research methods within and across academic institutions. For some, there is a deep-rooted and somewhat misguided belief that digital methods are flawed by methodological considerations relating to reliability and validity. For others, progress and greater awareness of the value of digital methods may stem from greater visibility of staff and research students partaking in research optimizing such methods (Roberts et al., 2013).

We hope that this collection goes some way to contributing to these efforts. The digital may still be viewed as peripheral by some, but in practice it is firmly embedded in and across our everyday lives. We have also suggested that this distinction between 'mainstream' and 'marginal' should not be necessarily be readily accepted, and indeed productive tensions emerge as notions of marginal and mainstream shift and as researchers move between different perspectives on phenomena of concern. It is at the intersection of the digital and the social that we can find a crucial opportunity for the social sciences not only for innovation but also to be placed at the centre of fundamental concerns for contemporary social life.

References

boyd, d., and Ellison, N.B. (2007) 'Social network sites: Definition, history, and scholarship', *Journal of Computer-Mediated Communication*, 13(1), 210–30.

Hine, C. (2007) 'Connective ethnography for the exploration of e-Science', *Journal of Computer-Mediated Communication*, 12(2): 618–34.

Markham, A. and Buchanan, E. (2012) *Ethical Decision-Making and Internet Research. Recommendations from the AoIR Ethics Working Committee* (version 2), http://www.aoir.org/reports/ethics2.pdf.

Marres, N. (2012) 'The redistribution of methods: On intervention in digital social research, broadly conceived', *The Sociological Review*, 60(S1), 139–65.

Naughton, J. (2000) *A Brief History of the Future: The Origins and Destiny of the Internet*. London: Phoenix.

Nind, M., Wiles, R., Bengry-Howell, A. and Crow, G. (2012) 'Methodological innovation and research ethics: Forces in tension or forces in harmony?', *Qualitative Research*, 13(6), 650–67.

Roberts, S., Hine, C., Morey, Y., Snee, H. and Watson, H. (2013) '*Digital Methods as Mainstream Methodology*': Building Capacity in the Research Community to Address the Challenges and Opportunities Presented by Digitally Inspired Methods, Discussion Paper, NCRM, http://eprints.ncrm.ac.uk/3156/.

Savage, M. (2013) 'The "Social Life of Methods": A critical introduction', *Theory, Culture and Society*, 30(4), 3–21.

Savage, M. and Burrows, R. (2007) 'The coming crisis of empirical sociology', *Sociology*, 41(5), 885–99.

Taylor, C. and Coffey, A. (2008) *Innovation in Qualitative Research Methods: Possibilities and Challenges*. Cardiff: Cardiff University.

van Dijck, J. (2013) *The Culture of Connectivity: A Critical History of Social Media*. New York: Oxford University Press.

Wiles, R., Bengry-Howell, A., Crowe, G. and Nind, M. (2013) 'But is it innovation?: The development of novel methodological approaches in qualitative research', *Methodological Innovations Online*, 8(1), 18–33.

Index